SAINT JOHN
OF THE CROSS

FATHER DONALD HAGGERTY

Saint John of the Cross

Master of Contemplation

IGNATIUS PRESS   SAN FRANCISCO

Cover art:
Drawing of the Crucifixion
by Saint John of the Cross (Detail)
Convento de la Encarnacion, Avila, Spain
Photograph © Album/Art Resource, New York

Cover design by Roxanne Mei Lum

© 2022 by Ignatius Press, San Francisco
All rights reserved
ISBN 978-1-62164-542-9 (PB)
ISBN 978-1-64229-187-2 (eBook)
Library of Congress Control Number 2021941891
Printed in the United States of America ∞

To Father Conrad de Meester, O.C.D.
(1936–2019)

Whoever hears the words *Be ye perfect* must not expect his nature to be "perfected" in any more comfortable fashion. Should one entertain such expectation, even though it be only by diminishing his natural desires in order to cultivate them in peace, he will succeed only in atrophying his nature in order to suffer less. . . . That is why St. John of the Cross so passionately reproaches those who fear to suffer, for their lack of ambition and magnanimity. When self-annihilation and suffering achieve their full dimensions, as in the Doctor of Night himself, then do love and perfection achieve theirs, also. To be sure, a hundred-fold reward is promised us even on this earth. But only on the conditions which have already been set down: "Since I have taken up my abode in nothing, I find that nothing is wanting to me."

—Jacques Maritain, *The Degrees of Knowledge*

The mystical grace bestows as experience what faith teaches: the indwelling of God in the soul. Whoever, led by the truth of faith, seeks God, will set out by his free effort precisely to there, where the mystically graced are drawn . . . into the empty solitude of his interior in order to linger there in dark faith—in a simply loving upward glance of the spirit to the hidden God who is presently veiled. Here he will remain in deep peace—as at the place of his rest until it pleases the Lord to transform faith into seeing. Indicated in a few strokes, this is the *ascent to* Mount Carmel as our holy father John of the Cross has taught it.

—Edith Stein
(Saint Teresa Benedicta of the Cross, O.C.D.),
Finite and Eternal Being

For fifteen years or so, I hated St. John of the Cross, and called him a Buddhist. I loved St. Teresa, and read her over and over again. . . . Then I found I had wasted fifteen years, so far as prayer was concerned!

—John Chapman, O.S.B.,
The Spiritual Letters of Dom John Chapman

CONTENTS

ABBREVIATIONS

AMC   *The Ascent of Mount Carmel* (books 1, 2, 3)

DN   *The Dark Night* (books 1, 2)

SC   *The Spiritual Canticle* (stanza commentaries, 1–40)

LF   *The Living Flame of Love* (stanza commentaries, 1–3)

SLL   *The Sayings of Light and Love*

L   The Letters

P   The Precautions in Special Counsels

CR   Counsels to a Religious in Special Counsels

INTRODUCTION

A small anecdote in the life of Saint John of the Cross (1542–1591) concerns a Carmelite Sister, Catalina de la Cruz, the cook at the convent in Beas, who was known as a simple person. One day she told him that she noticed at the pond in the monastery garden, whenever she passed by, the frogs at the edge of the pond leaped into the water to hide themselves as though they could hear her footsteps approaching on the soft ground. Saint John of the Cross replied that these frogs were going to the place where they were most secure. They preserved themselves by plunging into the depths of the water. He advised her to do likewise. She, too, should flee from creatures and descend into the depths where God is hiding, and where she could conceal her life in him. Years later he still remembered the conversation. He asked in a letter to the Mother Prioress at the Carmel of Beas to be remembered to "our sister Catalina and tell her to hide herself and seek the depths" (Brenan, 45).

This advice to hide oneself and seek the depths is a fitting image for introducing a work on Saint John of the Cross and his teaching on contemplation. In recounting this anecdote, we can take note also that Saint John of the Cross clearly understood the call to contemplation to be open to every openhearted and generous soul, including those living in the world. He wrote a major treatise, *The Living Flame of Love*, for a Spanish laywoman. His experience may have been that

13

the rugged souls of determination are those who advance most securely along the contemplative path to God. These seem often to be the most simple people, those not held back by ambitions for the enjoyment of their pride in this passing world. Indeed, nothing of spiritual elitism is compatible with the grace of contemplation. It is not a feat of acquired skills or of learned proficiency in prayer but, rather, an interior path of humility and deep faith and intense love for God. Are we perhaps invited in God's plan to this grace of contemplation? A consuming desire for God that will not release our soul is one sign that this grace may await us or is already present. But we must be ready, if that grace is to deepen its impact, to leave naked the depths of our soul for God. We must be willing to give to God an offering of love and sacrifice, seeking nothing more urgently in life than him. These are serious demands, certainly. For souls who may be attracted to such a life of deeper personal interiority with God, Saint John of the Cross is an incomparable mentor.

This book is focused with specific concentration on the teaching of Saint John of the Cross regarding contemplation. He is without parallel the Church's great teacher of contemplation. It is his subject of magisterial authority par excellence. There is arguably no one in the history of the Church who has written with his insight of personal experience and acumen on this subject, and that would include his good friend Saint Teresa of Ávila (1515–1582), who has her own great appeal. Contemplation is a challenging and difficult topic of study and, even more so, an arduous road to walk in the spiritual life. Saint John of the Cross was aware on both counts in taking up his pen. What we intend to do in this book is to reduce somewhat the difficulty of understanding contemplation in the Catholic tradition by making accessible the great pages and most penetrating passages of Saint John of the Cross on this subject. A commentary supported by abundant quotations that highlights his most prominent teachings and clarifies the unity of his overall thought can prove immensely useful in his case. His teaching on contemplation is invaluable, but it is also a subject that has various strands of requirements and repercussions that weave sometimes in a dispersed and unmethodical manner throughout his works. Bringing these strands together in a manageable and organized way for our deeper comprehension is one objective of this book. The four major treatises and minor works of Saint John of the Cross fill over 700 pages in his *Collected Works*. What we are providing is an effort of precision to bring the best of his teaching to the forefront for a wider, more accessible appreciation. Ideally, we may discover that a patient absorption of his thought is well worth the labor of love it requires. Exposure to his writings can change our lives permanently, as it evidently did the lives of some saints, beginning with our idea of prayer itself, but extending also to our perception of sanctity and its fundamental demands.

In a brief introductory remark, it might be mentioned that contemplation is a word often not understood properly. The reality of a more mysterious encounter with God in the silence of prayer is in part what is invoked by this word. But the real meaning of contemplation, as Saint John of the Cross teaches, is always more than a matter of an experience in prayer. The soul itself becomes more contemplative as we give ourselves more fully to God, just as it becomes more wise, more charitable, more humble. There is a link always between our conduct of life and our prayer. The prayer of contemplation is a grace, and all serious souls should aspire to it, but it depends on our effort to please God in love *outside* the silence of prayer. A refusal to say "no" to God, in whatever he asks of us, is necessary again and again if we want deeper relations with God in prayer. God carves depths of a different encounter with himself as we become more accessible to his mysterious advances both in and out of prayer. We learn over time that these advances are utterly personal and hidden within the mystery of God. As requests, they have much to do with generosity toward God, in the trials he allows, in the purifications he asks of us, in the opportunities for sacrificial charity he provides. Generosity of soul conditions spiritual advancement; holding back the gift of oneself, when God asks for more, impedes it. Not surprisingly, when God sees a serious desire for himself, and a constancy in self-offering, he acts mysteriously upon deeper regions in our soul. Then the great promise identified in Saint John's Gospel that God might abide in us, and we might abide in God (Jn 15:4–5), becomes an experienced truth within our soul. This possibility is at the heart of contemplation in prayer.

Crossing thresholds in our personal engagement with God, in which we experience in mystery his personal presence abiding within us, does not occur easily, not without a great surrender of our soul to God and his holy will. Unfortunately, this important truth is not acknowledged in many current books on prayer. It is easy to find written works suggesting that contemplation can be adopted simply as a preferred *method* of prayer, if one is so inclined. Contemplative prayer is then conceived as a matter of personal taste, an option available on a menu of prayer possibilities. This is a grave misconception. The true grace of contemplation, as already alluded, does not happen this way. Unless a soul is serious in giving itself away in sacrificial generosity, and decisive in living for others, there can be no grace of contemplation in prayer. An excessive tendency to "subjectivism" is the crutch carried by all dubious forms of self-oriented spirituality. They are recognized by the halting step of self-gazing and the descent into religious illusions. In contrast to every false understanding of contemplation, it is certainly informative to study the teaching of Saint John of the Cross. His instruction is far removed from a simple notion of lessons in a method of prayer. For him, contemplation is inseparable from a radical transformation of the soul in its entirety. The effect of reading Saint John of the Cross is to perceive a profound demand to live a *full* life of love for God, in prayer and outside of formal prayer. The perspective of this book will reflect that need.

The format of the topical treatments in this book does not follow a conventional schema, if we can speak as such in regard to Saint John of the Cross' teaching. A straightforward passage through his four major treatises is not the most helpful approach. The primary desire here is that a profound hunger for God take hold in the reader, which would seem consistent with this saint's own intentions in his writings. And so we exercise a certain amount of movement from one treatise to another in treating topics, shifting attention as needed, in order to seek a deepening comprehension. A recommendation might be suggested. Pondering for a moment the quotations from Saint John of the Cross in the text can only enhance their illuminating impact. His finest writing and most memorable passages are often found when he is expounding his most important teachings. We might point out as well that in the chapters on contemplation itself, what may seem to be reaffirmations and some repeated emphasis is deliberate. The subject poses difficulties, and a clear understanding is important. It may entail direct application for our lives. Fruitful teaching ordinarily requires some return on significant matters from different angles. And so that

tactic will be present at times in these chapters examining
contemplative prayer. Another comment might also be apropos. In matters of serious spirituality, it is better to plunge
into deeper waters at once. This does not mean introducing abstruse teaching that will not be understood; rather, it
means taking up matters from the start that are highly significant from a contemplative point of view and beneficial to
wrestle with immediately. If we hold an attentive gaze upon
the spiritual principles elucidated in the first three chapters,
all that follows becomes more easily recognized for its value
and truth. Saint John of the Cross, never one to delay in
exposing essential truths, invites such a treatment.

We begin, then, in chapter 1, with the first stanza commentary of *The Spiritual Canticle*, a rich portion of writing
that can have a profound impact on spiritual life and prayer.
It is a treatment of the concealed presence of God within
depths of the soul and explains in a striking way how this
truth can affect our life of prayer. We follow with a chapter
provoked by a section of *The Living Flame of Love* on the
effect of the theological virtues on the faculties of the soul.
What may sound in that phrase like a dry topic proves to
be again immensely important for the interior life of a soul
desirous to seek union with God. We turn then to a presen-
tation in *The Ascent of Mount Carmel* to examine the impact
of faith on the intellect and the dark obscurity it causes, a
crucial topic for contemplation. This chapter is followed by
an examination of aspects of experiential contact with God's
communications in prayer from the same treatise. Then, in
chapters 5 and 6, from larger sections of *The Ascent*, we
examine the ascetical principles of Saint John of the Cross
and his understanding of the purification of the will and
its great importance in the spiritual life. In chapter 7, we
take up Saint John of the Cross' lively discussion from the

beginning of *The Dark Night* in which the seven capital sins become analogues for spiritual impediments in prayer.

The next major portion of the book, beginning in chapter 8 and taking up several chapters, makes a coordinated use of three of the four major treatises and concentrates on contemplation itself: the extensive preliminary comments on the subject by Saint John of the Cross; his teaching on the signs and symptoms of its inception in a life; the conduct necessary for a soul responding to contemplative graces in prayer; the various repercussions that must be dealt with in this prayer to allow it to flourish; and the encounter with purifying experiences that advance the soul in contemplation. In these chapters on contemplation, we include a chapter that examines a magnificent letter Saint John of the Cross wrote on the role of the will in interior prayer. The latter portion of the book will make use once again of the various treatises of Saint John of the Cross to explore some of the deeper implications of contemplation as a life progresses: the beauty of love experienced in the wounds of love in contemplation; the reality of darkness in the spiritual life and prayer as a conduit to greater graces; and the role of suffering in the interior life for the sake of a more profound love for God. We conclude the book with a chapter presenting some of the memorable spiritual advice Saint John of the Cross gave to souls in letters and instructions. At the end is also a short selection of some notable aphorisms sent personally by Saint John of the Cross to individual Carmelite Sisters, and saved by them, known subsequently as *The Sayings of Light and Love*.

A last comment could be made. Most people have never visited a cloistered convent or a monastery, although surely we have all known someone who is a deeply prayerful person, perhaps in our own family. We may wonder how it happens that some souls become so enamored of God and love prayer in this manner? Is it possible in our lives? An answer might be to think of the soul of the contemplative as a young child much loved by a father and mother, who see something unusual and special while that child is still at an early age. They sense a gift present and envision for this son or daughter some possible unknown greatness, without knowing what that might be. God may not be so different from these parents, except that he does know what this possibility is. He gazes on some souls with an immense desire that they arrive at a greatness in the spiritual realm. This greatness is not for public recognition, but for the gift of a hidden union with himself in the contemplative path of sanctity. Souls inclined to prayer who begin to experience an intense need for a more personal closeness to God should consider that they, too, may be meant for such a hidden spiritual greatness. Perhaps God for some time has been trying to make them realize it.

And what would God desire especially for them? Not deeds of public achievement or a spiritual influence that visibly touches many lives in a clearly evident manner, but a concealed impact in the spiritual realm that will come from their secret relations of love with himself. Their steady encounter with him in the obscurity of an intense faith, their knowledge of his loving presence in the shadows of darkness, and their repeated acts of self-offering can become the source of a hidden influence upon others that cannot be measured. He treasures souls that never relinquish their passionate longing for him once they find him so undeniably near in the vicinity of a Catholic tabernacle. Saint John of the Cross teaches much that is not written down explicitly. Certainly a truth he teaches continually is that the contemplative soul is a beautiful secret of God's love for human lives. God shows special favor and love for these souls, but he also asks much from them in self-offering. These are souls chosen for a rare form of friendship. But it is never for this alone that they are chosen. Their friendship with him leads to their own Calvary, where they find a great love for Jesus in his crucifixion and for Mary his mother standing nearby and where they discover a power of intercession for others that they must never deny or neglect.

I

THE HIDING PLACE
OF THE BELOVED

Perhaps a sampling of the poetry of Saint John of the Cross should be explored privately as a first encounter with this Carmelite mystic and saint, who might otherwise be considered too severe in his spiritual demands and, for that reason, ignored and neglected. The beauty, for example, of "The Spiritual Canticle" as a poem ought to be savored in its forty stanzas before reading the stanza commentaries in the larger work of the same name. The poem is a dialogue between a bride and her Beloved, as in the biblical *Song of Songs*, and like that work it depicts anguished tensions in the relations of love between a soul and God, when a soul is truly in love with God. And, indeed, this is the central theme of Saint John of the Cross throughout his mystical compositions—to be *in love with God*. The repercussions that ensue from such a mysterious love are an endless source of provocation for him. What would it mean to have a lifetime love affair, as it were, with God? Let us take these words in their most sacred sense, without any vulgar connotation, and then we begin to sense the unheard-of possibilities that may seize our soul's desire in reading this mystical saint. The poem commences with these striking words from the first stanza:

> Where have you hidden,
> Beloved, and left me moaning?

You fled like the stag
after wounding me;
I went out calling you, but you were gone.

This initial stanza of "The Spiritual Canticle" unlocks
the bolt of a door, allowing us a first glimpse at the soul
of Saint John of the Cross and his intense love for God.
In these opening lines of a lengthy poem, we hear the ago-
nized voice of a lover tormented by her solitude, in a terrible
suffering after the departure of her Beloved. The piercing
lament of the bride, wounded in the depth of her soul, is
an image of the lover of God who seeks for his return after earlier enjoying his close presence. The mood of loneliness in the poem will shift over the course of its forty
stanzas to a recognition of the Beloved's presence even in
his concealment. But for now, as the poem commences, the
pain is strong and irremediable. Many of the stanzas of this
exquisite poem, full of lush natural images, were composed
by Saint John of the Cross without pen or paper, the stanzas
kept in his memory, while he was locked in a windowless,
six-by-ten-foot converted closet, with only a thin slit of light
high up in a wall. That room served as a makeshift prison
cell in the Calced Carmelite Friars' monastery in Toledo,
Spain, for nine months of his life, from December 1577
until August 1578. Only in the very last period of the nine
months did he receive pen and paper from a sympathetic
friar serving as his jailer and write down verses. He later
recounted to Carmelite nuns that another important poem,
"The Dark Night", was completed before he left that prison
cell.

He was thirty-five years old and ten years into his priesthood when he was taken captive during a period of tense
hostility against the Discalced Carmelite reform initiated by
Saint Teresa of Ávila in 1562. After meeting Saint Teresa

in September 1567, soon after his priestly ordination, and with her invitation to join her reform movement, he himself became a prominent figure at the start of the reform in the men's Carmelite branch and, eventually, a target of wrath for the higher superiors of the Calced Carmelites, who by that time deeply resented the reform. For five years until his arrest on December 2, 1577, he had been living a relatively quiet life as the confessor and chaplain to about 130 Carmelite nuns at the Carmel of the Incarnation in Ávila, where he shared a small cottage with another Carmelite friar on the edge of the property. Saint Teresa of Ávila was finishing a term as Mother Prioress during his first eight months there. The great commentary of *The Spiritual Canticle*, a stanza by stanza exposition of the poem, serving as a treatise of mystical theology to help toward an understanding of the mystical meanings hidden in the poem, was requested by Mother Ana de Jesús, prioress of the Carmel at Granada, and completed in 1584. This was six years after his escape from the Toledo imprisonment on a moonless night during the octave of the Assumption of Mary in 1578. His door had been left unlocked, allowing him to climb out a window in another room and lower himself down by tied blankets on to the ledge of a stone wall beyond which, if he did not land properly, was a long deadly plunge to the rocks below bordering the river Tagus. Saint John of the Cross, in his mid-thirties during the nine brutal months of isolated suffering and physical deprivation in the Toledo monastery, had written very little before this, only some aphorisms and letters. He became the mystical poet and writer we know after the dark desolation of those months of extreme trial. Exceptional fruitfulness arising from grave suffering is a unique mark of the man and his teaching.

Let us return to the provocative first lines of the poem: "Where have you hidden, Beloved . . . after wounding me;

I went out calling you, but you were gone." Are these words simply a verse from a poem or, more profoundly, a prayer overheard from a mystic in deep relations with God? In all the teaching of Saint John of the Cross, despite the forbidding features of its radical demands, hides a poet of sanctity who has fallen in love with God, even helplessly so. The Church may call him the Mystical Doctor in recognition of the superlative teaching in his four major treatises; yet the weight of that title is not entirely helpful. He is not proposing a speculative doctrine of mystical ascent to be mastered by careful study and strict application. Abstraction has little place or purpose in his writing, even as he makes every effort to clarify in precise language what may often be impossible lessons to convey to a reader lacking experience of what he is elucidating. Simply reading once through his work will never disclose his teaching adequately. At some point, he has to become a very loved mentor to whom one turns with increasing need over the course of years, or else he slips away quietly and will be forgotten, as he was apparently forgotten by many in his own lifetime. But if he is embraced as a trusted guide, and his direction is accepted, he can become a companion who pushes and prods us to a mysterious, unsettling desire for God, which is only a start toward greater effects over time. If he remains a friend for many years, a hunger and fire in our soul for God far beyond any initial expectation of spiritual pursuit is bound to ignite within us.

We learn, gradually, that his manner of persuasion, even in what can seem passages of dry expository commentary, is an appeal to our heart to become a beloved friend of God. Or, better, to come to know as he does the *crushing* experience of a love for God. This experience of being conquered by a love for God floods through his teaching. We hear it in the opening verse of the poem: "*Where have you hidden, Beloved . . . after wounding me?*" The pursuit of God, if passionate and determined, as expressed by these words, implies always vulnerable relations with a Beloved who is infinitely beyond the human lover's grasp. Every page written by this man assumes that a soul can be in love with God. But this is a most daunting prospect, since God remains for our lifetime an unseen presence of elusive mystery. And clearly no one can simply decide to fall in love with God. The reality of such a love, if it happens, is never planned by choice, but occurs if our soul is open to such a grace and gives way to God. And perhaps it requires as well that we spend enough time alone and silent in front of a crucifix and a tabernacle. Precisely the need for such a surrender and such hours alone with the crucified Lord Jesus may be why God rarely becomes the great passion in most lives. Without a passion for Jesus Christ crucified, and a great surrender to him, reading Saint John of the Cross may not be worth the trouble. But on the condition that, even to some extent, we fall in love with our God who became a brutalized criminal on a Roman cross, this saint becomes indispensable. He is absolutely needed for understanding the way to a greater love of God in the silence of contemplative prayer that some souls do seek in this life.

The first stanza commentary of *The Spiritual Canticle* begins, then, by turning a gaze on the bride's pain just heard in the poem's initial words. Her affliction in the poem concerns the loss of her bridegroom. Not that he has died; rather, he has disappeared, leaving her in dreadful loneliness and painful longing. In other circumstances of life, this scenario could be likened to a young soldier going off to war soon after a marriage and the suffering this departure would cause his beloved new wife. Separations of this kind, with all their tragic uncertainty, have been repeated countless times in the last hundred or more years. But the bride in this case is a poetic figure for the soul itself, and the one she loves, and who is absent to her, is the Lord himself. As Saint John of the Cross writes, she "complains to him of his absence . . . since his love wounds her . . . and yet she must suffer her Beloved's absence" (SC 1.2).

At first, according to the words of the commentary, the cry of the bride in the opening line of the poem—"Where have you hidden, Beloved"—identifies the Beloved's *absence* as her essential suffering. But Saint John of the Cross is quick to correct a misconception. The Beloved of the soul is not absent at all. Instead, he is hiding in concealment, and not far from the soul. This shift from a complaint of absence to a recognition of concealment is a subtle change and immensely significant. It alters the tone of the question— "Where have you hidden, Beloved?"—from a young bride's lament of pain in a poem to a soul's intense desire for the concealed presence of the hidden Lord. This concealment of God in his hidden presence to the soul cannot be overstated in its importance for Saint John of the Cross. The focus on suffering that initiates the commentary of *The Spiritual Canticle* is precisely the intense suffering of love in a soul pursuing union with a hidden God. The soul's encounter with a God who hides even as he is near is a source of ongoing, painful struggle. There is nothing a soul can do, no option or remedy, but to embrace this concealment of God as an essential aspect of relations with our Lord. And so the seemingly simple advice that follows: "A person should think of him as hidden and seek him as one who is hidden, saying: 'Where have You hidden?'" (SC 1.3).

For Saint John of the Cross, however, there is a kind of

spiritual appendage that must be attached to this stress on God's concealment to the human soul, which he addresses at this early stage in the first stanza commentary. He insists that the interior experiences we undergo in the long pursuit of prayer have a problematical quality about them, indeed, an unreliability of sorts. This uncertainty has nothing to do with the objective truth of our revealed Catholic faith. The God we are addressing in prayer, for instance, in the vicinity of a Catholic tabernacle, is the risen Jesus Christ, the incarnate Son of the living God, present in the mystery of the Blessed Sacrament. The problematic aspect is not the objective, unchanging truth of his divine presence. Rather, it is the subjective experience we may have of encounters with a God who remains concealed. On the one side, there is the possibility of interpreting consolation within our soul as evidence of a direct contact with God. On the other side, there is the possibility of misconstruing interior desolation as an indication of God's distaste for our soul. Perhaps the second possibility is even more common. In addressing the problematic risk of interpretations rooted in a misguided subjectivism, Saint John of the Cross directs our attention to the objective truth of the divine hiddenness. If God is infinite mystery in his divine nature, it follows that there is an unreliability in depending on our subjective experience as a measure of personal relations with God. Elevated experiences of God in prayer, if they occur, can be a gift of God and perhaps a reprieve from struggles in prayer. But they do not remove, even temporarily, the essential concealment of God in his presence to the soul. Always, as Saint John of the Cross insists, "he is still hidden to the soul" (SC 1.3). The following passage is instructive on this point and worthy of a longer quotation:

Neither the sublime communication nor the sensible awareness of his nearness is a sure testimony of his gracious presence, nor are dryness and the lack of these a reflection of
his absence. . . . It must be understood that if a person experiences some elevated spiritual communication or feeling or knowledge, it should not be thought that the experiences are similar to the clear and essential vision or
possession of God, or that the communication, no matter
how remarkable it is, signifies a more notable possession
of God or union with him. It should be known too that if
all these sensible and spiritual communications are wanting and individuals live in dryness, darkness, and derelic-
tion, they must not thereby think that God is any more
absent than in the former state. People, actually, cannot
have certain knowledge from the one state that they are
in God's grace or from the other that they are not. (SC
1.3, 4)

The concealment of God is as such a constant experiential
component within prayer itself. It is a factor of ambiguity
in prayer, an inescapable reality of prayer in its subjective
quality, because of the varying experiences of consolation
or desolation undergone from day to day in prayer. Whether
God is near to us or distant from us cannot be determined
by any subjective measure of experience. Nor should we
seek to make such a determination. To measure prayer by

means of the shifting inner experiences of prayer is to invite
an instability into our relations with God. The unchanging
truth is that God hides in the encounter we have with him
in prayer. The result is an inability to lay hold of him in a
manner that can be definitively ascertained in a subjective
sense. Yet for Saint John of the Cross, this truth is not so
consequential that it should discourage our efforts in prayer.

Another truth of consequence quickly arises in this treatment that is even more significant for the interior life of prayer. If God remains in concealment, hiding from us and eluding our grasp, the question naturally can be raised of where he may be hiding. And if he is hiding, rather than absent, where might he be found? Again, it may be helpful to repeat that an absence and a concealment are very distinct realities, not at all comparable. Concealment implies an actual presence in a location, but a presence under the cover of a disguise or enclosed within some hiding place. Every child who has played the game of hide-and-seek knows, while the game is in progress, that whoever is being sought is hiding somewhere out *there*, in an unknown place, perhaps very near, but not yet found.

Given the necessity of an encounter with God's concealment in prayer, Saint John of the Cross thus takes up the question of where the Son of God may be hiding, so that he can be sought by our soul. Our own answer might be to point to his presence in the Eucharist, where on any day an intimacy with him in prayer and in Mass and Holy Communion is possible. But this is not the location of the divine hiding that Saint John of the Cross will reference in this first stanza commentary. Rather, he declares the Catholic doctrine of the indwelling presence of the Holy Trinity "in the innermost being of the soul" (SC 1.6) to be the essential truth to remember avidly for "this thirsting soul" seeking a "union of love" with God. Thus a precise "location", as it were—"the innermost being of the soul"— has been identified as the hiding place of God. The discovery should enable us to pursue our Beloved in prayer with a sense of targeted focus. Stressing the importance of this inward realization in faith, Saint John of the Cross alludes as well to a passage now attributed to Pseudo-Augustine's *Soliloquies: "I did not find you without, Lord, because I wrongly sought you without, who were within"* (SC 1.6). In the view of Saint John of the Cross, the knowledge of the hiding place of God within the soul itself is an irreplaceable insight once it is embraced. We can hear this importance in the tone that Saint John of the Cross adopts at this point. A longer quotation from back to back paragraphs may be valuable, not only for its spiritual clarity, but even more for its insistent tone:

> Oh, then, soul, most beautiful among all creatures, so anxious to know the dwelling place of your Beloved so you may go in search of him and be united with him, now we are telling you that you yourself are his dwelling and his secret inner room and hiding place. There is reason for you to be elated and joyful in seeing that all your good and hope is so close as to be within you, or better, that you cannot be without him. . . . What more do you want, O soul! And what else do you search for outside, when within yourself you possess your riches, delights, satisfaction, fullness, and kingdom—your Beloved whom you desire and seek? Be joyful and gladdened in your interior recollection with him, for you have him so close to you. Desire him there, adore him there. Do not go in pursuit of him outside yourself. You will only become distracted and wearied thereby, and you shall not find him, or enjoy him more securely, or sooner, or more intimately than by seeking him within you. (SC 1.7, 8)

After this statement, so promising in its instruction, a caveat is quickly posed regarding the revelation of this "location" of the divine presence within the soul. The indwelling presence of God in our soul, while a wonderful truth of faith, remains nonetheless a *hidden* presence. And this concealment of God, precisely in his near proximity in the soul, becomes the source of a great affliction for a soul that loves him with intensity. In a marvelously understated tone, after the last sentences in the passage just quoted, Saint John of the Cross captures the dilemma in a single sentence: "There is but one difficulty: *Even though he does abide within you, he is hidden.* Nevertheless, it is vital for you to know his hiding place so you may search for him there with assuredness" (SC 1.8; emphasis added). Good news, followed by a hard truth not to be neglected. Saint John of the Cross refers here gently to the struggle that can be expected for the loving soul in its quest for God. Our Lord is exquisitely close, residing in the innermost depth of the soul, and yet perpetually hidden in the intimacy of his divine presence. It is as though a welcome truth, so enticing and necessary to know, is accompanied upon a closer look by a great barrier to its enjoyment. How hidden will our Lord's presence be? Can he ever be experienced within our soul if he hides? Is there a way to lift the veil of divine concealment and pierce through this barrier to direct encounters with him? The answer to these questions will not come by proposing a method or practice to be employed in prayer. The response of Saint John of the Cross is to urge an interior disposition in prayer that must be cultivated if we are to encounter the hidden Lord. The short comment that follows is truly at the heart of his teaching, reiterated in many contexts again and again: the need to conceal ourselves from our own attention, to escape from self-regard and preoccupation with our own experience in prayer if we are to encounter our Lord present in concealment within our soul. "Yet you inquire: Since he whom my soul loves is within me, why don't I find him or experience him? The reason is that he remains concealed and you do not also conceal yourself in order to find and experience him" (SC 1.9).

Clearly, with this statement, Saint John affirms the possibility of experiencing our Lord in prayer; soon he will take up the subject at greater length. The play on the word "conceal", however, deserves a remark, since the word has a dual purpose in the passage just quoted. The divine concealment refers to the hiddenness of an infinite God present in the innermost depths of the soul. God in his divine infinitude forever surpasses our limited grasp and comprehension. On the other hand, the notion of the soul concealing itself identifies, quite differently, the need for us to hide ourselves in self-forgetfulness during prayer. We need to let go and lose preoccupation with ourselves in the time of prayer. And how is this done? We forget ourselves inasmuch as we turn our attention with some intensity to our Lord himself. Self-forgetfulness in prayer is not accomplished by an effort of concentrated labor. Only an indirect means is availing. A turning from self will take place when our attention is drawn away from ourselves, which happens primarily because love for a Beloved draws our attention.

Saint John of the Cross already suggests here that a secret contemplative encounter with our Lord can occur only on the condition that the person praying disappears from view into an inner enclosure of hiddenness. Again, this forgetfulness of self can take place because love for Another has become the focus of attention. Every contemplative encounter with God in prayer happens only in a secrecy that does not allow the prying eyes of any self-observer. The only eyes necessary are God's eyes upon the soul. The turn away from self, due to love for Another, is a critical component. The soul must take care not to seek in any *self-conscious* manner to enjoy satisfactions in an experience of our Lord. All must take place without a possessive impulse to take hold of an experience and grasp it possessively for personal satisfaction. The following very significant words take the point farther and are worth pondering repeatedly. They begin to suggest the essential path that leads securely to the contemplative encounter in mystery with our Lord. "If you want to find a hidden treasure you must enter the hiding place secretly, and once you have discovered it, you will also be hidden just as the treasure is hidden" (SC 1.9).

The hidden treasure is, of course, our Lord himself, and his hiding place, as we know now, is the "innermost being of the soul". But what does it mean for our soul to enter secretly into that hiding place? And what is this experience of contemplative encounter in which the soul itself will likewise be hidden? Is there an instruction that must be followed in order to cross a threshold within our soul to this desired hiding place? These questions cannot be overstated in their importance. And, indeed, this will be the next focus of the commentary, namely, to expose the requirements necessary to pass in secrecy into the presence of our Lord dwelling within the depth of our soul. The secrecy of the passage into the divine presence within the soul is a crucial element in contemplative prayer. And what does this entail? The pronounced accent is on this taking place "*in hiding*"; namely, by a passage in prayer through the inward silence of self-forgetfulness to the secret place of hiding, leaving behind everything that might draw our particular attention. The soul has to become lost to its ordinary self-regard and consciousness of self if it is to enter the hiding place secretly. No method of mental training allows us to traverse this passage. Rather, some form of release from self-regard must take place by means of our love for God in response

to grace. Clearly we have our part to do as well, which is a
submissive entry into a self-emptying interior mode. How
this is to occur calls for an ongoing clarification, which can
be heard initially in these words:

> Since, then, your beloved Bridegroom is the treasure hid-
> den in a field for which the wise merchant sold all his pos-
> sessions [Mt. 13:44], and that field is your soul, in order
> to find him you should forget all your possessions and all
> creatures and hide in the secret inner room of your spirit
> and there, closing the door behind you (your will to all
> things), you should pray to your Father in secret [Mt. 6:6].
> Remaining hidden with him, you will experience him in
> hiding, that is, in a way transcending all language and feel-
> ing. . . . Since you know now that your desired Beloved
> lives hidden within your heart, strive to be really hidden
> with him, and you will embrace him within you and ex-
> perience him with loving affection. (SC 1.9, 10)

The last advice to "strive to be really hidden with him"
combines, in effect, a necessary interior disposition to be
pursued in prayer with the necessary truth of the divine
indwelling. Knowledge of the "place" of divine hiding is
one thing, but now the great stress is directed to the attitude
that our soul must adopt in its pursuit of the God who hides
himself within our soul. What will this hiding of our soul
actually entail as a chosen attitude of prayer? The answer is
a subtle but important teaching for Saint John of the Cross.
The hiding of the soul takes place, not simply by the self-
forgetfulness already mentioned, but by keeping a consistent
attitude of deep and certain faith while in prayer. The point
is easily missed. The tendency of a loving person may be
to try to leap the barrier of separation from God that may
be felt in prayer precisely by an attempt to cultivate feelings
of intimacy with God. The soul's desire to scale the wall

of a separation from God by means of its emotion, and so
to enter into an immediate experience of the presence with
God, is often pursued as an effort to *feel* his presence.

On the contrary, Saint John of the Cross insists that the
opposite, almost, must be done. We are to seek God in
faith as concealed in his transcendent mystery and beyond
our reach. Only in this way are we drawn into the personal
presence of the One who hides within our soul. We are led
to him by seeking him precisely as beyond our reach and
outside our feeling. The true experience of God is necessarily an experience of his transcendent mystery. This does
not mean that he is unknown; rather, that he is known more
deeply when he is known as One who is beyond our knowing. This experience is what takes the soul into its own
hiding and readies it for the mysterious encounter with the
hidden God. The following paragraph conveys the real paradoxical nature of the discovery of God in an experiential
manner. *Finding* God in the silence of prayer is *experiencing*
the concealment of God in his utter mystery. The following
statement is arguably one of the most significant passages in
all of Saint John of the Cross' writing:

> You do very well, O soul, to seek him ever as one hid-
> den, for you exalt God and approach very near him when
> you consider him higher and deeper than anything you
> can reach. Hence pay no attention, neither partially nor
> entirely, to anything your faculties can grasp. I mean that
> you should never seek satisfaction in what you under-
> stand about God, but in what you do not understand about
> him. Never pause to love and delight in your understand-
> ing and experience of God, but love and delight in what
> you cannot understand or experience of him. Such is the
> way, as we said, of seeking him in faith. However surely it
> may seem that you find, experience, and understand God,

because he is inaccessible and concealed you must always
regard him as hidden, and serve him who is hidden in a
secret way. (SC 1.12)

These words can be categorized as a brief exercise in
apophatic spiritual theology; yet that label risks missing the
importance of this powerful passage for the life of prayer.
Apophatic theology is essentially an acknowledgment that
God in his ultimate mystery is unknown to us. Despite all
that we can state accurately in conceptual propositions concerning the revealed truth of God—statements about his
attributes and his nature, of the Incarnation and Trinity, of
his divine actions as Creator and Redeemer and Sanctifier—
God remains a transcendent reality beyond the understanding of our human mind. Doctrinal propositions of divinely
revealed truths do indeed arrive at a knowledge of truth.
The mind in the act of faith assents to these revealed truths
by means of the doctrinal propositions formulated in precise language and exact vocabulary. But these same truths
of God extend in their actual reality infinitely beyond the
grasp of our understanding. It is one thing to assent to a
revealed truth of God; it is another matter to comprehend
it fully. Our comprehension is always limited and finite.

But is this all that Saint John of the Cross is teaching in
this passage? No, he is drawing out a great consequence for
prayer that results from an apophatic awareness of God's infinite mystery. The passage that we just heard is not a theological discourse on the incomprehensible nature of God.
Instead, Saint John of Cross is proposing a necessary interior *disposition* that must direct our pursuit of God in prayer
due to his incomprehensible nature. It is one thing to embrace in thought an apophatic awareness that God extends
beyond our intellect's grasp. It is quite another thing to make

our pursuit in prayer depend on seeking God as One who remains in perpetual concealment. This means to plunge more deeply over time into a recognition of the concealment of God to our experience precisely as we seek him in love. The last words of this recent quotation are worth repeating: "However surely it may seem that you find, experience, and understand God, because he is inaccessible and concealed, *you must always regard him as hidden*, and serve him who is hidden in a secret way" (SC 1.12; emphasis added).

We might not initially recognize the hard demand presented here. The usual approach in prayer for most people is to seek a personal encounter with God, and by that is meant ordinarily a felt experience of his presence. The desire for some form of personal contact with our Lord is strong for any soul of Christian faith. But Saint John of the Cross is challenging the soul to a much deeper act of faith. And a deeper faith leads us always to the truth of God's concealment—precisely in the encounter with his personal presence. We can note this by paying close attention to the words Saint John of the Cross uses. The phrase "to seek him *ever* as one hidden" does not imply that this effort terminates at some point. It does not suggest that it is an approach to take simply on difficult days of prayer. In a certain sense, the concealment of God does not lift after some point in time. There is no end point in the pursuit of God as One who hides. His mystery extends indefinitely into the future as we pursue him in love. And yet this does not mean that he is not encountered. He offers us his personal presence in deeper prayer even as he remains concealed in mystery. We must look to a depth within God to realize the nature of a concealed encounter with him.

Then, what kind of encounter takes place, if at all? Let us be clear. In no way does Saint John of the Cross place his stress only on a frustration that ensues from God's hiddenness. There is no suggestion of a hopeless incapacity to proceed farther in our pursuit of a concealed God. He urges, not a grudging submission to divine mystery, but rather a leap forward into the divine mystery by means of our love for an utterly personal and yet nonetheless hidden God. His accent is on the need to *seek* the ever hidden God in a daily effort of prayer. This disposition plants us in truth and bears fruit in prayer. The disposition to seek God precisely in his concealment opens prayer to a *true* encounter with God. We take a step closer to him each time we engage his personal presence as veiled behind shadow. This seeking of God in his hiddenness is what it means to seek him in truth. It is a difficult but all-important teaching.

To "seek him ever as one hidden" is perhaps clarified when we contrast this approach to silent prayer with what we might otherwise search for as experiences in prayer. The common desire to seek more tangible encounters of satisfaction in prayer is quite different from what is proposed here. Saint John of the Cross suggests that seeking experiences in prayer of any sort is a detour off from the genuine road of deeper prayer. Let us recall these words recently quoted about what *not* to do in prayer: "pay no attention, neither partially nor entirely, to anything your faculties can grasp . . . never seek satisfaction in what you understand about God . . . never pause to love and delight in your understanding and experience of God." On the contrary, as stated in the same passage, "you exalt God and approach very near him when you consider him higher and deeper than anything you can reach." And so, in consequence, we should seek to find our satisfaction in prayer in what amounts to a contradiction of our soul's inclination: "seek satisfaction . . . in what you do not understand about him . . . love and delight in what you cannot understand or experience of him" (SC 1.12). The instruction declares, in effect, that something much greater awaits us in the encounter with God in prayer than anything of tangible satisfaction. But we must be willing to enter depths of a new awareness to realize this different encounter with God. We must pass through a blindness and a sense of incapacity as a pathway to God, rather than find in them obstructions of a conclusive nature.

The strong emphasis here on desiring to arrive, as it were, at an experience of some form of dissatisfaction in prayer, to come to know strangely a spiritual delight in what is frustrating for the mind, can seem at first an unattractive teaching. It needs to be pondered, because this is clearly not all that the teaching proposes. As an approach to prayer, it may require traveling a long road of purification to accept its necessity in the life of prayer. It does not attract the soul that wants to taste experiences of immediate closeness and enjoy what seem to be direct encounters with God. The words of Saint John of the Cross can perhaps sound as though prayer should become a painful pursuit of self-contradictory impulses. And yet the initial words of this same longer passage we have been referencing contain a promise worth hearing again, namely, that you will "approach very *near* him when you consider him higher and deeper than anything you can reach" (SC 1.12; emphasis added). And is that not our goal? The effort to adjust our awareness in faith to the deeper mystery of God's personal presence and, even more, to assimilate an experience of God's mystery at the heart of prayer itself is the essential challenge here. Let us listen to further words from this same section. The stress is clearly on the possibility of approaching God in intimacy and drawing near to him in prayer:

Do not be like the many foolish ones who, in their lowly understanding of God, think that when they do not understand, taste, or experience him, he is far away and utterly concealed. The contrary belief would be truer. The less distinct is their understanding of him, the closer they approach him, since in the words of the prophet David, *he made darkness his hiding place* [Ps. 18:11]. Thus in drawing near him you will experience darkness because of the weakness of your eye. You do well, then, at all times, in both adversity and prosperity, whether spiritual or temporal, to consider God as hidden, and call after him thus:

> Where have you hidden,
> Beloved, and left me moaning? (SC 1.12)

It might be helpful, after this passage, to close this chapter with an essential recapitulation of the spiritual challenge in this teaching. The concealment of God in his transcendent mystery is, not primarily a theological affirmation in this saint's writings, but a proposal for prayer. As Saint John of the Cross expresses this truth, the concealment of God entails a presence of God hiding and certainly not an absence of God. His concealment does not undermine or strip the personal nature of an encounter with God in prayer. It rather provokes our soul to a more intense faith and love. The concealment of God, as such, is never a concluding word on the lips of Saint John of the Cross. If the concealment of God, on the other hand, becomes too exclusively a focus in prayer, the result might be that we will drift during our prayer into nebulous thoughts about an unknown God. God is not a vague entity enclosed under the cover of impenetrable shadows. He is known and encountered in the real identity of Jesus Christ and close to us physically in the proximity of a tabernacle or at the Holy Sacrifice of the Mass. Yet precisely there, in the Real Presence of the Eucharist, we encounter the great truth of how concealed he is.

Nonetheless, a significant consequence ensues from God's concealment within the soul, which has to do with our approach to God in prayer. Our soul, in seeking God as One who hides, should allow itself to be carried into the place of concealment where God resides in our soul. The seeking of God as hidden is akin to being drawn to the beauty of his infinitely expansive love. The utterly personal nature of God can never be forgotten, despite what can sound in apophatic language like the remoteness of God from our experience. We must allow ourselves to be drawn by God, experiencing him in a most personal way precisely as a mystery beyond our experience. Simply put, he is a mystery of personal love, and for the rest of our lives he remains beyond our full comprehension. This infinitude of his personal love for souls is the truth we repeatedly encounter in prayer. It is his infinite *love* that is the truth always beyond our grasp. In short, God chooses to dwell in a secrecy of vast love within our soul. To the degree we give way to God and are empty of unnecessary appetites and pleasure, as we will see, this secret presence of God in his mysterious love can become a more piercing truth to our soul. For the moment the following statement from *The Living Flame of Love* can be read as a striking last passage on this subject of his intimate presence of love dwelling within us in concealment. We will see its implications play out significantly in subsequent chapters:

> It is in the soul in which less of its own appetites and pleasures dwell where he dwells more alone, more pleased, and more as though in his own house, ruling and governing it. And he dwells more in secret, the more he dwells

alone. Thus in this soul in which neither any appetite nor other images or forms nor any affections for created things dwell, the Beloved dwells secretly with an embrace so much closer, more intimate and interior, the purer and more alone the soul is to everything other than God. (LF 4.14)

2

CAVERNS OF LONGING
WITHIN THE SOUL

In this second chapter, we introduce the teaching of Saint John of the Cross on the impact of the theological virtues of faith, hope, and charity upon the soul in pursuit of God. Once again, like the concealment of God within the innermost being of the soul, this teaching pervades his understanding of interior prayer. Each of the theological virtues inhabits a faculty of the soul: faith in the intellect, hope in the memory (a variation from Saint Thomas Aquinas, who places hope in the will, but consistent with the thought of Saint Bonaventure), charity in the will. The union of a soul with God depends on the manner in which these theological virtues serve to unite the faculties of the soul with God. The human faculties are "divinized" by means of the theological virtues if a true advancement into sanctity takes place. They can enjoy as such a direct, immediate union with God himself. This is not simply, however, a general theological affirmation. It is important to keep in mind that Saint John of the Cross is writing for souls who aspire to contemplation and ultimately to saintliness. The union in prayer with God that contemplation fosters is the context for the discussion of the theological virtues that follows in this chapter. Contemplation, in turn, is a primary component on the path to sanctity and union with God. Saint John of the Cross makes use again of a poem as a point of departure for his teaching.

This time we turn to the third stanza of "The Living Flame of Love":

> O lamps of fire!
> in whose splendors
> the deep caverns of feeling,
> once obscure and blind,
> now give forth, so rarely, so exquisitely,
> both warmth and light to their Beloved.

"Deep caverns of feeling" is the phrase chosen by Saint John of the Cross in his commentary on *The Living Flame of Love* to describe the human faculties of intellect, memory, and will in their capacity for contemplative graces and for sanctity. "Caverns of feeling" is hardly a typical description for these faculties of the human soul. The metaphor of a deep cavern suggests an interior space without limits, an emptiness that has no end point. "They are as deep as the boundless goods of which they are capable since *anything less than the infinite fails to fill them*" (LF 3.18; emphasis added). The last phrase implies an extraordinary possibility: inner regions of endless depth in the soul that can be permeated with the presence of God himself; places of boundless immensity in the soul that can be filled by the infinite love of God; vast spaces inside the soul that await the fire of God to burn within them. Each of these faculties—intellect, memory, will—has a limitless capacity of hunger and thirst for God.

This depiction, in contrast to a more abstract treatment of the "faculties of the soul", is a central insight in the spiritual theology of Saint John of the Cross. His essential challenge is also present here. Unless the interior regions within the intellect, will, and memory undergo over time an emptying and purging, "they do not feel *the vast emptiness of their deep capacity*" (LF 3.18; emphasis added). Contemplative life, as we shall increasingly see, demands a courageous effort of denying, losing, and renouncing, never simply for an ascetical discipline of self-denial, but in order to carve a vast emptiness within the hidden inner regions of the soul, so that they can be filled with God himself. There is no deeper union with God in prayer without a progressive entry into an inward emptiness within these faculties. What this means and how it leads to God will require careful elucidation and avoidance of misinterpretation. For the idea of emptiness is vulnerable as an image; it suggests deficiency, vacancy, or an absence. And yet in tandem with the image of "deep caverns of feeling", where God can be mysteriously met, the notion of a *"vast emptiness"* within the soul waiting to receive the infinite *love* of God describes the radiant possibility of supernatural transformation in contemplation.

The need in deeper prayer for this emptying of the intellect, memory, and will for God by means of the theological virtues is also on display at the beginning of book 2 of *The Ascent of Mount Carmel*. There Saint John of the Cross teaches that the theological virtues of faith, hope, and charity perfect these faculties of the soul by producing "emptiness and darkness in them" (AMC 2.6.1). The reference to darkness is pertinent and deserves a brief comment, since this image of darkness plays so keenly into the thought of Saint John of the Cross on contemplation. Again, let us reiterate that the context of these comments is a teaching on the interior depths of relations with God in prayer. The intellect, memory, and will must be led into a "spiritual night" that becomes their "means to divine union" (AMC 2.6.1). The theological virtues of faith, hope, and charity, as they deepen their impact on a soul pursuing serious interior prayer, will each cause an emptiness and darkness in their respective faculties: "The intellect must be perfected in the darkness of faith, the memory in the emptiness of hope, and the will in the nakedness and absence of every affection" (AMC 2.6.1). The images of darkness, of emptiness, of nakedness and absence all refer to an "emptying" in these faculties caused by the presence of the theological virtues inhabiting them in grace. We will observe in time the great importance of this teaching for contemplation.

Clarifying his expressions further, Saint John of the Cross teaches that these theological virtues "void the faculties" (AMC 2.6.2). By this, he means that in silent prayer they take from the faculties their capacity for enjoying satisfaction and leave them barren and vacant in prayer. In each case, their natural inclination as a faculty is frustrated because of the presence of the theological virtue permeating the faculty. In other words, the faculty cannot arrive at a satisfaction in silent prayer that would ordinarily be available to it in other forms of activity. This is perhaps a surprising thought for us. These faculties, in effect, cannot find a stable or lasting satisfaction in God. The reason is that they do not arrive at God in a manner that the intellect, memory, or will can enjoy in any complete sense. Their natural capacity cannot assimilate the gift that God gives of himself. On the other hand, we *can* choose to seek satisfactions in prayer to which these faculties are inclined—whether in thoughts or feelings. Indeed, most people would think that satisfactions in prayer must necessarily be a sign of being united more closely to God. But in Saint John of the Cross' teaching, this assumption is erroneous. These satisfactions in prayer do not in themselves unite us to God. And why not?

Saint John of the Cross invites us to ponder more deeply the nature of a personal engagement with God in prayer.

God is a mystery of infinite love, and nothing experienced as a satisfaction in prayer by our intellect, memory, or will is in itself a reliable means that we can say unites us to him in his truth as infinite love. Rather, the theological virtues of faith, hope, and love are themselves the means by which the faculties of the soul are directly joined to God. This union takes place accompanied by an experiential emptying of the faculties. Satisfactions that may be experienced in prayer are only secondary aspects. The more important effect of deeper prayer is an emptying purification of the faculties. This teaching arises from the truth of God's infinite transcendence; a consequence of which is the incapacity of knowledge, feeling, or any experience to take hold of God. In his actual truth, God remains always beyond the grasp of any human experience. This truth sheds light on the image of the faculties as "caverns" of the soul. The faculties as caverns of endless depth have always, as it were, greater extension within them in which God still remains concealed in his love. The experience of emptiness and barrenness in the faculties coincides with the entry into greater depths of God's hidden presence within the "caverns" of the faculties. A passage from Saint John of the Cross' treatment on faith in this section of *The Ascent* is illustrative of this teaching and can perhaps help a bit at this point:

> It is told of our Father Elijah that on the mount he covered his face (blinded his intellect) in the presence of God [1 Kgs. 19:11−13]. He did this because, in his lowliness, he did not dare to gaze on something so lofty, and he clearly realized that anything he might behold or understand particularly would be far distant from God and most unlike him. In this mortal life no supernatural knowledge or apprehension can serve as a proximate means for high union with God through love. Everything the intellect can

understand, the will enjoy, and the imagination picture is
most unlike and disproportioned to God. (AMC 2.8.4–5)

The teaching can sound subtle and daunting, and perhaps
not very comprehensible at this point. Nonetheless, a clear
contrast is being presented between what can be a particular satisfaction sought by our intellect, memory, or will
in prayer and the greater spiritual possibility of a union of
these faculties with the hidden presence of God himself. As
recently stated but worth repeating, God in his infinite being is always beyond the grasp or enjoyment of the human
capacity of these faculties. Only in a manner that exceeds
their natural capacity do they encounter God in his truth.
But this will mean an encounter in a mysterious manner
beyond the ordinary operation of the faculty. Such an encounter with God always means an overwhelming excess
of contact with God that cannot be assimilated by the faculties in their usual mode of understanding or enjoyment.
Saint John of the Cross states emphatically: "The soul is
not united with God in this life through understanding, or
through enjoyment, or through imagination, or through any
other sense; but only faith, hope, and charity (according to
the intellect, memory, and will) can unite the soul with God
in this life" (AMC 2.6.1).

One thing, in other words, is the satisfaction in an hour
of prayer that can be enjoyed by the intellect, memory, or
will. This can come, for instance, to the intellect in prayer
through an act of understanding a scriptural passage with
some new insight. Quite another thing is for the intellect
itself to arrive by means of supernatural faith at union with
God. This union does not come through an elevation of
understanding or any other natural act exercised by the intellect. It occurs because faith in its naked purity unites the

intellect to God, as we will see. The same pattern holds for the other two faculties and their respective theological virtues. A crucial implication is present in this teaching: the necessity, for the sake of purification, that the intellect, memory, and will do not obstruct the effects of faith, hope, and charity. And how would that happen? It can happen by seeking in prayer some satisfaction of insight or image or feeling toward which the intellect, memory, or will are naturally inclined, thus resisting the emptying of the faculty. An effort of emptying the intellect, memory, and will of natural satisfactions is required in the interior life of deeper prayer, so that these faculties respond to the graces of the theological virtues operating within them. Saint John of the Cross summarizes the necessity of this purification in prayer in this manner: "Faith causes darkness and a void of understanding in the intellect, hope begets an emptiness of possessions in the memory, and charity produces the nakedness and emptiness of affection and joy in all that is not God. . . . We must lead the faculties of the soul, then, to these three virtues and inform each faculty with one of them by stripping and darkening it of everything that is not conformable to these virtues" (AMC 2.6.2, 6).

Let us remember what was presented in the previous chapter by Saint John of the Cross regarding the hidden presence of God in the soul. This teaching casts a light on the reason for the necessity of a radical purification of these faculties. In a fundamental way, we remain ignorant of the limitless capacity of our soul for union with the infinite love of a hidden God if we resist the need for the interior purification of the soul in prayer. And what kind of purification is necessary? This is not a proposal of ascetical practices addressing bodily desires. The purification involves, instead, the hard *interior* task within prayer itself of emptying ourselves of our ingrained habits to strive for satisfactions other than in God himself. The God we seek is a God who hides in concealment within the innermost being of the soul. He is a God who must be sought as *ever* hidden. And we ourselves, as we have seen, must hide from ourselves in seeking only for him. On the other hand, prayer does offer the possibility of seeking personal satisfactions pleasing to our own spirit, satisfactions that are less than God and that sometimes can turn us back on ourselves. We can choose to occupy ourselves in the pursuit of perceptions, insights, or feelings sought for themselves rather than as stepping-stones leading to God himself. We may claim that we are seeking the experience only of God, but actually we are often seeking our own satisfaction in these spiritual experiences.

In various places, Saint John of the Cross identifies this tendency of a self-interested motive in prayer as a target of reproach. In fact, it is rather common to direct desires in prayer toward an enjoyment sought for ourselves. The desire for a tangible sense of a felt closeness to God is a typical example. The feeling of love in prayer—whether rooted in emotion or as an experience more deeply resonating in one's spirit—can be easily identified as a direct experience of God's presence. This satisfaction in feeling conveys a sense of fulfillment, an arrival of sorts, in which the soul can momentarily find its repose. There seems to be no need to look farther now that we have "found" love. Our desire is satiated, at least for the moment, in a satisfying experience. In the view of Saint John of the Cross, this tendency poses an impediment to contemplation and to a deeper union with God. Unwittingly, we settle for enjoying a satisfaction vastly inferior to the pursuit of God himself. An illusion takes place in identifying the satisfaction enjoyed in some tangible manner with the soul taking possession of God to some degree. The contrast in prayer is enormous when we make every effort not to halt at a sense of satisfaction and, instead, maintain a pure pursuit of God, not stopping at the satisfactions that might be enjoyed by the faculties. In short, the immense capacity of these faculties for a reception of the infinite is discovered only by keeping to the forefront of our spiritual awareness "*the vast emptiness of their deep capacity*" (LF 3.18; emphasis added). Indeed, it is an amazing possibility we are being offered, as we hear in these words from *The Living Flame of Love*:

> The capacity of these caverns [intellect, memory, and will] is deep because the object of this capacity, namely God, is profound and infinite. Thus in a certain fashion their capacity is infinite, their thirst is infinite, their hunger is also deep and infinite, and their languishing and suffering are infinite death. Although the suffering is not as intense as is the suffering of the next life, yet the soul is a living image of that infinite privation, since it is in a certain way disposed to receive its plenitude. This suffering, however, is of another quality because it lies within the recesses of the will's love; and love is not what alleviates the pain, since the greater the love, so much more impatient are such persons for the possession of God, for whom they hope at times with intense longing. (LF 3.22)

For Saint John of the Cross, the challenge of interior prayer is exposed to a large extent in this passage. The infinitude of divine love demands a release by these faculties from all grasping at experiences of God. Parallel patterns of purification take place in the intellect, memory, and will as they allow themselves to be emptied for God alone. Faith unites us to God only more deeply when we are experiencing a blindness of the intellect; hope unites us to God only in voiding any support of recollected memories; charity unites us to God only by an adherence in pure desire to God himself. Satisfactions as experiences in prayer tend by contrast to deflect us from desiring God purely in himself. This teaching is not, of course, advocating a kind of nihilistic approach to prayer. For Saint John of the Cross, it is never an experience of satisfaction or enjoyment in itself that is so problematic in prayer. The problem he is addressing arises when the faculties of intellect, memory, and will occupy themselves in *pursuing* experiences of enjoyment in prayer —even the experience of love, when it is sought for its own satisfaction. Let us remember again that all these comments assume a serious committed life of silent interior prayer. When the purpose of such prayer is for something other than God himself, the faculties of intellect, memory, and will forfeit their innate capacity for being filled by the infinite love of God. The spiritual demands upon a soul are admittedly great, but the reward is also great. The readiness to be content with nothing but God himself can transform prayer into an endless quest of longing for God himself. And this should be our goal in prayer, an ultimate love for the Beloved. Nothing else can surpass a pure desire for God alone. As Saint John of the Cross writes in a selection from *The Sayings of Light and Love*: "Souls will be unable to reach perfection who do not strive to be content with having nothing, in such fashion that their natural and spiritual desire is satisfied with emptiness; for this is necessary in order to reach the highest tranquility and peace of spirit. Hence the love of God in the pure and simple soul is almost continually in act" (SLL 54).

We encounter the importance of seeking a contentment with nothing other than God in many places in Saint John of the Cross' writings. Shortly after introducing the image of the faculties as "deep caverns of feeling" in *The Living*

Flame of Love, for instance, he affirms that a primary impediment to contemplation occurs when attachments cling to us and are repeatedly sought instead of our seeking God himself. These attachments are always contrary to accepting a contentment with having nothing: "Any little thing that adheres to them in this life is sufficient to so burden and bewitch them that they do not perceive the harm or note the lack of their immense goods, or know their own capacity" (LF 3.18). The words are a strong admonition. It takes very little to upset and block the proper dynamism of a holy pursuit of God in or out of the life of prayer. We can end up living unaware of the harm inflicted by very common tendencies that, in effect, keep us from being content with having nothing, that is, nothing but God. We have a capacity for greatness, for being filled with the love of God in our prayer. Yet we may live our hours of prayer like restless marauders in a search for prizes or enjoyments worth very little, seeking for delights that satisfy us only in negligible and fleeting ways. Without an awakening by which God becomes a passionate pursuit engaging our life's entire intensity, our soul can descend easily to a dull caricature of its actual potency. As Saint John of the Cross writes:

> It is an amazing thing that the least of these goods is enough so to encumber these faculties, capable of infinite goods, that they cannot receive these infinite goods until they are completely empty, as we shall see. Yet when these caverns are empty and pure, the thirst, hunger, and yearning of the spiritual feeling is intolerable. Since these caverns have deep stomachs, they suffer profoundly; for the food they lack, which as I say is God, is also profound. (LF 3.18)

The goal of serious interior prayer in silence, as such, is to enter more deeply into a great hunger and thirst for the hidden God of vast love. All the preliminary conditions that can provoke this hunger, inside and outside prayer, must be observed as strict spiritual laws. Flouting them always hinders our movement forward in prayer and in our love for God. The purification of these faculties, if we want deeper relations with God, is without option. It is resisted at the cost of halting spiritual progress. This purification can take place only by depriving the faculties of their natural desire for satisfaction until ultimately, after a long perseverance in self-emptying and with the help of grace, one desire alone inflames our soul's hunger and thirst. We should not miss the stress in this teaching on losing ourselves for love of God. For Saint John of the Cross, the effort of self-renunciation is never exclusively directed toward the things outside us, but it extends its impact into the depths of the soul. A heart empty of desire except for God himself may come to know eventually a profound fulfillment of its deepest desire: "Deny your desires and you will find what your heart longs for", writes Saint John of the Cross in an aphorism. "For how do you know if any desire of yours is according to God?" (SLL 15).

The pure "yes" of a soul to God alone, like the *fiat* of the Virgin Mary at the Annunciation, is really what opens the floodgates to contemplative graces. The purity of that "yes" reflects a desire not to stop in love until we arrive at God himself. But this consent to God must necessarily include a great spirit of abnegation toward ourselves and all secondary desires. The consent to belong entirely to God becomes a refusal toward everything that would pull us back into self and our own self-interest. To be clear, Saint John of the Cross is urging a far-reaching willingness to become in love all that God desires and to desire ultimately only him. The emptying of the faculties in prayer must be accompanied

by a surrender of our will and all our desire to God's will.
The firm choice to seek only God entails many refusals to
seek satisfactions in what is not God. This exclusiveness in
our love for God does not mean, of course, that we love no
other persons in this life; rather, that all love flows from a
deeper undercurrent of an intense love for God. God, from
his end, so to speak, responds to intense love for himself
and fills the soul with his own presence. He fills what he
finds, by means of our love, empty for himself. All this takes
place under the dynamic thrust of a pure, unstinting "yes"
to God, which is the great word of love in a soul. As Saint
John of the Cross writes in *The Living Flame of Love*:

> When the soul has reached such purity in itself and its fac-
> ulties that the will is very pure and purged of other alien
> satisfactions and appetites . . . and has rendered its "yes"
> to God concerning all of this, since now God's will and
> the soul's are one through their own free consent, then the
> soul has attained possession of God insofar as this is pos-
> sible by way of the will and grace. And this means that in
> the "yes" of the soul, God has given the true and com-
> plete "yes" of his grace. (LF 3.24)

Much of the treatment of contemplative purification in the
writings of Saint John of the Cross is directed toward the
intellect's response in faith to a purification by an experiential darkness and to the will's purification in charity by
the absence of desire for anything but for God and his will.
These matters will be taken up in time. It can be instructive
as part of this chapter, however, to observe for a moment,
in an illustrative manner, how the purification of memory
by the theological virtue of hope occurs and the proper

response of the memory to this action of grace. The pattern for one faculty is the pattern for all three. The purification of all three faculties is for the union in love of the soul with God. The emptying of the faculties of their natural operations and capacities, and of their natural apprehensions and satisfactions, is likewise a necessity for the sake of contemplation. These two goals, in the pages of Saint John of the Cross, go hand in hand. As he writes, "we are imparting instructions here for advancing in contemplation to union with God" (AMC 3.2.2). In the case of each faculty, a kind of disengagement from the ordinary operation of the faculty must take place to allow the action of God to move it in a supernatural manner during prayer: "All these sensory means and exercises of the faculties must consequently be left behind and in silence so that God himself may effect divine union in the soul" (AMC 3.2.2). The soul in its prayer cannot remain simply passive in this work of grace; it has to cooperate in the self-emptying of the faculty. Unfortunately, it is precisely the activity of the faculties in deeper prayer, when exercised apart from God's grace, that can be a primary obstacle to the reception of contemplative graces. On the other hand, there is a "method" of receptivity that must be voluntarily practiced, as Saint John of the Cross writes: "One has to follow this method of disencumbering, emptying, and depriving the faculties of their natural authority and operations to make room for the inflow and illumination of the supernatural. Those who do not turn their eyes from their natural capacity will not attain to so lofty a communication; rather they will hinder it" (AMC 3.2.2).

In the case of the memory, then, in which the theological virtue of hope resides in the schema of Saint John of the Cross, the great need for union with God and for contemplation is a dispossession of all clear knowledge in prayer. Such knowledge, by its very clarity, would only be a barrier to an encounter with the truth of God's incomprehensibility. If the faculty of memory is, like the other faculties, a "cavern" of limitless depth, the pathway to that inner depth is a passage in prayer through a dark emptiness of knowledge. "If it is true—as indeed it is—that the soul must journey by knowing God through what he is not rather than through what he is, it must journey, insofar as possible, by way of the denial and rejection of natural and supernatural apprehensions" (AMC 3.2.3). This teaching coincides with the treatment of faith and the intellect. The intellect, too, in faith, must accept a dark path of obscurity in prayer, a dispossession of both natural and supernatural knowledge. This teaching, to be clear, pertains to the inner life of prayer. It is in no way a description of a general condition of incapacitation in the faculty.

We might especially note in this last quotation the reference to *supernatural* knowledge, which may seem odd to us. Yet this knowledge, too, is included in the need for dispossession in prayer. The idea, of course, is not to suggest a rejection or loss of the knowledge of faith. It is rather, once again, to insist on the realization that God's infinitude extends beyond any particular knowledge of God that might be enjoyed in prayer. God by his nature is incomprehensible for us. These faculties of the soul can approach God only by accepting an incapacity of the faculty's operation to embrace a fuller knowledge of God. For the memory, this will mean the choice of not turning to distinct remembrances of any kind in prayer. "We must draw it away from its natural props and boundaries and raise it above itself (above all distinct knowledge and apprehensible possession) to supreme hope for the incomprehensible God" (AMC 3.2.3). The requirement is to forgo thoughts culled from our memory that might seem to elevate the soul to some perception of God, but which actually compete with the truth of God as One who is beyond any particular thought. The memory in deeper prayer must leave thoughts aside because they do not aid, but rather obstruct, the reception of contemplative graces. As Saint John of the Cross writes in regard to the exercise of a time of silent prayer:

> There is no way to union with God without annihilating the memory as to all forms [i.e., items of knowledge]. This union cannot be wrought without a complete separation of the memory from all forms that are not God. As we mentioned in the night of the intellect, God cannot be encompassed by any form or distinct knowledge. . . . Since the memory cannot at the same time be united with God and with forms and distinct knowledge, and since God has no form or image comprehensible to the memory, the memory is without form and without figure when united with God. Its imagination being lost in great forgetfulness without the remembrance of anything, it is absorbed in a supreme good. (AMC 3.2.4)

An important understanding about deeper interior prayer is being conveyed here. Even though contemplation always has an element of passive receptivity to grace, as will be examined later more fully, it is nonetheless necessary that the faculties of the soul exercise a suitable effort of their own in denying and rejecting their inclination to seek easier satisfactions in prayer. These faculties play a key role by their own choice in accepting the purgative darkness that descends upon the faculty, particularly in a deeper prayer of contemplation. A spirit of surrender to effects that may be hard to manage, and difficult to understand at first as a benefit, is necessary for the contemplative path to God. It is a misconception to think that contemplation is entirely under the action of God and that the soul simply soaks itself contentedly in the reception of grace. Rather, a need, at least initially, for certain interior exercises of spiritual mortification will arise. Without watching ourselves self-consciously, our faculties of intellect and memory must nonetheless be aware not to embrace thoughts about God or to seek reflections that would appeal as an immediate satisfaction in prayer. God in his infinite reality of love is always beyond such reflections. "It is extremely easy", admonishes Saint John of the Cross, "to judge the being and height of God less worthily and sublimely than befits his incomprehensibility" (AMC 3.12.1). With specific regard to the memory, the necessary approach in deeper prayer will be to deny the inclination to recall all that could be of provocative interest to the mind. A refusal in prayer to go in search of insightful or stimulating thoughts is the hard demand being proposed. The stress is strong in the following passage on this need to temper and tame any inclination to seek food for thought and reflection. It would seem almost unnatural and contrary to good spiritual sense. Yet Saint John of the Cross is clear enough: "Through the spiritual person's own efforts, the memory must be brought into this night and purgation. . . . The memory, as though it were nonexistent, should be left free and disencumbered and unattached to any earthly or heavenly consideration. It should be freely left in oblivion, as though it were a hindrance, since everything natural is an obstacle rather than a help to anyone who would desire to use it in the supernatural" (AMC 3.2.14).

What we are encountering again in this teaching are fundamental tenets of apophatic theology, but in the context of the prayer of contemplation. The God we seek in prayer is a personal Being of infinite Love, a Trinity of Persons who

can be known and loved, but never known or loved adequately and never taken hold of in possession. Our knowledge in prayer, however sublime, or even mystical, always
falls exceedingly short of arriving at the reality of Almighty
God. The apophatic stress on the inadequacy of our *knowledge* in confronting the infinitude of God's being is paral-
leled by the contemplative accent on the dark insufficiency
of our *experience* of God in prayer. We can encounter God
in the deeper realms of prayer only in a manner that draws
us ever more into the abyss of his mystery. As Saint John of
the Cross writes in this section on the memory: "Souls must
go to God by not comprehending rather than by comprehending, and they must exchange the mutable and comprehensible for the Immutable and Incomprehensible" (AMC
3.5.3).

Indeed, Saint John of the Cross, throughout his writings,
repeats this apophatic principle that what is comprehensible about God must be viewed as an inferior knowledge to
what is incomprehensible. The latter is the truer knowledge
of God, and, equally so, it is the more genuine experience
of God in contemplative prayer. Advancement in prayer signifies, on the one hand, a more personal encounter with the
presence of God. But it signifies as well a more profound
encounter with his incomprehensibility as God. We do not
bring God down, as it were, to the limitations of our capacity. But it is also true that God does not diminish himself or
renounce his own infinite magnitude in drawing closer to
the soul that he loves much. He remains the God of infinite
love and always beyond our grasp or experience. This truth
governs the constant teaching of Saint John of the Cross.
The experiential poverty of the soul in prayer before the
transcendent majesty of God's love is never overcome. This
truth applicable to contemplation must be accompanied by
a deliberate rejection of lesser pursuits in the time of prayer.

Once again, from the section on the memory, we hear this emphasis: "The highest recollection . . . consists in concentrating all the faculties on the incomprehensible Good and withdrawing them from all apprehensible things, for these apprehensible things are not a good that is beyond comprehension" (AMC 3.4.2).

Dispossession of the faculties becomes as such a key condition for assimilating the apophatic truth of God's incomprehensibility that must accompany the contemplative encounter with God. These faculties must, indeed, become *empty caverns* for God to fill them with his presence of immense love. If this happens, it does not mean special experiences of God. Quite the contrary, for contemplation is experientially apophatic. God is known and experienced and loved as One who is unknown in the fullness of his infinite being and love. This is the great interpretative insight that Saint John of the Cross continually reaffirms. The dispossession he urges for the faculties in prayer is, as it implies, an experiential emptiness of the faculty in the time of prayer. Not as though emptiness should be cultivated as an end in itself; rather, it should be cultivated with the apophatic understanding that letting go of a clear knowledge of God releases an obstacle and opens the way to the graced awareness that God in his incomprehensible reality extends beyond all knowledge even as he is near to the soul in the present hour. This kind of dispossession requires, to some extent, a deliberate effort of purgation because it involves a condition contrary to the natural operation and inclination of the faculty. As Saint John of the Cross teaches: "It is better to learn to silence and quiet the faculties so that God may speak. For in this state, . . . the natural operations must fade from sight. This is realized when the soul arrives at solitude in these faculties, and God speaks to its heart" (AMC 3.3.4).

The solitude just mentioned is, indeed, another useful

image for the emptying and dispossession of the faculties. The emptiness of being, as it were, in a solitary state is necessary for the intellect, memory, and will in order that they become capable of absorbing supernatural graces that convey an experiential encounter with God in contemplative prayer. Emptiness within the faculty means to be alone in the faculty without any other "companion" or object to occupy it. This emptiness is precisely the condition for the immediacy of an apophatic contemplative encounter with God: "The soul must empty itself of all that is not God in order to go to God" (AMC 3.7.2). In another sense, the emptiness simply means non-activity in the natural operation that the faculty ordinarily pursues. Non-activity is wrongly interpreted, however, if it is thought to be a mere passivity. There is always the implication that the exercise of the faculty is sometimes required to resist interference from its natural inclination to seek the comfort of other possible satisfactions. Instead, it must choose to surrender itself to an interior state of poverty and dispossession. The insistence in this teaching of an engagement of the faculty is illustrated in the following objection and response that Saint John of the Cross makes in regard to the memory's necessary emptiness in the time of prayer.

> If you still insist, claiming that a person will obtain no benefits if the memory does not consider and reflect about God, and that many distractions and weaknesses will gradually find entrance, I answer that this is impossible. If the memory is recollected [silent and empty] as to both heavenly and earthly things, there is no entry for evils, distractions, fancies, or vices—all of which enter through the wandering of the memory. Distractions would result if, on closing the door to reflections and discursive meditation, we opened it to thoughts about earthly matters. But in our

case we close the memory to all things—from which distractions and evils arise—by rendering it silent and mute, and listening to God in silence with the hearing of the spirit, saying with the prophet: *Speak Lord, for your servant is listening* [1 Sam. 3:10]. (AMC 3.3.5)

Lastly, in concluding this chapter, it can be asked how hope plays a role in this contemplative advancement of the soul. The theological virtue of hope enters into the gap of emptiness that ensues with the memory undergoing a dispossession of things that might occupy its activity and focus. Hope is the purifying virtue permeating the memory in order to empty it for the reception of God. This teaching offers a uniquely contemplative interpretation of hope as a virtue of the memory. For Saint Thomas Aquinas, as we mentioned, hope is located in the will. For both saints, hope as a virtue, and as a natural inclination, is directed toward what has still not been reached, not yet attained, and waits still in the future to be possessed. It implies always a longing for something. We can gain insight into what Saint John of the Cross is doing by placing hope in the memory if we consider what happens to the memory when a person is "in love". The memory is likely then to recall the beloved person often to mind, never forgetting for any prolonged length of time the presence of the beloved in this world. A natural return to the thought of this loved person takes place. This does not entail thinking of memories from the past but simply involves the repeated calling back of one's attention to that loved person, which happens easily and without an effort of thought. All love tends to have this effect on the attention. We find ourselves returning in thought to whatever or whomever is loved. This fixation on God as the Beloved who is still beyond our reach becomes an immediate effect on the memory due to hope in the faculty. As Saint John of the Cross writes, it has a profound effect:

> The following must be kept in mind: Our aim is union with God in the memory through hope; the object of hope is something unpossessed; the less other objects are possessed, the more capacity and ability there is to hope for this one object, and consequently the more hope; the greater the possessions, the less capacity and ability for hoping, and consequently so much less of hope; accordingly, in the measure that individuals dispossess their memory of forms and objects, which are not God, they will fix it on God and preserve it empty, so as to hope for the fullness of their memory from him. (AMC 3.15.1)

Again, we hear the "emptying" or purging effect of the theological virtue upon the human faculty. When the memory is empty of other "things" that could draw and preoccupy it, supernatural hope unites the faculty more intensely over time to God himself. Yet even with this progressive advancement, God remains an unattained love, an unreachable presence, and is known as such. The graced impact of hope is to place the memory in a kind of quiet fixation or "holy obsession" with God in the silent time of prayer, without allowing for an ultimate union. Contemplative graces, mediated for the memory through the virtue of hope, have this deepening effect of transfixing the inner desire of the soul for a Beloved who is not yet attained, not possessed, not encountered sufficiently. This amounts to another aspect of apophatic *experience* in prayer, similar to the incomprehension that the intellect undergoes in contemplation. In this case, hope purges the memory by what can seem an extreme sense of God's unattainability. The impoverishment that takes place due to hope purifies the faculty of memory for the reception of God alone. When hope is permeating the memory, nothing but the desire to be united one day to God alone can take a possessive grip on it. Such is the nature of a deep love for God. The effect is always that thoughts, desires, and the memory are continually returning to him.

3

CONTEMPLATIVE FAITH: CERTITUDE IN DARKNESS

We turn now to the initial chapters in book 2 of *The Ascent of Mount Carmel*, which contain a rich, important treatise on the theological virtue of faith. It will be helpful to explore this section immediately after the previous chapter on the theological virtues and their respective faculties, and after our examination of the memory and the virtue of hope. Incidentally, Karol Wojtyła, the future Pope Saint John Paul II, in writing his doctoral dissertation as a young priest in the late 1940s under the direction of Father Reginald Garrigou-Lagrange, O.P., at the Angelicum in Rome, concentrated most of the pages of his dissertation, entitled *Faith according to Saint John of the Cross*, on this relatively short section in *The Ascent* that we are about to examine. The teaching of Saint John of the Cross on faith in these chapters is directed primarily toward the role of faith in contemplation, not just to the knowledge of God that faith provides to every Christian believer.

The effect that deeper faith has on the intellect, when the soul is receiving contemplative graces, is to plunge the intellect into a purifying experience of interior darkness during the time of prayer. This experience is almost always contrary to a soul's expectation and a surprising paradox. With the soul's life of faith advancing, we would likely anticipate a sharper, clearer vision toward the Catholic truths we

know in faith. A more penetrating understanding of revealed
truths should ensue, we think, a greater luminosity in our
awareness of divine truths. Instead, according to Saint John
of the Cross, the opposite effect occurs during the prayer
of contemplation. A darkness and obscurity pervade the intellect in prayer itself, due to a more intense faith. This is
not a question of confusion or doubt in thought, but rather
a reluctance to think at all while in the silence of prayer.
The preference of the mind in the prayer of contemplation
becomes a desire to remain silent, not seeking thoughts, but
simply to turn an attentive gaze to the presence of God. Recognizing this phenomenon becomes a significant element in
responding properly to the graces of contemplation, as we
will see in due time. Indeed, the teaching on faith is an absolute necessity for understanding the effects of contemplative graces in prayer. For the moment, the nature of faith's
deeper impact on the intellect is our subject.

It is worthwhile to ponder this teaching carefully, since
it affects the soul so strongly in the life of silent prayer and
contemplation. With the advancement of faith and the onset of contemplative graces, the intellect, as mentioned, does
not experience greater clarity of insight but, rather, a dark
blinding of its ordinary capacities during prayer. The blindness is not merely a temporary condition, an obstacle that
passes after a time or one that can be overcome by adopting remedies. It cannot be evaded or successfully resisted;
on the other hand, it can be easily misconceived. It is not
a sign of a diminution in faith that one seems to "see" less
in faith than previously during the time of prayer. Faith has
not diminished because thoughts seem to die away in prayer
and a desire for a silence of the mind attracts the soul more
strongly. Then what is happening?

The theological virtue of faith places our intellect in an

immediate proximity with the presence of God as we pray in silence. This is even more deeply true when faith advances and contemplative graces begin to show effects. The greater closeness with God, however, does not remove a barrier of mystery from our relations with God. On the contrary, it thrusts our soul more vigorously in the direction of his infinite mystery. We meet here again the apophatic consequence of advancement in relations with God. The result of deeper faith is not to *see* better, but to *know* more certainly. In a very striking sentence, Saint John of the Cross writes: "Though faith brings certitude to the intellect, it does not produce clarity, but only darkness" (AMC 2.6.2). A more intense certitude that revealed Christian truth is absolute truth becomes the primary consequence of increased faith. But this certitude is not synonymous with clear vision. The soul experiences a blind but certain knowledge that it is embracing truth in its faith, yet with no increase of insightful understanding during the time of prayer. The certitude, however, is not simply our conviction in regard to doctrinal truth. It is experienced especially as a certitude of the personal presence of God during prayer, but without any clear thought. This experience of a blind certitude, as we shall see, is an essential aspect of the path of pure, naked faith that must be the road walked in the contemplative life of prayer. A turn to another stanza in the poetry of Saint John of the Cross can be useful, this time from the second stanza of his short poem "The Dark Night":

> In darkness, and secure,
> by the secret ladder, disguised,
> —ah, the sheer grace!—
> in darkness and concealment,
> my house being now all stilled.

Saint John of the Cross initiates his discussion on faith in book 2 of *The Ascent* with this stanza. It is important always to keep in mind the context for his treatment of faith in this section. His purpose is to expose the influence of deeper faith on the intellect when the grace of contemplation is present. Wasting no time, he writes immediately of the necessity of "leaning on *pure faith alone*" (AMC 2.1.1; emphasis added). An exercise of pure faith is an essential requirement for contemplation, but the phrase needs some explication. A kind of interior asceticism of the spirit is necessary if the intellect is to respond properly to the graced purification that it undergoes in prayer. The cause of the purification is the influence of infused faith on the intellect when the grace of contemplation is being given. Unlike the asceticism of bodily self-denial, a more subtle abnegation must take place. The asceticism in this case is not directed at denying the senses some opportunity for indulgent gratification. Rather than such a concrete goal, the need now is for the intellect to exercise a kind of mental austerity in adjusting itself to a changed interior ambiance in prayer itself. In a manner beyond the control of the intellect, the effect of deeper faith upon prayer itself when the grace of contemplation ensues is to enclose the intellect in an experience of obscurity and emptiness. A purification is taking place, which always entails a stripping down or emptying of a faculty or appetite. In one sense, every purification must be received passively from grace; in another sense, it requires a cooperation on our part.

In this case, under the influence of deeper faith, the cooperation involves a mortification by the intellect: an emptying of the desire for spiritual gratifications that can be enjoyed by the intellect in the life of prayer. These can be sought in a way that becomes an impediment to the pure pursuit of God for himself alone. A "complete pacification of the spiritual house" (AMC 2.1.2) is required that will "quiet down" the impulse to pursue experiences of an intellectual or imaginative satisfaction in prayer. This "ascetical" task for the intellect in the interior life of prayer entails, in a telling phrase, "the negation through pure faith of all the spiritual faculties and gratifications and appetites" (AMC 2.1.2). What this "*pure* faith" will mean as a virtue of the intellect in contemplation needs to be explained with some care. For the intellect must cooperate in its own purification precisely through this exercise of pure faith. Taking us farther along in explanation, and referring to the stanza of his poem, Saint John of the Cross comments: "The soul, consequently, affirms that it departed 'in darkness, and secure.' For anyone fortunate enough to possess the ability to journey in the obscurity of faith, as do the blind with their guide, and depart from all natural phantasms [images] and intellectual reasonings, walks securely. . . . For the less a soul works with its own abilities, the more securely it proceeds, because its progress in faith is greater" (AMC 2.1.2, 3).

This last sentence, in particular, captures the dilemma at hand. The intellect by natural inclination—like all the faculties and appetites—wants to work in pursuit of a satisfying experience for itself. And what might that be in prayer? The acquisition of insightful thoughts about God and his relation to one's own life, new perceptions about scriptural passages, or fresh intuitive flashes of spiritual awareness— all these gratifying experiences can be sought in prayer. Obviously, they are not in themselves wrongful to experience. But the discussion here concerns the experience of the soul in prayer when it is receiving the grace of contemplation. And in that context, a possessive impulse to search for these kinds of satisfaction in prayer does harm to a contemplative invitation in grace. Why so? These experiences of satisfaction may be fine to pursue at an earlier time in a spiritual life. But the pursuit of them now is contrary to the impact of supernatural faith on the intellect when the grace of contemplation is affecting the silence of prayer. A purification of the intellect by means of spiritual darkness is a distinctive feature of contemplation. A sense of obscurity toward what is known in faith begins to enclose the intellect in a cloud of incomprehension. It is a purification by grace of the intellect's natural operation, which ordinarily seeks the satisfaction of taking hold of knowledge that it can savor and enjoy. Now this is no longer possible, due to the effect of contemplative graces.

What can be the reason for this experience in prayer? Saint John of the Cross affirms that supernatural faith, inasmuch as it places us in an immediate contact with God, affects the intellect in a strangely painful way with the onset of contemplative graces. The truths of revelation that the intellect embraces in faith now seem to surpass comprehension in a manner unlike any previous experience in prayer. A deeper understanding of theological faith can explain why this occurs. It is inadequate to conceive of our faith as simply an assent by our mind to truths that are then held securely with personal conviction. This is not at all the full picture. On a very personal level, in our relations with God himself, faith is a kind of real conduit into the actual mystery of God. As a theological virtue, it unites the intellect quite directly and immediately to the mystery of God. The effect of this union, depending on a soul's closeness to God, is to stretch the intellect beyond what it can assimilate in its natural capacity. The result in the time of interior prayer is a painful experience of obscurity within the intellect toward the God of ultimate mystery known personally in faith. This is not an experience of dark doubts about God. Rather, it is as though a light has begun to shine too brightly, preventing our eyes from seeing what is there in front of us. The closer we approach the light of God, the more his presence blinds us. The ordinary act of comprehension in regard to natural objects of knowledge does not function in this way. But when the knowledge is of God himself in his immediate personal presence to the soul, the consequence is vastly different. The following words of Saint John of the Cross may require some pondering. They convey the issue at stake and provide a theological background to this teaching:

> Faith, the theologians say, is a certain and obscure habit of soul. It is an obscure habit because it brings us to believe divinely revealed truths that transcend every natural light and infinitely exceed all human understanding. As a result the excessive light of faith bestowed on a soul is darkness for it; a brighter light will eclipse and suppress a dimmer one. The sun so obscures all other lights that they do not seem to be lights at all when it is shining, and instead of affording vision to the eyes, it overwhelms, blinds, and deprives them of vision since its light is excessive and unproportioned to the visual faculty. Similarly the light of faith in its abundance suppresses and overwhelms that of the intellect. For the intellect, by its own power, extends only to natural knowledge, though it has the potency to be raised to a supernatural act whenever our Lord wishes. (AMC 2.3.1)

This teaching of Saint John of the Cross on faith and the intellect can easily be misunderstood. Some will be tempted to perceive a damaging effect being described, inasmuch as the description seems to portray a reduction in the intellect's ability to function properly as a consequence of deeper faith. But, again, it must be remembered that the context of the discussion is an explanation of the effects of the grace of contemplation on the intellect. A blinding of the intellect to some extent is an experiential element in such prayer. The blinding is a reduced capacity for fruitful thought or reflection. A silencing of the mind, not by a deliberate choice or by the adoption of a prayer method, but as a result of faith's spiritual impact on the intellect, becomes unavoidable in such prayer. It is admittedly a difficult teaching to embrace, because it strongly contradicts early expectations in a life of prayer. The knowledge of God that faith grants in contemplation does not become a stimulant to more expansive thoughts about God. It does not enliven the energies of the mind for the sake of intellectual pondering, at least in the time of prayer itself. What it does instead, most fruitfully, is to intensify the *certitude* of God's *presence* while one prays.

In other words, two quite different effects take place in the intellect due to the advancement of faith as a supernatural virtue. An intense certitude of his mysterious presence can be accompanied at the same time by an inescapable sense of painful obscurity in knowing God. The metaphor of blindness in the face of an excessive light is thus fitting. Deeper faith embraces God more certainly and takes hold of revealed truth more securely, but it does so blindly. It *knows*, and yet it knows without the support of clear thought and vision. The paradox is strong, but more than a paradox is being presented. There is a need for the intellect to be blinded and to accept a blinding experience of darkness in its faith if prayer is going to take us more deeply into the *mystery* of God. The person who receives contemplative graces must cooperate with the effects of faith in the silent hours of prayer. This teaching on faith in the context of contemplation poses dual aspects: an objective effect by the very nature of faith and a personal response necessary for the soul in prayer: "Faith nullifies the light of the intellect; and if this light is not darkened, the knowledge of faith is lost. . . . Faith, manifestly, is a dark night for souls, but in this way it gives them light. The more darkness it brings on them, the more light it sheds. For by blinding, it illumines them" (AMC 2.3.4).

The tenor of such a description does require that a careful distinction be maintained between faith as belief in the revealed truths of Catholic doctrinal profession and faith in its experiential dimension within a particular soul. The objective reality of faith as a knowledge of God brings us to know transcendent truths beyond the grasp of our intellect. These are truths of revelation that we embrace in Christianity with firm, unwavering conviction. But the actual reality of these transcendent truths has immediate subjective repercussions for our relations with the God of mystery whom we know in prayer by means of faith. Even with great fervor of heart, we do not bring God down to our limited capacity of comprehension. Rather, we are lifted up to heights where, so to speak, it becomes harder to breathe and more difficult to see. The person who accepts this effect, and realizes that a different interior ambiance is now being experienced, opens the inner caverns of the soul wider to contemplative graces. It is incumbent upon a soul receiving contemplative graces that it should walk straight ahead into the path of darkness that begins to enclose it in the experiential dimension of prayer. In that sense, Saint John of the Cross does not simply declare that "faith is a dark night for the soul" (AMC 2.4.1) as a metaphor for the limitations of our knowledge of God. He is urging the soul in its prayer to undergo willingly, voluntarily, an entry into this subjective experience of darkness. This takes place by detaching ourselves from the satisfactions that may have formerly occupied prayer. As he writes of a soul in this deeper experience of prayer:

> They must also darken and blind themselves in that part of their nature that bears relation to God and spiritual things . . . the rational and higher part of their nature. . . . The soul must perfectly and voluntarily empty itself—I mean in its affection and will—of all the earthly and heavenly things it can grasp. It must do this insofar as it can. As for God, who will stop him from accomplishing his desires in the soul that is resigned, annihilated, and despoiled? (AMC 2.4.2)

Let us step back a moment and clarify any possible misconception. It is an axiom of Saint John of the Cross that a soul must suffer for the love of God in seeking God as the Beloved. What does this entail for the intellect in the silence of prayer? He does not suggest that silent prayer should take place in a vacuum of mental emptiness, or, surely, that we must be locked up emotionally in a cage, cut off from all affection, feeling, or desire. Neither mental starvation nor emotional barrenness are advisable states to cultivate in prayer. It is impossible not to encounter at times satisfaction in our love for God, which is a wonderful thing. Rather, what Saint John of the Cross identifies as a spiritual danger, when a purer effort of faith is not exercised in prayer, is the possessiveness that can take hold in our soul because of the pleasant experiences that prayer can bestow. From motives of self-interest, these experiences can be pursued as ends in themselves. A kind of rivalry between created things and the singular greatness of God occurs not just in the excessive pursuit of worldly ambitions or pleasures. It happens as well in prayer itself, namely, in the pursuit of consolations or special insights. Indeed, in prayer there can be almost a kind of mismatch in the competition between created things and God himself because the satisfactions received in prayer can be immediate and quite strong. Often these satisfactions in prayer are thought to contain the measure of our closeness to God, and so in many lives they are sought avidly.

All this is contrary to the acceptance of a blinding obscurity that a purer faith elicits. We forget or perhaps never realize the infinite capacity of the human faculties of intellect, memory, and will for receiving the hidden loving presence of a concealed God. The "vast emptiness of their deep capacity" (LF 3.18) is a good phrase to recall from the last chapter. If we can maintain the effort of a pure seeking of God alone, the hidden God who eludes the grasp of our possession, we move forward on the path to him alone as our Beloved. We plunge more deeply by the help of grace toward the mystery of God waiting for us within our soul. Much depends on a refinement of our desire so that God alone is sought in prayer. As Saint John of the Cross writes in *The Living Flame of Love*: "The more the soul desires God the more it possesses him, and the possession of God delights and satisfies it" (LF 3.23). But this is a possession of God precisely in his divine hiddenness. The infinite presence of love in God remains always a mystery of concealment for our intellect. An illustrative passage may be useful. The importance of an interior emptying of the intellect by means of faith is explicitly proposed in the following passage. Intensity of faith unleashes an experiential emptying of the intellect in prayer as the intellect encounters in prayer the actual reality of God. The reason for this spiritual consequence is also stated in the passage. The disproportion between an infinite God and the finite human soul must necessarily impact the intellect in prayer when a soul is drawing closer to the mystery of God. The intellect in prayer will always find itself dazzled into a blinding experience of darkness as it draws nearer to the light of God.

> We can gather from what has been said that to be prepared for this divine union the intellect must be cleansed and emptied of everything relating to sense, divested and liberated of everything clearly intelligible, inwardly pacified and silenced, and supported by faith alone, which is the only proximate and proportionate means to union with God. For the likeness between faith and God is so close that no other difference exists than that between believing in God and seeing him. Just as God is infinite, faith proposes him to us as infinite. Just as there are three Persons in one God, it presents him to us in this way. And just as God is darkness to our intellect, so faith dazzles and blinds us. Only by means of faith, in divine light exceeding all understanding, does God manifest himself to the soul. *The greater one's faith the closer is one's union with God.* (AMC 2.9.1; emphasis added)

As we read here, the task of emptying ourselves of the intellectual lights that can be sought in prayer, while a serious demand, is also accompanied by a great promise. The mystery of God himself—Father, Son, and Holy Spirit—can fill what has been left vacant and empty in a soul. It is a well-known truism that nature abhors a vacuum. In a similar fashion, God does not leave unrewarded the effort to empty ourselves out of a pure desire for him alone. No longer to go in pursuit of satisfactions in prayer may seem an extreme demand until we realize that anything less than God himself is unworthy of our desire in prayer. The exclusive passion for God alone in prayer leaves our soul alone with God. This becomes the inner ambiance for meeting God silently in the hidden mystery of contemplation. In a telling image, Saint John of the Cross writes that our soul becomes then like a

blind man led by the hand of another. This blind man, that
is, the soul in the prayer of contemplation, cannot know
where he is at present, in what direction he is heading, or
how he is to arrive at a destination. He must simply allow
himself to be led. But this is precisely what does happen
when our soul willingly accepts the need in deeper faith to
be blindly led by the God of infinite love who hides himself
within the caverns of our soul in prayer. In a passage from
The Spiritual Canticle, Saint John of the Cross writes a striking comment on the soul led in blindness by faith and love
to the place of God's hiding. "Listen to a word abounding
in substance and inaccessible truth: seek him in faith and
love, without desiring to find satisfaction in anything, or
delight, or desiring to understand anything other than what
you ought to know. Faith and love are like the blind person's
guides. They will lead you along a path unknown to you,
to the place where God is hidden" (SC 1.11).

The image of the blind person is very dear to Saint John
of the Cross. It captures, not so much a helpless quality of
the soul in prayer, but the need to be taken by the hand and
guided by another. Leading ourselves would mean to follow
our own lights, to direct and navigate the course of our own
prayer, while perhaps looking for discoveries that seem to
justify and reward the pursuit of interior prayer. The search
for particular insights to feed our intellect in prayer would
be an example. What is then found by means of thought
or imagination, while perhaps uplifting and profitable in a
certain way, is not God himself. The deeper response of the
prayer of contemplation requires, instead, a purification of
the intellect where by means of pure faith we aim toward
God himself, and nothing less than God. We need to lean on
a pure faith in order to arrive at what only a pure faith can
encounter in prayer. The accent on an exercise of a "dark

faith'', a faith empty of self-seeking, blind in vision, stripped of satisfaction, is strong in the following passage from this section on faith in *The Ascent*:

> People must empty themselves of all, insofar as they can, so that however many supernatural communications they receive, they will continually live as though denuded of them and in darkness. Like the blind, they must lean on dark faith, accept it for their guide and light, and rest on nothing of what they understand, taste, feel, or imagine. All these perceptions are darkness that will lead them astray. Faith lies beyond all this understanding, taste, feeling, and imagining. If they do not blind themselves in these things and abide in total darkness, they will not reach what is greater: the teaching of faith. (AMC 2.4.2)

There is an almost repetitive insistence by Saint John of the Cross on the importance of this teaching of the sublime nature of faith. One can surmise that he recognized it as a troubled area of subtlety that many spiritual people do not confront properly. The customary method in silent meditative prayer to seek knowledge, insight, images, tastes, feelings, perceptions, and so forth, is at odds with the clear direction presented here to drop this approach in prayer once the grace of contemplation is given. We might think at first that the target of the remarks just quoted is directed at the impulse to exercise our own autonomy in prayer. Or it might seem a rebuke toward the neglect of a need to depend on grace if we are to arrive at God. We can see now that a deeper purpose, a more vital consequence, is at stake. The arrival at a knowledge *about* God in prayer is not comparable in value to even a mere step toward union *with* God himself. The experience of some degree of closeness with God in any taste, feeling, or sense of possession is not a union with God himself. Resting in these experiences is either to stop on the path or, worse, to detour off the path. The human tendency is to exaggerate the significance of these experiences and to measure our relations with God by them when he infinitely surpasses anything we can encounter in prayer. Saint John of the Cross can be quite dismissive in tone toward such experiences: "If the soul in traveling this road leans on any elements of its own knowledge or of its experience or knowledge of God, it will easily go astray or be detained because it did not desire to abide in complete blindness, in the faith that is its guide. However impressive may be one's knowledge or experience of God, that knowledge or experience will have no resemblance to God and amount to very little" (AMC 2.4.3).

The urgent need of the soul in prayer must be, as such, to adopt a radical exercise of pure faith in its approach to God. At the point in the spiritual life when contemplative graces are beginning to stir, it is time to lift anchor, as it were, and plunge into deeper waters of faith: "Those who want to reach union with God should advance neither by understanding, nor by the support of their own experience, nor by feeling or imagination, but by belief in God's being" (AMC 2.4.4). The last phrase "belief in God's being" may seem ordinary enough. Is that not simply what faith is—to believe in God? But quickly we should recall the real demand in the deeper act of faith—a *pure* faith—that must take place in contemplative prayer. We must believe *in* God precisely as One who is *beyond* our measure or grasp or comprehension. We must adhere to him, search and seek for him, as infinite mystery *and* as a personal presence of love immediately engaged with us in the current hour of silent prayer. In short, we must enter into faith itself, into the mystery of believing, to approach the personal mystery of God. We believe *in* him in the prayer of contemplation as we surrender our being *into* him. We give way to him and allow him to abide in us: "For God's being cannot be grasped by the intellect, appetite, imagination, or any other sense; nor can it be known in this life. The most that can be felt and tasted of God in this life is infinitely distant from God and the pure possession of him" (AMC 2.4.4).

The need of the soul, or, more precisely, the need of the intellect in contemplative prayer, is, then, to "live in darkness" toward "everything comprehensible to the heart, which signifies the soul" (AMC 2.4.4). This is the repeated refrain in this discussion. The teaching on a practical level is largely a demand to release ourselves from former habits of seeking satisfaction in prayer, which we have heard now with some insistence. Saint John of the Cross asks that we detach ourselves from a habit of finding satisfaction in what is comprehensible, so that we may lean out toward a goal that transcends all that can be comprehended. The exercise of faith in contemplative prayer is a dynamic turn of the intellect toward a limitless vista, toward the ultimate reality of God. The soul must encounter in mystery what cannot be known. In a pointed phrase, Saint John of the Cross teaches prayerful souls: "Consequently, they must pass beyond everything to unknowing" (AMC 2.4.4). What is proposed is not an "unknowing" that would be a confused staring into the darkness of doubt. Rather, it signifies a steady gaze of certitude lifted up toward an unseen horizon of light and love. The need of the intellect is essentially to plunge into *faith itself*, in all its purity and in deep certitude, as an immeasurable leaning of the soul toward God himself. "The intellect must be blind and dark and abide in faith alone, because it is joined with God under this cloud" (AMC 2.9.1). Methods or modes of prayer do not achieve this. Nonetheless, there must be a refusal to practice prayer as though just following customary routines, locked in place, looking to satisfy ourselves in ways that have become familiar and mildly rewarding. Our motivation should not be to recover satisfying experiences of God if on any day we are consoled. Above all, perhaps, we should not go to prayer with an illusion of proficiency. God's unpredictability must direct the soul on the path of prayer, which in effect makes prayer quite new on each day. As Saint John of the Cross affirms:

> As regards this road to union, entering on the road means leaving one's own road; or better, moving on to the goal. And turning from one's own mode implies entry into what has no mode, that is, God. Individuals who reach this state no longer have any modes or methods, still less are they attached to them, nor can they be. I am referring to modes of understanding, tasting, and feeling. Within themselves, though, they possess all methods, like one who though having nothing yet possesses all things [2 Cor. 6:10]. (AMC 2.4.5)

A courage of soul is clearly needed to go forward on this contemplative path of pure faith. The underlying challenge of darkness, in particular, implies a need to cross a threshold of insecurity in prayer in which there may seem initially no support for the intellect, no footing in ideas to plant our spirit, nothing in thought to brace ourselves in familiar surroundings. Blindness becomes more than a metaphor in this teaching. The intellect's state of incomprehension toward God is a real ambiance of difficult interior experience. It must be a blindness that is willingly accepted if it is to bring spiritual benefit. In a very striking phrase, Saint John of the Cross writes farther on in this section: "In order to draw nearer the divine ray, the intellect must advance by unknowing rather than by the desire to know, and by blinding itself

and remaining in darkness rather than by opening its eyes"
(AMC 2.8.5).

The initial insecurity of a darkened experience in faith,
advancing by unknowing, surely requires some adjustment
and an assimilation. However, the insecurity need not continue interminably. The deliberate refusal of satisfaction for
the intellect in prayer may be for a certain period of purification a radical austerity for the intellect. But the result in time
can be to sense a door opening into a purer encounter with
God himself. He who is infinite mystery in his being must
be approached in the unknown truth of his infinitude as
Someone known and loved. Intensity of faith accompanies
the more intense love that unites us personally to God. As
heard earlier in this chapter and worth repeating: "Only by
means of faith, in divine light exceeding all understanding,
does God manifest himself to the soul. The greater one's
faith, the closer is one's union with God" (AMC 2.9.1). A
pure, naked faith will come to know the presence of God
in a more intense certitude of love. Every other sense of understanding God must be subjugated in prayer to the truth
of God as the exceedingly Almighty One who is loved. In
the following passage, Saint John of the Cross insists on the
vigor of an intense desire needed for the pursuit of God
precisely when our intellect in faith is submerged in an incomprehension of God's ultimate mystery. This longer quotation conveys how narrow and serious is the road into the
night of contemplation where a blessed contact with God
awaits the depths of a soul in its prayer.

> Passing beyond all that is naturally and spiritually intelligi-
> ble or comprehensible, souls ought to desire with all their
> might to attain what in this life could never be known
> or enter the human heart. And parting company with all
> they can or do taste and feel, temporally and spiritually,

they must ardently long to acquire what surpasses all taste and feeling. To be empty and free for the achievement of this, they should by no means seize on what they receive spiritually or sensitively . . . , but consider it of little import. The higher the rank and esteem they give to all this knowledge, experience, and imagining (whether spiritual or not), the more they subtract from the Supreme Good and the more they delay in their journey toward him. And the less they esteem what they can possess—however estimable it may be relative to the Supreme Good—the more they value and prize him, and, consequently, the closer they come to him. In this way, in obscurity, souls approach union swiftly by means of faith, which is also dark. (AMC 2.4.6)

A concluding word can be offered at the end of this chapter. Perhaps, in a first serious encounter with Saint John of the Cross, we might be tempted to think that a kind of humiliation of the intellect is being asked of us in the incomprehension that we must experience in faith toward God, at least in regard to contemplation. The first exposure to this doctrine may seem almost to propose an impersonal sense of God, who would be too far away and remote, hidden behind a wall of distant silence. The humiliation would consist in the frustration of wanting some definite experience of his real presence, some thoughts of deeper insight into God, and being told bluntly not to seek such things. Perhaps the helpful corrective to these misgivings would be to remember the name of this saintly Doctor of the Church. His appellation Saint John *of the Cross* implies a deep attachment in his own life to the crucified Lord Jesus. He was well-known for carving wooden crucifixes. He may have sketched the remarkable drawing of Christ crucified on the book's cover as a meditation on the Father gazing upon his Son's suffering at Calvary. The incomprehension we encounter in prayer can be fed steadily by remembrance of the singular event in history when our God died as a man in the horror of a Roman crucifixion. Any longer gaze at a crucifix plunges us into an incomprehension of the infinitude of divine love nailed to a Roman cross. The abandonment of Christ to his Father's will finds a parallel in our own incapacity to comprehend his infinite love. We have no option then but to abandon ourselves blindly to a love beyond our understanding.

4

DIVINE COMMUNICATIONS?
CAUTION AND CARE

This next chapter extends the previous discussion on the role of faith in the interior life of prayer. It is a chapter of some indirect interest, we might say, not bearing explicitly on contemplative concerns, but addressing secondary matters involving faith that can take place in prayer. The purity of faith essential for contemplation and for advancing toward union with God, which we examined in the last chapter, leads Saint John of the Cross to treat in a later portion of book 2 of *The Ascent of Mount Carmel* the question of possible communications by God to the soul during prayer, or even outside formal prayer. These communications can be of various sorts; the issue at stake is a proper attitude and discernment in their regard. The teaching serves to underscore the critical need for a *pure* exercise of faith in the pursuit of God in prayer. We will hear again in this discussion the importance of an experiential darkness that accompanies the path into deeper faith. All other forms of experience and communication that may seem to come from God cannot compare to the need for a *pure* faith toward God and his immediate mysterious presence to us in prayer.

The subject we are going to explore now certainly has some pertinence today, when the claim is not infrequently heard that a person has received particular messages from

God or prophetic inspirations about the future or is convinced by charismatic experiences of divine directions for a
personal life or for that of others. Saint John of the Cross is
strongly adverse to this tendency to embrace these communications as direct revelations by God to the soul. His opposition is not primarily due to skepticism that God can speak
to a soul if the Lord so desires; or to a caution about their ambiguity and the chance for erroneous interpretations, which
indeed are possible; or even due to the difficulty of discernment whether a communication is genuinely from God or
perhaps from the devil. His great resistance is due to the fact
that a dependency on these communications is contrary to
the purity of faith that we have now seen to be of such
importance, by which alone a soul truly advances to God.
These other possibilities of spiritual experience, in their various forms, are deceptively attractive. Souls easily become
attached to them, inasmuch as they seem to be a privileged
encounter with God. On the contrary, they may deflect the
soul from the purer path of deeper faith or, as Saint John of
the Cross likes to say, from the abyss of faith. The following short statement is a good introductory remark for this
subject. Referring to the Second Letter of Saint Peter that
faith is like a candle shining in a dark place (2 Pet 1:19),
Saint John of the Cross writes of the importance of holding
to the dark certitudes of faith:

> He asserts that we should live in darkness, with our eyes
> closed to all other lights, and that in this darkness faith
> alone—which is dark also—should be the light we use.
> If we want to employ these other bright lights of distinct
> knowledge, we cease to make use of faith, the dark light,
> and we cease to be enlightened in the dark place men-
> tioned by St. Peter. This place (the intellect—the holder
> on which the candle of faith is placed) must remain in

darkness until the day, in the next life, when the clear vision of God dawns upon the soul. (AMC 2.16.15)

Fundamentally, Saint John of the Cross opposes the pursuit of particular, clear apprehensions of any sort as the means for a supposed direct entry into the knowledge of God. This is always contrary to the deeper path of pure faith: "One cannot advance in faith without closing one's eyes to everything pertaining to the senses and to clear, particular knowledge" (AMC 2.16.15). His first reference in this regard is to communications to the imagination through some image or idea of what can seem to be a direct experience of God. This might come through a visual apprehension of Jesus during prayer, by what seems to be a clear spoken word from him, or through some spiritual insight that seems clearly from a source outside oneself. Even when a communication of this kind comes in prayer by means of grace, this is always, insists Saint John of the Cross, a lesser form of knowledge than the knowledge that comes by naked and pure faith. The latter implies always a knowledge without dependency on images, words, or particular ideas. "The eyes of the soul . . . should be fixed on the invisible, on what belongs not to sense but to spirit, and on what, as it is not contained in a sensible figure, brings the soul to union with God in faith" (AMC 2.16.12). Saint John of the Cross is thus blunt in urging the soul not to overvalue any image or particular idea given in prayer to the imagination or intellect. "Individuals should neither feed upon nor encumber themselves with them" (AMC 2.16.6). Rather, they should be renounced and avoided as a spiritual hindrance. "Individuals must have no desire to admit them even though they come from God" (AMC 2.17.7). The last phrase is striking . . . "even though they come from God". Why, we might wonder, does he warn so sharply against this if possibly these ideas or images have a source in grace?

The reason has to do with the demands of a genuine contemplative faith. Indeed, the demands of contemplation hover always in the background on all pages in the writings of Saint John of the Cross. The path of a purer faith necessary for contemplation requires that souls "remain detached, divested, pure, simple, and without any mode or method as the union demands" (AMC 2.16.6). This is a recommendation we have heard already in the treatment on faith in the last chapter. An absence of images and ideas from the intellect accompanies the grace of contemplation because of the effect of faith on the intellect. The things we grasp by some particular communication through imaginative vision, in a thought, or by some interior words will always be represented to the intellect "in some limited mode or manner" (AMC 2.16.7). Leaning on these communications, we risk halting on the path of a deeper faith. The goal of prayer for a lifetime is to seek the infinite purity of God. This is the only path to eventual union with God. A pure and naked intellect, devoid of distinct or clear thoughts or images, is the proper ambiance for pursuing God in faith: "In this high state of union God does not communicate himself to the soul—nor is this possible—through the disguise of any imaginative vision, likeness, or figure, but mouth to mouth: the pure and naked essence of God (the mouth of God in love) with the pure and naked essence of the soul (the mouth of the soul in the love of God)" (AMC 2.16.9).

The requirement for contemplation is boldly stated in these words, namely, that the intellect should not encumber itself with thoughts and apprehensions that offer some particular appeal in their clarity. The effort must be, rather, to stretch beyond the comprehensible and clear idea or the attractive image and to face the truth of an infinite, unseen God in the purity of faith. It is necessary to resist being held back by what is less important, thereby halting advancement on the road to God. This teaching is consistent with the apophatic principles we have exposed earlier. The reality of God is disproportionate to any limited apprehension that the mind can embrace. Advancement to God in deeper prayer is by means of faith. But this movement into the mysterious presence of the God of hiddenness must come by means of a pure and naked faith. There is a dual need to leave the intellect empty of a clear object of focus and yet burning with certitude toward the immediate presence of God in prayer. In the following passage, Saint John of the Cross writes of the need not to latch onto any particular knowledge of God if we are to be united to his surpassing truth in prayer. The apophatic dimension is so often for him, not a theological premise, but an experiential path to union with God.

> God's wisdom, to which the intellect must be united, has neither mode nor manner, neither does it have limits nor does it pertain to distinct and particular knowledge, because it is totally pure and simple. That the two extremes, the soul and divine Wisdom, may be united, they will have to come to accord by means of a certain likeness. As a result the soul must also be pure and simple, unlimited and unattached to any particular knowledge, and unmodified by the boundaries of form, species, and image. Since God cannot be encompassed by any image, form, or particular knowledge, in order to be united with him the soul should not be limited by any particular form or knowledge. (AMC 2.16.7)

Saint John of the Cross goes on to affirm further reasons why we do not need special communications from God by images or particular ideas as a way to gain closer relations to

God. First, he says, because God does not need this means of an interior visual image or of particular thoughts to communicate to the deeper layers of the soul. His communication to these deeper layers of the soul in contemplation is rather by means of silence. Secondly, this other way is a source of "spiritual stagnancy since a person is not then employed with the more important things and disencumbered of the trifles of particular apprehensions and knowledge" (AMC 2.17.7). The vividness at times of visual communications upon the internal senses of the imagination can make it hard to realize their lesser worth. We are disinclined to treat these lesser experiences with a proper discernment and even with a spirit of dismissal. Their value is limited at best; yet the initial impression is to exaggerate their importance. Saint John of the Cross offers the more penetrating interpretation. The sense appeal of such imaginative experiences indicates their inferior status in comparison to the deeper path of faith: "It is regrettable that a soul, having as it were an infinite capacity, should be fed, because of its limited spirituality and sensory incapacity, with morsels for the senses" (AMC 2.17.8). Saint John of the Cross comments further that when imaginative visions of any kind occur, it is common that souls are tempted to exalt themselves: "They go about feeling pleased and somewhat satisfied with themselves, which is against humility" (AMC 2.18.3). Attachment to these experiences takes place easily, and they are treated as excessively significant and sometimes talked about with spiritual directors, who may take too much interest in such matters. According to Saint John of the Cross, these experiences would be better treated with an indifference that might diminish their importance to the soul, including an indifference that should come from the spiritual directors of these souls. As he writes: "Neither do these directors ground their disciples in faith, for they frequently make these visions a topic of conversation. Consequently, the individuals get the idea that their directors are setting store by their visions, and as a result they do the same and stay attached to them, instead of being built up in faith, detached, emptied, and divested of apprehensions so as to soar to the heights of dark faith" (AMC 2.18.2).

Another form of communication can be what seem to be special messages or particular revelations from God. At times these are requested by souls for enlightenment about matters to be done or choices to be made. An open door to erroneous interpretations presents itself here. Saint John of the Cross spends a bit of time teaching that the words given in such messages or the instructions that may be discerned with some sense of immediate clarity, or the expectations that are aroused based on the literal meaning of what is heard may all turn out not to occur in the manner anticipated. Saint John of the Cross refers here especially to instructions regarding future actions based on predictions about what is to happen. Often people dependent on this mode of communication from God, trusting too confidently in them, believe that everything is to take place in accord with what they think they have heard from God. The thought is that events will take place in the manner that God has spoken to them, since, if God has spoken, it cannot be otherwise. Saint John of the Cross has a strong rebuttal to that notion. He does not deny that God may communicate to a soul. He insists, rather, that God's communication can easily be misunderstood in its true meaning because of the soul's inability to perceive a deeper spiritual interpretation. "Not all revelations turn out according to what we understand by the words" (AMC 2.19.1). The literal meaning is in fact rarely the actual significance of the communication.

The result can be mistakes and delusions. "Since God is immense and profound, he usually includes in his prophecies, locutions, and revelations other ways, concepts, and ideas remarkably different from the meaning we generally find in them" (AMC 2.19.1). The idea of events or predictions taking place as stated literally in the reception of an inner word from God is a presumption that often proves wrong. "God's revelations or locutions do not always turn out according to people's understanding of them or according to what seems to be the meaning of the words. One should neither find assurance in them nor believe them blindly, even though one knows they are God's revelations, responses, or words. Though they may in themselves be certain and true, they are not always so in their causes or in our way of understanding them" (AMC 2.18.9).

The comments here speak of an essential difficulty in our relations with God due to the apophatic truth of his infinite transcendence. God's personal communications to a soul, when they are indeed from him, are not deceptive or misleading in themselves; yet we are quite capable of being misled by them. This can happen "by understanding God's locutions and revelations according to the letter, according to the outer rind" (AMC 2.19.5). It should be pointed out that Saint John of the Cross uses the terminology of locutions and revelations here, not necessarily as extraordinary mystical experiences, but in the sense of communications to the intellect or imagination that give every indication of coming from a source beyond ourselves. In Saint John of the Cross' view, the divine purpose of these communications is often not at all in the literal meaning of the words or images communicated. "God's chief objective in conferring these revelations is to express and impart the spirit that is enclosed within the outer rind. This spirit is difficult to understand, much richer and more plentiful, very extraordinary and far beyond the boundaries of the letter" (AMC 2.19.5).

Prudence dictates, as such, a need to discard an easy interpretation of these communications understood at face value. The opportunity for presumption and a subsequent deception is all-too-real. We hear again the great importance of returning to a pure exercise of faith: "The soul should renounce, then, the literal sense in these cases, and live in the darkness of faith, for faith is the spirit that is incomprehensible to the senses" (AMC 2.19.5). Saint John of the Cross may have been commenting on the basis of his own experience with souls. The expectation that events will occur, a turn in circumstances will take place, or an idea will be fruitful, in accord with an apparent communication given by God, is typically not fulfilled as anticipated. The reason is not due to a change or reconsideration on God's part, but because of a misunderstanding of meaning on the soul's part. The following words are a strong corrective in this regard: "Evidently, then, even though the words and revelations are from God, we cannot find assurance in them, since in our understanding of them we can easily be deluded, and very much so. They embody an abyss and depth of spirit, and to want to limit them to our interpretation and to what our senses can apprehend is like wanting to grasp a handful of air that will escape the hand entirely, leaving only a particle of dust" (AMC 2.19.10).

An illustration used by Saint John of the Cross may be instructive. A soul is experiencing intense longings to be a martyr and then in prayer hears a communication from God —"You shall be a martyr." At the same time, God grants to the soul "deep interior consolation and confidence in the truth of this promise" (AMC 2.19.13). And so that person begins to live with this thought of an inevitable death by martyrdom. Nonetheless, the person does not end up dying as a martyr. What happened? Did the person fail to live up to a standard of virtue necessary for the prize of martyrdom? This is not a correct understanding, according to Saint John of the Cross, if indeed a holy life ensued. Instead, Saint John of the Cross comments that the promise of God heard in these words was true, and it was a promise that was kept, even with no literal fulfillment. However, it was fulfilled in truth in a far better way. How can that be if a person did not die a martyr's death? He answers:

> Regardless of the promise, this person in the end does not die a martyr; yet the promise will have been true. . . . Because it will be fulfilled in its chief, essential meaning: the bestowal of the essential love and reward of a martyr. God truly grants the soul what it formally desired and what he promised it because the formal desire of the soul was not a manner of death but the service of God through martyrdom and the exercise of a martyr's love for him. Death through martyrdom in itself is of no value without this love, and God bestows martyrdom's love and reward perfectly by other means. Even though the soul does not die a martyr, it is profoundly satisfied since God has fulfilled its desire. (AMC 2.19.13)

The essential teaching here is to take care with what can appear to be forms of direct communication from God. The initial reaction of exuberant receptivity to supposed divine communications needs to be tempered lest misunderstandings ensue. A wise understanding flows through this teaching: "God usually affirms, teaches, and promises many things, not so there will be an immediate understanding of them, but so that afterward at the proper time, or when the effect is produced, one may receive light about them" (AMC 2.20.3). These are secret truths, we should assume, in God's dealings with our soul, which we are incapable of comprehending for what might be a long period of time. The tendency to interpret them with immediate clarity leads easily to misconceptions of God's actual intent and meaning in any communication.

Saint John of the Cross raises the rhetorical objection: "If we are not to understand or get involved with these locutions and revelations, why does God communicate them?" (AMC 2.20.6). His answer is that everything can be understood in due time as God desires it to be understood, but this implies a need for patience and humility. The risk of error is strong to the extent that we are impetuous and presume a special understanding due to our closeness with God. "Believe me," writes Saint John of the Cross, "people cannot completely grasp the meaning of God's locutions and deeds; nor, without much error and confusion, can they determine this meaning by what appears to be so" (AMC 2.20.6). There should be no surprise that God's communications "do not materialize as expected" (AMC 2.20.8). The mistake is to think we have comprehended God quite clearly, when in truth we may have walked into a dark corner of misinterpretation. "One should seek assurance, therefore, not in one's understanding but in faith" (AMC 2.20.8). Always the return in the discussion is to the importance of a purer exercise of faith.

Another issue of interest that Saint John of the Cross addresses is the thought of some people that God must be pleased when a soul petitions him to know certain things by supernatural messages, precisely because he does seem to answer at times such requests. Saint John of the Cross expresses a contrary view: "Yet the truth is that, regardless of his reply, such behavior is neither good nor pleasing to God. Rather he is displeased; not only displeased but

frequently angered and deeply offended" (AMC 2.21.1).
The reason for God's displeasure is the illicit crossing of
boundaries when we seek to know things by supernatural
messages when the proper way is to use our faith and reason to exercise discernment about what God wants from
us. It is a presumptuous act to try to arrive at immediate,
unambiguous knowledge of divine matters by some special
supernatural favor instead of humbly walking the path of
faith. The former tendency is a way of tempting God: "For
to tempt God is to desire communication with him in extraordinary ways, supernatural ways" (AMC 2.21.1). If God
at times gives an answer, it is only "because of the weakness of the individual who desires to advance in that way"
(AMC 2.21.2). If God does not condescend to reply, such
persons withdraw into sadness and will "imagine that God
is unhappy with them, and become overwhelmed" (AMC
2.21.2). God is not desirous or pleased "that communication
with him be carried on in such a manner" (AMC 2.21.2).
He is a loving God who can be indulgent to his children,
"since they are good and simple". "But the fact that he answers them does not mean he is pleased with this practice"
(AMC 2.21.2).

The problem with this spiritual approach echoes what has
been heard earlier about the seeking of our own satisfaction
in prayer. Saint John of the Cross admonishes again strongly
in this matter: "I consider a desire to know things through
supernatural means far worse than a desire for spiritual gratifications in the sensitive part of the soul" (AMC 2.21.4).
Saint John of the Cross is adamant in stressing that there is
no need to go beyond or outside the path of faith. Faith, as
it advances, urges upon the soul an increasing submission to
God's will in all things, even when the comfort of clarity
is absent from our perspective. Surrender to God, even in

obscure darkness, is always a superior act to a search for direct guidance by means of a special message from God. It should always be assumed that the leap of faith in seeking the will of God is far more pleasing to him than dependency on a special message telling us what to do next in life. The following warning of Saint John of the Cross, if it is correct, indicates that God is not happy at all with our seeking special supernatural communications from him. The repercussion of such practices is often seen in regrettable fruits in a life. "God, though angered, condescends in this and many other ways to the desires of souls. Scripture provides many testimonies and examples of this. . . . I only say that the desire to communicate with God in this way is extremely dangerous—more so than I can say. The person attached to such ways will go far astray and often become greatly bewildered. Anyone who has esteemed them will understand through experience what I mean" (AMC 2.21.7).

Saint John of the Cross brings this particular discussion to an end with comments on what he calls supernatural locutions received by the inner spirit. Again, he does not mean extraordinary mystical locutions, but three categories of interior experience that need discernment and proper understanding. The first he terms "successive locutions". These are not so unusual in the life of prayer, since they take place during the time of meditative reflections in the quiet of prayer. Persons doing a discursive meditation with an attentive absorption, proceeding from point to point in thought, may find at times that they are encountering unknown truths never before considered "with so much ease and clarity that it will seem to them they are doing nothing and another person is interiorly reasoning, answering, and teaching them" (AMC 2.29.1). All this takes place as though the soul is "carrying on a dialogue". The Holy Spirit is present to help

the person to form these "concepts, words, and judgments",
but the truth is that the person utters these statements to
himself. The intellect, recollected and united to the truth,
and assisted by the Holy Spirit, is enlightened in this way
in truths. The mistake is to think that these statements are
coming completely from God alone, as though God from
on high, as it were, is speaking from the heavens to the
soul. "Anyone having this experience cannot help but think
that these statements or words come from another. They do
not know about the ease with which the intellect, in deal-
ing with concepts and truths communicated by another, can
form words for itself that also seem to come from another"
(AMC 2.29.2).

The problem in this matter is that although the Holy Spirit
does not deceive, the person may be deceived inasmuch as
the intellect, in forming its propositions and words, is capable of embracing incomplete and partial truths and missing
other aspects of truth. A defective reception of the communication is quite possible. Saint John of the Cross writes, for
instance: "I knew a person who in experiencing these successive locutions formed, among some very true and solid
ones about the Blessed Sacrament, others that were outright
heresies" (AMC 2.29.4). More commonly, and perhaps of
pertinence today, souls will take words or messages received
in the quiet recollection of prayer as direct locutions from
God himself, when in reality the person is the origin of the
statement purportedly spoken by God. Saint John of the
Cross could be speaking to our own day in these words:
"I greatly fear what is happening in these times of ours: If
any soul whatever after a few pennies worth of reflection
experiences one of these locutions in some recollection, it
will immediately baptize all as coming from God and, sup-
posing this, say, 'God told me', 'God answered me.' Yet this

will not be true but, as we pointed out, these persons will themselves more often be the ones who speak the words" (AMC 2.29.4).

The actual truth is that in a desire for such "locutions" and an attachment to them, souls often answer themselves in prayer and "think that God is responding and speaking to them" (AMC 2.29.5). Clearly restraint and self-discipline are needed to correct what can prove to be a serious harm to the spiritual life. The danger is especially serious if instructions heard in prayer are viewed as divine directions when in fact the path proposed for some choice of action is contrary to God's will. The human person is easily gullible to the thought of receiving divine favors in this manner: "They think something extraordinary has occurred and that God has spoken, whereas in reality little more than nothing will have happened, or nothing at all, or even less than nothing" (AMC 2.29.5).

The main objection to dependency on this spiritual approach to God is once again that it is a barrier to the true path of deeper faith. By paying attention to such "locutions", or seeking them out, a person does not live in the "abyss of faith" (AMC 2.29.7). Seeking these kinds of special instructions is an impediment to deeper faith. As Saint John of the Cross writes, "the intellect should remain in obscurity and journey by love in darkness of faith and not by much reasoning" (AMC 2.29.5). Saint John of the Cross goes on to ask rhetorically why the intellect should deprive itself of such truths if the Holy Spirit illumines the intellect through them. His answer is that the superior illumination will always come by a recollection "purer and more refined" in faith, "in which there is no clear understanding" (AMC 2.29.6). Paying attention to the distinct or clear instruction is contrary to embracing "the communication of the abyss of faith" (AMC 2.29.7). This is far superior in worth, even though not immediately satisfying to the mind or spirit. "In this faith God supernaturally and secretly teaches the soul and raises it up in virtues and gifts in a way unknown to it" (AMC 2.29.7). The path of humility likewise demands a recognition that any assumption of special communications from God may simply feed a soul's vanity. As Saint John of the Cross observes with a certain pungency:

> Yet some intellects are so lively and subtle that, while recollected in meditation, they reason naturally and easily about some concepts, and form locutions and statements very vividly, and think that these are indeed from God. But that notion is false, for an intellect somewhat freed from the operation of the senses has the capacity to do this and even more with its own natural light and without any other supernatural help. Such an occurrence is frequent. And many are deluded by it into thinking that theirs is the enjoyment of a high degree of prayer and communion from God; consequently they either write the words down themselves or have others do so. But it comes about that the experience amounts to nothing, nothing substantial in the line of virtue comes from it, and it serves for no more than to induce vainglory. (AMC 2.29.8)

After what has been said, the question of the second and third types of interior locutions can be dealt with more quickly. The second kind is called a formal interior locution and takes place outside of any spiritual recollection in meditative prayer. It gives the appearance of an utterance coming independently from the person who receives it. A person has in no way been pondering the matter, and the thought or some words suddenly come to the mind, clearly present and, as it were, heard. Again, this does not mean an extraordinary mystical experience, but some word heard in the inner spirit. There can be explicit words, or sometimes not, or ideas and inspirations spoken to the inner spirit. "All these words come without any intervention of the spirit because they are received as though one person were speaking to another" (AMC 2.30.2). If they are from God, they are usually for the sake of teaching some truth or shedding some light of direction in a person's life. The same care of possible exaggeration or deception needs to be observed as in the previous instructions. The third kind of interior locution is less problematic; it is called a substantial locution and involves God bestowing a virtue or strength to the soul by means of the expression spoken in words. "For example, if our Lord should say formally to the soul, 'Be good,' it would immediately be substantially good; or if he should say, 'Love me,' it would at once have and experience within itself the substance of the love of God; or if he should say to a soul in much fear, 'Do not fear,' it would without delay feel great fortitude and tranquility" (AMC 2.31.1). This third type of internal locution is generally unproblematic because the focus is on a virtuous command. Unlike the third type, however, the problem of the second form of interior locution includes the possibility that diabolic communications occur in this manner. That alone is a reason to exercise a serious caution. The following instruction of Saint John of the Cross is emphatic about rejecting such communications, whether or not such a communication comes from God. The danger is that the soul is indeed deceived and might bring harm upon itself.

> A person should pay no more attention to all these formal locutions than to the other kind, for besides occupying the spirit with matters irrelevant to faith, the legitimate and proximate means to union with God, they will make one an easy victim for the devil's deceits. At times one

can hardly discern the locutions spoken by a good spirit or those coming from a bad one. . . . Individuals should not do what these words tell them, nor should they pay attention to them—whether they be from a good or bad spirit. Nevertheless, these locutions should be manifested to a mature confessor or to a discreet and wise person who will give instructions and counsel and consider the appropriate thing to do. But a person's attitude toward them ought to be one of resignation and negation. (AMC 2.30.5)

The concluding remarks in this chapter can turn fittingly to the middle section of this treatment on special communications from God. Saint John of the Cross initially contrasts the licit and necessary approach by which inquiries were made of God in the Old Testament for visions and revelations and such tendencies after the revelation of Jesus Christ. Prophets in the Old Testament desired revelations and at times questioned God to inform them of unknown matters, and God responded. "But in this era of grace, now that the faith is established through Christ and the Gospel law made manifest, there is no reason for inquiring of him in this way, or expecting him to answer as before" (AMC 2.22.3). We have all we need in Jesus Christ: "In giving us his Son, his only Word (for he possesses no other), *he spoke everything to us at once in this sole Word—and he has no more to say*" (AMC 2.22.3; emphasis added). It is a striking reply to the desire for additional light from God. The attempt to question God or to desire a special revelation on some matter is foolish behavior and offensive to God. The path of humility and self-effacement is the safe and sure road. The following long quotation is quite severe in its rejection of the desire for special communications from God out of curiosity or even with some supposed great need for personal guidance. But it is also a beautiful statement of faith. In Jesus

Christ we have everything and more. His presence in the Eucharist is enough to feed our soul and communicate the deep mystery of his desires for our lives.

> God could answer as follows: If I have already told you all things in my Word, my Son, and if I have no other word, what answer or revelation can I now make that would surpass this? Fasten your eyes on him alone because in him I have spoken and revealed all and in him you will discover even more than you ask for and desire. You are making an appeal for locutions and revelations that are incomplete, but if you turn your eyes to him you will find them complete. For he is my entire locution and response, vision and revelation, which I have already spoken, answered, manifested, and revealed to you by giving him to you as a brother, companion, master, ransom, and reward. . . . If you desire me to answer with a word of comfort, behold my Son subject to me and to others out of love for me, and afflicted, and you will see how much he answers you. If you desire me to declare some secret truths or events to you, fix your eyes only on him and you will discern hidden in him the most secret mysteries, and wisdom, and wonders of God. (AMC 2.22.5, 6)

5

ASCETICISM: RECOVERY OF
A NEGLECTED VALUE

In this chapter we take up a subject planted more firmly on the ground, namely, Saint John of the Cross' instructions in book 1 of *The Ascent of Mount Carmel* on asceticism and self-denial. This teaching will make better sense now after we have seen his understanding of the great role of purification in the human faculties for the sake of union with God. Unfortunately, asceticism is a largely forgotten word in contemporary spirituality, despite its importance in the Catholic tradition. In truth, it has never been a treasured topic or a popular Catholic pursuit. It has always been subject to exaggerated notions that distort it and empty it of value. Today another reason may exist for its virtual disappearance from spiritual teaching, which is the excessive focus on the inward path of silent meditative practices that has lately preoccupied spirituality. Writings on the quest for God through methods of meditative mindfulness typically ignore self-denial or bodily discipline as a prerequisite for spiritual growth. This is not to say that these writings encourage moral laxity, but simply that a need for some commitment to asceticism and to real practices of self-denial is nowhere to be found in them. Frankly, this is not a good sign of their value as a teaching for souls seeking a closer relationship with God. The neglect of an ascetical element in the pursuit of God leaves unaddressed the retention of indulgent tendencies in a life. The effort of seeking God ends up then often as a self-absorbed quest, instead of a pure and sacrificial pursuit in response to Jesus' own words in the Gospel and in imitation of saintly lives.

Before examining the teaching of Saint John of the Cross, let us first say that asceticism does not mean taking up extreme practices of austerity or severe penances, although saintly lives have often given examples of this, including the lives of Saint John of the Cross and some of his companions in the Carmelite reform. Nonetheless, some evidence of an ascetical quality is surely a necessity in every healthy spiritual life, given the alluring attraction that human nature, wounded by original sin, will experience toward the pleasures of the senses. Asceticism is a response, a counterweight, to the moral danger of sensual temptation and to all tendencies to selfishness. In practice, it entails voluntarily depriving oneself of easy comforts and pleasures in exchange for a graced increase in spiritual strength. In all traditional spirituality, it is taught as a means to the greater end of union with God. A training in habits of mortification has always been an essential preparation for a serious pursuit of God. It has never been taught that asceticism assures an arrival at God, but it does serve the preliminary function of helping one to shed indulgent tendencies and forge a purer desire for God.

Indeed, the idea goes back for centuries that ascetical practices of self-denial inculcate in the soul a manly spirit ready to meet the rigors of spiritual testing that are bound to come later in a life. Naturally, not everyone, even in Trappist monasteries or Carmelite cloistered convents, succeeds in all the demands of personal privations, but some proficiency in self-denial has been generally assumed for a dedicated spiritual life. In the past, there was no such thing as a monastery or convent, and actually no seminary in older days, that did not foster practices of mortification regarding sleep, food, clothing, schedule, comforts, and so forth. Communal deprivations combined with personal penances. All that has vastly diminished in the last decades, and in many cases it has disappeared entirely in places where we would expect to find it, namely, in the religious congregations. It is no exaggeration to say that the traditional tomes of spirituality have become dusty volumes lining the shelves of unused sections of seminary and religious house libraries. In many diocesan seminaries a recreation room with a well-stocked refrigerator and wine cabinet has replaced the chapel for the late evening hour. Spiritual directors in these houses of formation, with some exceptions, generally avoid the expressions "self-renunciation" or "self-denial", except at times to urge the self-denying practice of a nonjudgmental tolerance toward the sexual proclivities of others. Saint John of the Cross takes a rather different tack, to say the least. Only at the risk of underestimating the demands for a holy life can one presume that he expresses an antiquated requirement for spiritual advancement in these uncompromising words:

> Mortification of the appetites is necessary for one's spiritual fruitfulness. I venture to say that without this mortification all that is done for the sake of advancement in perfection and in knowledge of God and of oneself is no more profitable than seed sown on uncultivated ground. Accordingly, darkness and coarseness will always be with a soul until its appetites are extinguished. The appetites are like a cataract on the eye or specks of dust in it; until removed they obstruct vision. (AMC 1.8.4)

Certainly, on the basis of this passage alone, we can say that Saint John of the Cross shows no signs of an allergic reaction to the value of self-renunciation and mortification.

Indeed, he could be called, instead of the Mystical Doctor, the Church's Doctor of self-denial. For him, the theme of self-denial threads through all stages of the spiritual life. Not only does he propose mortification of the appetites in the strict sense of bodily discipline as a preliminary work of the spiritual life. The principle of self-denial, in a wider application of the term, also plays a key role for him in the interior life of prayer itself, as we have already observed. The spirit of self-renunciation helps to carve a swath of purification into the depths of the soul, readying it for the grace of contemplation and aiding as well in a proper response to contemplative graces. The essential importance of purification for a soul's advancement in love explains the essential need for self-denial, first learned in physical privations, but then transferred to the interior desires of the soul.

For Saint John of the Cross, union with God is the great goal of *everything* in life. It demands an ongoing journey of purification, a vast dying to self, fueled by a dynamic of self-emptying that will touch all areas of exterior and interior life. Through all types of purification, the need is to die to self by denying oneself. Let us recall that Jesus himself proclaims just this same need in the Gospel: "Unless a grain of wheat falls into the earth and dies, it remains alone; but if it dies, it bears much fruit" (Jn 12:24). The dying proposed in this Gospel passage is not death at the conclusion of a life, but death as a giving away of self, as an immolation of self for another, the death that can be a long martyrdom of many years in a life. In another statement, Jesus proclaims: "If any man would come after me, let him deny himself and take up his cross and follow me" (Mk 8:34). All serious spiritual life has this one goal—union with God—and that can only mean in some mysterious manner an identification with the crucified Lord Jesus Christ. An opening phrase in *The Ascent of Mount Carmel*, prior to his Prologue, announces the kind of spiritual mentoring we can expect to receive from Saint John of the Cross—a consuming, intense, uncompromising direction, with no time to waste. Union with Christ crucified will not be possible without "complete nakedness" in the offering of our love to our Lord: "This treatise explains *how to reach divine union quickly.* It presents instruction and doctrine valuable for beginners and proficients alike that they may learn how to unburden themselves of all earthly things, avoid spiritual obstacles, and live in that complete nakedness and freedom of spirit necessary for divine union" (AMC Prologue; emphasis added).

The exercise of self-denial presupposes, then, a profound objective: dying to self for the sake of union with God. What is necessary in this pursuit, in the loss of self demanded by love, at least as regards ascetical self-denial? Clearly, it is not to starve oneself to death. Rather, initially and difficult enough, it is to accept voluntary privations in one's life; the more radical the better, albeit with common sense and a certain respect for moderation. A breaking free from attachments to comfort and pleasure calls for decisive choices. The task is not to search for painful experiences or harsh penances, but more to step back voluntarily from an easy life of pleasant enjoyments. This reduction of pleasure-seeking, of gratification of our impulsive desires, is always at first an exacting work. Saint John of the Cross comments on the darkness this causes within the inner spirit, as desires are tempered and disciplined: "To deprive oneself of the gratification of the appetites in all things is like living in darkness and in a void" (AMC 1.3.1). Deprivation leads inevitably to this experience of an interior darkness. In renunciations directed at the pleasures of the senses, a first taste of a spiritual hunger can arise that in time can be stretched into far deeper regions of the soul.

Most people, until they begin to deprive themselves, have little awareness of how indulgent our senses can be in satisfying our immediate desires. This is particularly true of pleasures in food, which makes food a good place to start in the matter of ascetical restraint. Restricting ourselves to eating only at meals and taking nothing else in between, tempering our intake, not always choosing in accord with preference, mild steady fasting in predictable routines—these are hardly extreme measures. But quickly they begin to teach us how to say "no" to desires that would otherwise be indulged without a thought. These lessons of self-denial, first learned in physical privations, can carry over for use into many areas of the spiritual life, especially in exercising charity or conquering pride, but also in the life of prayer when prayer is difficult, as we shall see. The power to command, and the strength to refuse, are indispensable for virtue but are essential as well for contemplative life, as we will also see. All self-denial becomes a form of dying to self, which in itself is a core principle of spirituality, but it also fosters a vibrant will that is able to give freely and generously to God. The interior freedom to love without restraint depends on embracing an ultimate spiritual principle that "He must increase, but I must decrease" (Jn 3:30), as Saint John the Baptist famously taught, and without which there is no open path to God.

By contrast, the absence of a virtuous habit of self-denial will almost always mean that bodily satisfactions and pleasurable experiences are identified to some extent with personal happiness. This tendency to seek pleasure for the sake of happiness, even when these pleasures are not gravely sinful, has no small effect on our spiritual life. We do not lose ourselves, as Jesus asks, while preoccupied with pleasing ourselves. A life taken up with the habitual chase after sense enjoyment may not be a bad life, but it is bound to suffer a dullness spiritually. Little hunger of soul can be felt when the desire for sense gratification rules us daily to some degree. A fire of love for God can hardly catch flame before it smolders again, replaced by inferior desires. Perhaps the following statement from book 2 of *The Ascent of Mount Carmel* ought to be presented at this point and pondered. What Saint John of the Cross is saying here, which is largely about prayer, is rarely embraced, no doubt in part because the habit of self-denial in physical privations is never adopted in any serious manner. The importance of this striking statement will become more evident in later discussions on prayer, but its admonition regarding self-denial, if unheeded, warns of inevitable harm to the spiritual path.

> I should like to persuade spiritual persons that the road leading to God . . . demands only the one thing necessary: true self-denial, exterior and interior, through surrender of self both to suffering for Christ and to annihilation in all things. In the exercise of this self-denial everything else, and even more, is discovered and accomplished. If one fails in this exercise, the root and sum total of all the virtues, the other methods would amount to no more than going around in circles without getting anywhere. . . . I would not consider any spirituality worthwhile that wants to walk in sweetness and ease and run from the imitation of Christ. (AMC 2.7.8)

For Saint John of the Cross, it is not simply the pleasures and enjoyments of the senses in themselves that are the crux of the problem. The human experience of sense satisfaction is unavoidable. Even the desert monks of the early Christian centuries, who took on extreme physical hardships, no doubt preferred the taste of one cooked leaf to another or found one cool spring of water a better choice over another. The Gospel recounts that Saint John the Baptist, in his desert, along with his consumption of the unpalatable locusts, survived also on honey. The Christian perspective in this matter, when it is healthy, advocates a balanced approach. It does not propose a denigration of bodily life to the point of destroying or damaging it. We are an inseparable unity of body and soul as human persons, and bodily life has a sacred dimension, a truth that has far-reaching consequences in morality. But that unity of body and soul is precisely the point and the issue of importance in asceticism. Nothing of bodily life can be lived as though detached from the soul's existence.

Even more to the point, bodily pursuits inevitably engage the will. The will and its desires remain always in a kind of dynamic consort with bodily, emotional, and intellectual activity. At the same time, the will is a primary reality in our lives by the manner in which it cooperates with or rebels against the graced invitations of God. Seeking union with God demands a deeply rooted determination of our soul to give our will fully in love to God. This cannot be accomplished without the desires of the will aligning themselves with the goal of a union with God's will in all facets of bodily, emotional, and intellectual life. Most importantly, the will is the faculty of love in the soul. The will must be empty of desires for gratification if by a great love it is to seek for God as a primary desire. All that touches and enters into the desires of the will is crucial for the possibility of a union with God by means of love. It remains now to explain how the will in its capacity for love is affected by the principles of self-denial and asceticism. These two statements from book 2 of *The Ascent to Mount Carmel* in effect define the nature of sanctity and at the same time express the essential importance of the will's purification in sanctity.

> Supernatural union exists when God's will and the soul's are in conformity, so that nothing in the one is repugnant to the other. When the soul rids itself completely of what is repugnant and unconformed to the divine will, it rests transformed in God through love. . . . A soul makes room for God by wiping away all the smudges and smears of creatures, by uniting its will perfectly to God's; for to love is to labor to divest and deprive oneself for God of all that is not God. When this is done the soul will be illumined by and transformed in God. (AMC 2.5.3, 7)

Saint John of the Cross will teach repeatedly a particular lesson that must be mastered over time. The refusal to give into the *desire* for the gratification of the appetites is the underlying principle that must motivate all practices of self-denial. Deprivation of the senses has value only inasmuch as it purges and purifies the will in its craving and coveting for immediate satisfactions. The goal is a nakedness of desire, a poverty of desire, so that interior desire is consumed, instead, with an intense longing for God. Desire does not die like a fire with no fuel to feed it; rather, it becomes a *concentrated* fire of greater desire that can be directed to God and *his* pleasure. Self-denial of all kinds can pave the way to this inner transformation. Ideally, the interior act of refusal —the "no" to something—is accompanied by an interior "yes" of the will to offer to God this sacrifice out of love in a desire to be united to God. When this sacrificial practice becomes more habitual toward gratifications that could be enjoyed in sense pleasure, an emptiness ensues that Saint John of the Cross describes as entering a night of darkness: "Any individuals who may have denied and rejected the gratification that all things afford them, by mortifying their appetite for them, live as though in the night—in darkness, which is nothing else than a void within them of all things" (AMC 1.3.2).

The focus, again, is not simply on denying pleasure in itself but on overcoming persistent *desire* for the gratification of our appetites. Insistent appetites, when indulged and disordered, cause spiritual stagnation. When we give in to them thoughtlessly or impulsively, they have a dissipating effect on the will, making our souls thereby restless, harried, hard to please. "This is the characteristic of those with appetites; they are always dissatisfied and bitter, like someone who is hungry" (AMC 1.6.3). On the other hand, when we deny our appetites and refuse to gratify them, leaving ourselves empty, the will is energized and opened to grace. Again, the critical target is not simply pleasure but the *craving* for pleasure and gratification. The desire for gratification weighs down the will when it longs for something that is not God's will. If some pleasurable thing is indulged in a choice, it is chosen for our own delight and sought for ourselves. The habit of indulging ourselves in pleasure invariably produces attachments to particular pleasures. We end up craving and coveting in consuming ways; the lingering effect on the will is a spiritually damaging heaviness of soul. There can be a heavy bloating of the soul just as there can be of the body. Saint John of the Cross will comment astutely that even without the opportunity to choose pleasures of the senses, the desire in itself for these pleasures can have a harmful effect.

> We are not discussing the mere lack of things; this lack will not divest the soul if it craves for all these objects. We are dealing with the denudation of the soul's appetites and gratifications. This is what leaves it free and empty of all things, even though it possesses them. Since the things of

the world cannot enter the soul, they are not in themselves
an encumbrance or harm to it; rather, it is the will and appetite dwelling within that cause the damage when set on
these things. (AMC 1.3.4)

It might be useful in a brief excursus to explain the understanding of the will and its operations that Saint John of
the Cross would have imbibed from his theological studies
at the Thomistic grounded University of Salamanca in the
mid-1560s. This teaching on the will is central to his own
spiritual doctrine. Succinctly stated, the will displays three
distinct types of operation, three different ways of being
"in act". Just as our arm, as a physical organ, can throw an
object, can lift it, or can pull it, so the will is exercising
itself, or is "in act", in three different ways of operation.
The first operation is the will in a state of desire, before
any choice: that is, the will wanting something, inclined
and drawn toward something, longing for it, full of desire
for it. This initial operation of desire in the will is always
dependent on the intellect. A fundamental law of the spiritual life is at work here: What attracts the intellect draws
the will in desire. Jesus himself pointed to this truth in the
Sermon on the Mount: "For where your treasure is, there
will your heart be also" (Mt 6:21). In other words, what
our mind extols and values, our will is drawn to seek. The
converse applies as well: What is perceived as repugnant by
the intellect, or fearful and threatening, provokes aversion
in the will, that is, a withdrawal of desire, a desire to evade
or avoid something.

This teaching contains a spiritual implication of vast importance. The appetitive life of desire in the will submits
to the attractions or aversions fed to it by the intellect. The
more compulsively and obsessively the mind dwells on an

object of desire, the more the will is invaded by desire for it. The more the mind is in fear or anxiety about an object of aversion, the more the will suffers a painful contraction and withdrawal in any remembrance of it. On that basis, the importance of "mental austerity" arises as a critical element of training in the practice of asceticism and all self-renunciation. When the mind no longer occupies itself in thought about something, there is little or no desire for it or aversion toward it. That is true of God, baseball, wine, or prayer. The desires for gratification, which Saint John of the Cross identifies as so problematic, are corrected, if possible, by turning the mind from the attraction that feeds these desires. The aversion toward what is difficult to bear in our lives likewise lifts when the mind gives less attention to it. Mental austerity—the calming of a mental need for impulsive gratification or the mental fear of suffering something —opens the way in turn to the will turning its desire to God more wholeheartedly. The emptiness of an unencumbered will, that is, a will not dominated by unhealthy desire in this first operation of the will, is an absolute requirement for spiritual transformation.

Before continuing with the two other operations of the will, perhaps it is beneficial to hear a very challenging passage from book 1 of *The Ascent of Mount Carmel* that proposes how the will in this first operation of desire can be quickly purified and refined and the soul prepared in turn for the grace of contemplation. We should take special note that the statement begins with the phrase—"endeavor to be inclined always". The first operation of the will in its inclination needs to be narrowed and focused in a sacrificial manner if our lives are to be conformed to God's desires. The following statement is an example of the rigor of Saint John of the Cross' teaching, but it is also a striking testimony to the importance of the will in its first operation of desire.

> Endeavor to be inclined always:
>> not to the easiest, but to the most difficult;
>> not to the most delightful, but to the most distasteful;
>> not to the most gratifying, but to the less pleasant;
>> not to what means rest for you, but to hard work;
>> not to the consoling, but to the unconsoling;
>> not to the most, but to the least;
>> not to the highest and most precious, but to the lowest and most despised;
>>> not to wanting something, but to wanting nothing.
>> (AMC 1.13.6)

The second operation of the will, familiar to all, is when the will actually chooses an action, exercising a power to accept or to refuse, to let go or to pursue, to take hold or to release, and so on. In every choice we make, as Saint Thomas Aquinas teaches, we are always choosing something desirable. It may not be the entire reality of a choice that is desirable, for no sin is desirable in itself as an offense against God. But by its nature, in the teaching of Aquinas, the will cannot exercise a choice for an action except that some aspect of a choice is perceived as desirable and offers some prospect of satisfaction if chosen. It is easy to perceive that the pleasure enticing us in a temptation to sin meets this criterion for a desirable choice. Again, we can see that the desire fed to the will by the intellect's attractions can affect an eventual choice. What is desired strongly is often what is chosen indulgently, unless we live with some degree of disciplined awareness. Ideally, we should desire to give delight to God in our choices, and our actions should follow from this desire to please God and ultimately to fulfill his will. If that desire to please God becomes the primary desire compelling our will, we are on the path to union with God. But, of course, a lifetime of spiritual perseverance is needed to follow this hard path.

The third operation is the delight or satiation that the will undergoes when, after desiring something, and then choosing it, the will experiences a satisfaction in that choice. Or, conversely, this operation will entail the frustration the will experiences in dissatisfaction by not being able to choose what attracts it in desire or in finding no satisfaction in what it has chosen. What we hear in these descriptions is again the link of one operation to the other. It should be noted at this point that the interconnection of these three operations is the fundamental teaching of Saint Thomas Aquinas on the habitus of virtue and vice. How so? What gives delight to the will ordinarily returns again in a predictable manner to arouse desire in the will for the same enjoyment. This teaching, which assumes an interplay of movement and flow through these three operations, is decisive for confronting the real challenge of union with the will of God. All three operations must be more and more permeated by divine grace and supernatural charity. A saintly life is one in which the will desires the desires of God, chooses in action the will of God, and finds delight in what delights God. Sanctity is indeed literally a state of soul, one in which the will in these three operations is inflamed by theological charity.

With this understanding, it should not be surprising that Saint John of the Cross, in addressing an essential obstacle to holiness, writes that the will in its *desire* is easily subject to a scattered and dissipated condition. The desire of the will is like a fire of energy in the human person. But it leaks away through various cracks, as it were, when diverse objects claim a pressing need for gratification.

> Because the force of the desire is divided, the appetite be-
> comes weaker than if it were completely fixed on one ob-
> ject. The more objects there are dividing an appetite, the
> weaker this appetite becomes for each. This is why the
> philosophers say that virtue when united is stronger than
> when scattered. It is therefore clear that if the appetite of
> the will pours itself out on something other than virtue,
> it grows weaker in the practice of virtue. A person whose
> will is divided among trifles is like water that, leaking out
> at the bottom, will not rise higher and is therefore useless.
> (AMC 1.10.1).

The implication in this passage is that if God could be the
"one object" we desire, a life would be affected dramatically.
But such a state of soul requires a sustained tempering and
purging of the multiple and diverse desires that can divide
the will's strength and energy. "The soul that is not recollected in one appetite alone, the desire for God, loses heat
and strength in the practice of virtue" (AMC 1.10.1). The
interest of this last statement is especially in the use of the
word "recollected". A vigor of mental austerity is needed
to release ourselves from the clinging effect of desires and
of their repetitive tapping on our mind for attention, so that
in time we may approach a day when God alone draws our
desire more exclusively. The contrary possibility draws a
sharp warning: "The unmortified appetites result in killing
the soul in its relationship with God" (AMC 1.10.3).

Saint John of the Cross insists in particular on the spiritual harm that is incurred by desires repeatedly indulged and
satisfied. The heavy weight that bears down on the will due
to undisciplined habits of choice is noteworthy. A person
indulgent in needless desires "is like someone with a fever
whose thirst increases by the minute, and who feels ill until

the fever leaves" (AMC 1.6.6). The return of insistent desires, whenever we choose indulgently, is predictable. Fatigue and weariness of spirit are the consequence, rather
than real satisfaction. "The soul [is] wearied and tired by
all its appetites and their fulfillment, because the fulfillment
only causes more hunger and emptiness" (AMC 1.6.6). The
appetites, he writes, end up ruling the person and "resemble little children, restless and hard to please, always whining
to their mother for this thing or that, and never satisfied"
(AMC 1.6.6). There can be no spirit of deeper recollection
in the person subject to the demands of insistent appetites,
and this does not mean just sense desire. Any indulgent behavior whereby we mindlessly satisfy our immediate needs
—in speech, taste, distractions, entertainments—is enough
to keep us from the path of self-emptying. When we indulge these appetites frivolously, unthinkingly, we become
attached to the delight they promise. "They agitate and disturb one just as wind disturbs water. And they so upset the
soul that they do not let it rest in any place or thing" (AMC
1.6.6).

What is perhaps most perceptive in this treatment is the
understanding of the harm in attachments as an impediment
to spiritual growth. Habitual attachments, even when they
do not involve a clear sin, can be more damaging, in Saint
John of the Cross' view, than "the daily commission of
many other imperfections and sporadic venial sins that do
not result from a bad habit. These latter will not hinder a
person as much as will the attachment to something" (AMC
1.11.4). The reason for the harm has to do with the effect of
habitual attachments on the operation of desire in the will.
The desire for something that delights us or appeases some
obsessive need returns repeatedly and ends up stealing from
us a desire for God. The following statement is a strong

justification for the need to conquer attachments, even in small areas of indulged pleasure, in order to free our soul's deeper desire for God.

> It makes little difference whether a bird is tied by a thin thread or by a cord. Even if it is tied by thread, the bird will be held bound just as surely as if it were tied by cord; that is, it will be impeded from flying as long as it does not break the thread. Admittedly the thread is easier to break, but no matter how easily this may be done, the bird will not fly away without first doing so. This is the lot of those who are attached to something: No matter how much virtue they have they will not reach the freedom of the divine union. (AMC 1.11.4)

In bringing this discussion on asceticism to a close, we can note the radicality of the teaching and simultaneously the evident spiritual logic behind it. The demands of self-denial are inseparable from the will's central role in spiritual advancement. The highlighting of the danger of appetites and attachments when they are indulged voluntarily is because these habits immerse the faculty of the will in a contrarian manner of opposition to the will of God. They clog the will's operations, just as our arteries can be clogged and blocked, with the result that healthy blood is impeded from flowing freely. "A person has only one will and if that is encumbered or occupied by anything, the person will not possess the freedom, solitude, and purity requisite for divine transformation" (AMC 1.11.6). The first operation of desire in the will is of utmost importance in the spiritual life. It is compromised and harmed when desires are indulged. The will's operation of desire does not turn toward God in a loving need and inclination to please him when other created realities, some quite trifling, or others clearly sinful and indulgent, take captive the will's desire. We cannot advance toward God, indeed, we cannot be released from the entanglement of appetites and attachments, without a consuming desire for God, or, as Saint John of the Cross writes, "if the spiritual part of the soul is not fired with other, more urgent longings for spiritual things" (AMC 1.14.2).

The series of verses that follows is a fitting conclusion to this discussion. They epitomize the deeper demands of a spirit of self-denial. The spiritual effort to seek nothing but God himself, radically on display in these verses, is a proposition that extends far beyond mere practices of self-denial. A naked purity of desire is necessary to drive the soul forward on the contemplative path to God. These verses are worth committing to memory. They can be read as a quintessential commentary on Saint John the Baptist's words—"He must increase, but I must decrease" (Jn 3:30). And what do they teach us? An intense desire for God is not distinct from an intense love for God. The dynamic emptying of desire, letting it remain unsatisfied, opens us to an all-consuming passion for God. When we desire only him as our ultimate love, this purity of desire necessarily takes the will deeply into the mystery of God. We will see in time the significance that these verses have on the will's role in the prayer of contemplation. Ideally, prayer burns inwardly with a single great desire for nothing but God himself.

> To reach satisfaction in all
> desire satisfaction in nothing.
> To come to possess all
> desire the possession of nothing.
> To arrive at being all
> desire to be nothing.
> To come to the knowledge of all
> desire the knowledge of nothing.

To come to enjoy what you have not
you must go by a way in which you enjoy not.
To come to the knowledge you have not
you must go by a way in which you know not.
To come to the possession you have not
you must go by a way in which you possess not.
To come to be what you are not
you must go by a way in which you are not.

When you delay in something
you cease to rush toward the all.
For to go from the all to the all
you must deny yourself of all in all.
And when you come to the possession of the all
you must possess it without wanting anything.
Because if you desire to have something in all
your treasure in God is not purely your all.

In this nakedness the spirit finds its quietude and rest. For in coveting nothing, nothing tires it by pulling it up and nothing oppresses it by pushing it down, because it is in the center of its humility. When it covets something, by this very fact it tires itself. (AMC 1.13.11–13)

6

THE PURIFICATION OF
THE WILL FOR LOVE ALONE

After exposing these principles of asceticism, we turn to the purification of the will by the theological virtue of charity. Saint John of the Cross treats this subject in the last section of book 3 of *The Ascent of Mount Carmel*. The teaching is not a matter simply of self-denial leading to an emptying of the will for God. While the ascetical task is important and required, what is indispensable for the grace of contemplation is a developed capacity for deeper *self*-emptying. No grace of contemplation can be expected as long as we indulge coveting tendencies in our lives. A release from immoderate, self-oriented desires that turn us inwardly upon ourselves is therefore a necessary preparation for any deeper life of prayer. Seeking to please ourselves as a motive for choices is always some variation of this damaging inward turn. In the view of Saint John of the Cross, this tendency demands serious efforts of reversal. If we aspire to the grace of contemplation, our will has to give itself with vigor to the will of God. We have to strive to give delight to God by our choices and by our renunciations, not seeking to find pleasure and delight simply for ourselves. As we turn away from pleasing ourselves, we become more empty and receptive inwardly to God's promptings. The grace of contemplation in prayer then has an open window, if God chooses to bestow it. Otherwise, that window is sealed tight. The purpose of this chapter is to understand the deeper challenges in this purification of the will for the sake of contemplative graces. As the will exercises itself in interior self-renunciation, it opens itself to a loving union with the will of God. This increasing bond with the will of God is a necessary prerequisite for the prayer of contemplation.

Saint John of the Cross views the will as the *unitive* faculty in the contemplative path of the soul to union with God. In itself, that emphasis makes this subject of the will's purification by charity an essential component in spirituality. The response by Jesus Christ himself in the Gospel, answering the question "which commandment is the first of all?" (Mk 12:28), is to "love the Lord your God with *all* your heart, and with *all* your soul, and with *all* your mind, and with *all* your strength" (Mk 12:30; emphasis added). Interestingly, in the passage of Saint Mark's Gospel, Jesus quotes the Book of Deuteronomy (Deut 6:5), in which heart, soul, and strength are identified, but Jesus adds a need also to love "with all your mind". The mind, too, must give itself to the love of God in a complete manner. This does not imply, naturally, constant study, but rather reaffirms the necessary link between the mind and the will as explained in the last chapter. The attractions that draw the intellect provoke desires in the will. A loving attention to God and his will forges a flame of desire in the will for giving itself in a daily effort of love to him. The will never operates in an isolated manner; the intellect must accompany it. For that reason, mental austerity becomes a primary factor in shaping the will to love God in a total manner.

God asks for *all*; but do we give him all? This is a clear challenge if we aspire to contemplative graces. It does not mean, of course, selling everything and giving away all our possessions—in a material sense. But it may demand a need for a spirit of greater self-offering as our life continues. The contemplative soul is surely formed by the interior longing to forget self and give more fully to God. The manner in which the will is central to this disposition is our current focus. Granted the importance of the mind in its influence on the will, as already stated, it is nonetheless essential to affirm that the effort to love with all our being and strength is ultimately a question of our will. The presence of theological charity, i.e., supernatural *love*, resides in the will and its three operations. The strength of the soul to love, for better or worse, is always subject to the will. As our will rules and as it chooses, so our soul is shaped and fashioned, with the help of grace. And what does the will rule exactly? All the bodily and mental and emotional life of the human person is under the governance of the will—all the faculties, passions, and appetites. The thoughts and mental life, the feelings indulged, savored, and pursued, the choices adopted in action, all this is under the mastery of the will. A short paragraph in the opening section on the will in book 3 of *The Ascent to Mount Carmel* attests to the importance of the will in determining how fully the soul responds to grace and turns all its strength of love toward God. Inasmuch as contemplation is dependent on love, the purification of the will for greater love is an essential condition for any deeper contemplative union with God. "The strength of the soul comprises the faculties, passions, and appetites. All this strength is ruled by the will. When the will directs these faculties, passions, and appetites toward God, turning away from all that is not God, the soul preserves its strength for God, and comes to love him with all its might" (AMC 3.16.2).

Saint John of the Cross places great importance in particular on the exercise of the will in the purification of so-called inordinate feelings. What he means by feelings are the passions of the soul, which, if uncontrolled or regularly indulged, cause constant turbulence and disruption in our lives. The reason is that the passions, if not tempered, cling heavily to the will and weigh down the three operations of the will. No deeper interiority with God can be maintained without a discipline of the passions. These feelings, if not governed by an exercised strength of the will, tend to dominate a life by cleaving oppressively to the will, influencing its desires, its choices, and its pursuit of delights. The passions can lead us to continual instability in the spiritual life, including the life of prayer. In the treatment of Saint John of the Cross, there are four primary passions or feelings: joy, hope, sorrow, and fear. The challenge is to rule these passions in such a manner that "a person rejoices only in what is purely for God's honor and glory, hopes for nothing else, feels sorrow only about matters pertaining to this, and fears only God" (AMC 3.16.2). That statement in itself presents an immensely difficult demand. But the result of exercising or not exercising a control over these passions and directing them toward God is consequential: "When these emotions are unbridled they are the source of all vices and imperfections, but when they are put in order and calmed they give rise to all the virtues" (AMC 3.16.5).

Clearly, as we hear in these words, the will's engagement with the passions is a significant challenge for growth in spirituality. The will cannot be permeated by charity without a concentrated effort of purging and restraining immoderate passions, so that we can direct a single fire of concentrated passion within the soul to God himself. If we recall that the will is a "cavern" of vast emptiness capable of being filled by the infinite love of God, we appreciate better this teaching. The inner regions of depth in the will must be emptied of a kind of heavy, subversive influence coming from undisciplined passions. If the purification of the will by supernatural charity is to succeed as God desires, the passions must submit to a governance of self-control. This purification is inseparable from an intensifying presence of charity in the will as a person exercises renunciation toward self-indulgent tendencies. This work entails the concrete effort to subdue the impact of the passions upon the will so that they do not interfere with the will giving itself more fully to God. The centrality of this effort for holiness is evident in these brief words: "The *entire matter of reaching union with God* consists in purging the will of its appetites and emotions so that from a human and lowly will it may be changed into the divine will, made identical with the will of God" (AMC 3.16.3; emphasis added).

Saint John of the Cross lays much stress particularly on the passion of joy as it affects the will. It is an interesting corrective to what may be, without our conscious awareness, a common impediment to spiritual advancement. Saint John of the Cross is not advocating joylessness, naturally. Every saint gives evidence of a deep contentment and a radiant attraction flowing from his life of close relations with God. As the saying goes, there is no such thing as a sad saint. On the other hand, we who are not saints tend to seek our joys and delight in all manner of temporal enticements that have no link to God. We chase after joys and delight in the enjoyment of pleasure and possessions and in pursuing experiences of fleeting happiness instead of seeking an abiding state of joy found in the soul itself when we are giving ourselves more fully to God. And what is the nature of such a joy of soul; or, rather, what ought to be the cause of spiritual joy in our lives? Saint John of the Cross is rather strong in presenting what he calls a fundamental spiritual principle: "The will should rejoice only in what is for the honor and

glory of God, and the greatest honor we can give him is to
serve him according to evangelical perfection; anything un-
included in such service is without value to human beings"
(AMC 3.17.2). We might temper that statement a bit. Not
everyone will have a vocation to take up the vows of religious life, with their rigorous demands, but everyone can
pursue a serious hunger for the will of God in life. In that
hunger for God and his will, we can find our ultimate spiritual joy in this life. If, indeed, we do aspire to a union with
God, the following words near the end of *The Dark Night*
express starkly the serious demand of love that is required,
no matter what our state in life. They are worth including
as an additional comment in this discussion:

> One cannot reach this union without remarkable purity,
> and this purity is unattainable without vigorous mortifi-
> cation and nakedness regarding all creatures. . . . Persons
> who refuse to go out at night in search for the Beloved
> and to divest and mortify their will, but rather seek the
> Beloved in their own bed and comfort, as did the bride
> [Sg. 3:1], will not succeed in finding him. As this soul de-
> clares, she found him when she departed in darkness and
> with longings of love. (DN 2.24.4)

Let us recall, before we proceed further, that the degree
of our union with the will of God determines the measure
of love in our soul. It is our love united to the will of God
that is the source of the deep abiding joy in our soul. But
a will united to God requires a will emptied and purified
for God in the three operations of the will. Everything else
sought in excessive ways apart from the will of God that
seems to bring happiness has some deceptive quality. If we
are in conflict with the will of God, any semblance of happiness we seem to enjoy dissipates eventually or disappears
entirely. The principle that Saint John of the Cross advo-

cates is a concrete recommendation for daily use, although our whole life depends on this observance: a determination to seek our satisfactions in life, and in the immediate day, by esteeming what is pleasing to God. This focus on a desire for giving delight to God aligns us to the pursuit of God's will. To find joy in giving delight to God can return to animate desire in all our activities, in the most relaxed settings and in the most tense circumstances of any trial.

This same advice is also a matter of exercising a deep faith, inasmuch as it requires that we actually *believe* we can touch the Heart of God and give delight to him by our choices, particularly by our sacrificial choices. It is helpful to observe that Saint John of the Cross is often teaching an asceticism of love in the interior life. Self-denial and renunciation must be exercised in the interior life in response to the passions and our inmost thoughts. Mental austerity as a strength of mind to turn our attention away from what *interiorly* in our thought provokes the passions is always a mark of a serious spiritual quality. This same mental austerity is capable of directing our attention in love to God himself and the desire to please him. In this sense, the struggle against the passions is preparation for a wholehearted turning of our desire to God himself in prayer. On the other hand, neglect in this regard is consequential. Without some effort of mental austerity and interior restraint, the passions tend to catch flame easily and can burn like uncontrolled brush fires within the soul. In many lives, they wreak havoc, making a life subject to unstable, pressing demands. Unless a conversion then takes place and the will exercises some exacting governance, a life of deeper prayer will never draw attraction. All the instruction we are hearing in this chapter is an extension of the importance of an asceticism of love into a greater depth of application within the interiority of our lives. This effort of self-emptying within our inner life for God is an essential discipline if the grace of contemplation is to find a proper hunger and longing in the soul.

Saint John of the Cross proceeds to enumerate various aspects of worldliness that can take captive our passion of joy and that God would prefer that we not pursue so energetically as a cause of joy in our lives. The first category is what he calls temporal goods sought for the delight and satisfaction they bring to our lives. The pursuit of "riches, status, positions, and other things claiming prestige" (AMC 3.18.1), sought out of worldly desire and ambition, is a way of ignoring and resisting the will of God. To achieve satisfaction in these vanities that elevate our status in life is to embrace at times a permanent tension with God. We may achieve our ambitions, but a success in the world is perhaps not at all what God wanted us primarily to desire in life, which was rather to seek him first above all other things. The very delight experienced in worldly achievement often beclouds the spirit with an egoism that takes over a sense of personal identity and for many people is never overcome. We become obtuse and spiritually dull, unable to discern the transiency of our lives as we proceed each day closer to our final judgment and an entry into eternity. In Saint John of the Cross' view, status and success are not to be rejoiced in except insofar as they can be employed in the service of God. Perhaps these thoughts offer an invitation to rethink and modify our worldly attitudes if we have pursued worldly achievements and now can see through the deception of seeking our happiness in them. There may be things that are part of our lives that cannot be reversed or eliminated, but we should make an effort so that they may be turned to some degree to the service of God. To continue to seek joys in the indulged pleasures of a worldly life is to misconceive the purpose of life. Saint John of the Cross expresses in the following statement a difficult demand, but in the context of seeking union with God, it is not surprising. What he is referring to is an excessive joy in worldly satisfaction:

> The heart of the fool, states the Wise Man, is where there is gladness; but the heart of the wise is where there is sadness [Eccl. 7:4]. Gladness is blinding to the heart and does not allow it to consider and ponder things, while sadness makes people open their eyes and see the advantage or harm in things. . . . Nothing but what belongs to the service of God should be the object of our joy. Any other joy would be vain and worthless, for joy that is out of harmony with God is of no value to the soul. (AMC 3.18.5, 6)

It may be difficult for us to assimilate or perhaps to accept at face value what Saint John of the Cross is addressing in such strong terms. If we live in the world, not in a monastery, these demands may seem unreasonable. Such remarks, for Saint John of the Cross, are not directed toward winning over a general audience. He was writing for dedicated Carmelites and preferred a blunt exposé of the demands of holiness. In effect, however, even for us, he is affirming the crucial role of our will in sanctity and describing what happens by means of the three operations of the will. Saint John of the Cross goes on to explain more fully the harm to the soul in the embrace of joys that are sought solely for human satisfaction, without a reference to God. The essential harm is due to the nature of the will in its operations. The will that is divided and scattered in its pursuit of many self-centered desires is a will dissipated at its center. If we covet things other than God, while unconcerned for God, and find fleeting delights in them with no thought for God, we cannot but weaken our desire for God. It is as though the will has a single thrust of energetic drive in any hour, one force and momentum, which propels it in any hour toward the target of an object of desire. If we turn the desire of the will toward enticements offered by the things of this world, we turn at the same time away from God. A withdrawal from God takes place, often inadvertently, because we are fixated on attaining delights and satisfactions that do not align with God's will for us and that, indeed, may be directly opposed to his will. All harm to the soul has some connection to the desires of the will and the delights that the soul embraces in choices. We tear ourselves away from God for the sake of created things that have little value next to the pursuit of God. Saint John of the Cross begins the following passage with a warning about how slight the beginnings can be by which we turn our desires away from the pursuit of God as the primary love in our lives.

> We would run out of ink, paper, and time were we to describe the harm that beleaguers the soul because it turns its affection to temporal goods. Something very small can lead into great evils and destroy remarkable blessings, just as an unextinguished spark can kindle immense fires capable of burning up the world.
>
> All this harm has its origin and root in one main private harm embodied in this joy: withdrawal from God. Just as approaching God through the affection of the will gives rise to every good, so withdrawal from him through creature affection breeds every harm and evil in the soul. The measure of the harm reflects the intensity of the joy and affection with which the will is joined to the creature, for in that proportion does it withdraw from God. (AMC 3.19.1)

There is a clear interpretative key for this teaching in what we have already exposed regarding the threefold operations of the will. By the nature of its three operations working together, the will ordinarily finds itself "rotating back" in its desire to the things that have given delight in any particular choice. The pattern is repeated consistently: desire for something, followed by a choice for it, followed by a subsequent satisfaction in that choice. The momentum does not stop on its own; once activated, it returns and repeats itself. Desire is felt again for what has previously been chosen with some delight. The pattern tends to repeat itself. This is precisely the nature of all vice. Habits of repetitive sin, especially involving sensual matters, follow this pattern of a rotation through desire, indulged choice, temporary and fleeting delight, and the return again of desire. The great harm that takes place, if desires are indulged and delight is experienced in this repeated manner, is that the mind itself dulls in its relationship with God. The pursuit of satisfaction can dominate the soul in ways that do not necessarily involve grave sin but, nonetheless, pour sand, as it were, upon what could otherwise be a fire of longing for God. If a soul is indulging itself in attached ways in this manner, it is very unlikely to experience much desire at all for God and, therefore, little desire for prayer. And how common is this truth to this very day, even among those dedicated by a chosen profession as priests or religious to the service of God. Saint John of the Cross thus identifies a principal harm when a soul takes joy in self-centered and self-oriented delights: "dullness of mind and darkness of judgment in understanding truth and judging well of each thing as it is in itself" (AMC 3.19.3). That dullness of mind translates into a tepidity toward God and spiritual matters. The things of spirituality do not attract desire when the delights of the will are being indulged elsewhere. There tends to be a progressive momentum to these tendencies inasmuch as the will is a faculty of energy. The more that an appetite and thirst increase for one thing, the less there is attraction or hunger for another. For instance, the desire for money, writes Saint John of the Cross in the sixteenth century, as gold poured into Spain from the Spanish colonies in the New World, can become an idol and a god, dominating the desire for satisfaction and leading, if pursued to excess, to the loss of God. His words are just as pertinent in our own day: "Out there in the world, their reason darkened as to spiritual matters through covetousness, they serve money and not God, and they are moved by money rather than by God, and they give first consideration to the temporal price and not to the divine value and reward. In countless ways they make money their principal god and goal and give it precedence over God, their ultimate end" (AMC 3.19.9).

The primary harm to the will through indulging our desires is in the strength of attachment to a created thing that then takes captive the soul. Attachments are a consequence of all avaricious pursuit. We may get what we want, but the cost is to have a kind of foreign presence invading our soul and holding sway over our thoughts and desires. A spirit of possessiveness takes over the interior life. We do not want to lose what we have or renounce what we continue to desire for enjoyment. For Saint John of the Cross, the seeking of our joy in the things of this world leads often rather quickly to a possessive attachment toward them: "For there can be no voluntary joy over creatures without voluntary possessiveness, just as there can be no joy, insofar as it is a passion, unaccompanied by habitual possessiveness of heart. The denial and purgation of such joy leaves the judgment as clear as the air when vapors vanish" (AMC 3.20.2). This habit of possessiveness toward anything is a quality of steady, excessive desire in the will. It is the desire to hold onto something, to claim it for one's own, to have it readily available for consumption and enjoyment. The habit enters the soul like a heavy presence weighing down the soul to the degree that an indulged pursuit of any delight continues to repeat itself. This amounts to a will knocked off the path, out of kilter, dominated by self-centered needs, in its operation of desire. Possessiveness of this sort is always a sign of avarice in a soul.

Detachment, on the other hand, is a much favored quality of soul for Saint John of the Cross. It likewise enters into the three operations of the will. He writes, impressively, that detachment is "freedom of the heart for God. With this the soul is disposed for all the favors God will grant it. Without it, he does not bestow them" (AMC 3.20.4). Detachment of soul means that a soul is truly at liberty, free to take delight in things without a consuming need for them; free to refuse an enjoyment without excessive pain; not dominated by desire and the need to find satisfaction. In the detached soul, nothing is sought simply for the sake of self-satisfaction. Desires are not indulged as though the demand for a satisfaction *must* be met. Not surprisingly, detachment grows in a soul to the degree that God himself is the great desire of the soul. It is a natural consequence to treat things other than God with less importance as God becomes a more serious pursuit in our lives. Admittedly, there can seem to be an uncompromising severity in this teaching of Saint John of the Cross. But it is justified by the absolute purity that a true freedom of heart presumes. Nothing must cling to our soul, entrapping it, if we want God as the Beloved of our lives. An attachment to something that offers delight and pleasure can be the most deceptive obstacle because it appears to offer us happiness. Yet often the same thing promising happiness brings some form of lingering dependency on it for intermittent satisfactions. By contrast,

an interior freedom to love more fully is felt as our heart
refuses to be weighed down by any single thing or person
apart from God. As we shall see, prayer demands precisely
this cultivated quality of detachment in a soul. Prayer thrives
or struggles depending on detachment, because the latter is
present always in a great love for God. A powerful statement
taken from *The Spiritual Canticle* admonishes us that what is
ultimately at stake in detachment is whether Jesus our Lord
becomes Jesus the true Beloved of our life:

> You can truthfully call God Beloved when you are wholly
> with him, do not allow your heart attachment to anything
> outside of him, and thereby ordinarily center your mind
> on him. . . . Some call the Bridegroom beloved when he
> is not really their beloved because their heart is not wholly
> set on him. As a result their petition is not of much value
> in his sight. They do not obtain their request until they
> keep their spirit more continually with God through per-
> severance in prayer, and their heart with its affectionate
> love more entirely set on him. Nothing is obtained from
> God except by love. (SC 1.13)

In expounding his teaching on detachment as intrinsic to
greater love, Saint John of the Cross writes as well in book
3 of *The Ascent of Mount Carmel* about the seductive appeal
that the allurement of beauty can pose to the soul. He is
addressing, not the obvious dangers of sensual temptation,
but rather the spontaneous manner in which we are affected
so quickly by the attractions we find in the physical appear-
ances of people. The tendency to be deceived by beauty and
to find ourselves drawn in by an attractive appearance is a
common experience. We easily identify goodness with an
appealing outward demeanor, but that may not be an accu-
rate assessment. Saint John of the Cross offers his own can-
did comment on this tendency: "Beauty and all other nat-

ural endowments are but earth, arising from the earth and returning to it; grace and elegance are but the smoke and air of this earth" (AMC 3.21.2). He warns us not to be fooled by beauty. His words are apt for anyone who possesses natural beauty and for the one who beholds beauty in another: "These natural graces and gifts are such a provocation and occasion of sin both to the possessor and the beholder that there is scarcely a heart that escapes from this snare" (AMC 3.21.1). The realism of Saint John of the Cross, who spent five years as the confessor and spiritual guide to 130 Sisters in the convent of the Incarnation in Ávila and encountered many young Sisters in his work, is evident in these words: "So few will be found, no matter how holy, who have not been somewhat ravished and perplexed by this drink of joy and pleasure in natural beauty and graces" (AMC 3.22.4). The effort must be to maintain a calm awareness in our human encounters, remaining unpossessive toward others, detached from seeking our own conquests in human relations. This does not mean to be cold and distant from others, but at liberty to love as God desires that we love others. "By not becoming attached to anyone, despite these apparent and deceptive natural goods, a person remains unencumbered and free to love all rationally and spiritually, which is the way God wants them to be loved. As a result one realizes that no one merits love except for virtue. And when one loves with this motive, the love is according to God and exceedingly free" (AMC 3.23.1).

The essential point that Saint John of the Cross is making is the need to keep God at the center of our lives, not only as someone who is worshiped and adored, but as the Beloved we desire to please in all things at all hours. Naturally, there are sense satisfactions and innocent enjoyments in life, in food and eating and good company, for instance, that do not require elimination from our lives. Saint John of the Cross offers the simple instruction that in the encounter with any satisfaction given to our senses, we should try to turn our gratitude and awareness to God. There is no need to avoid all satisfactions, but rather the need to use them for a greater love of God. "For when the will, in becoming aware of the delight afforded by an object of sight, hearing, or touch, does not stop with this joy but immediately elevates itself to God, being moved and strengthened for this by that delight, it is doing something very good" (AMC 3.24.4). The real question here is the type of gratification sought, whether it is self-oriented toward our own pleasure or used innocently to praise and love God for his gifts; and, of course, whether or not it is sinful. The effort should be to make these joys and satisfactions inseparable from our love for God, never forgetting gratitude to him. A habit can be cultivated of remembering God even in sense enjoyments, giving him thanks for what is experienced. In his lifetime, Saint John of the Cross was well-known for basking in the beauty of natural settings of mountains, forests, and running streams; his poetry is likewise full of this sensual delight. "Spiritual persons, then, in whatever sensory gratification comes their way, whether by chance or through their own intention, ought to benefit from it only for the sake of going to God" (AMC 3.24.7). Otherwise, there is harm and hindrance in the spiritual life as we allow the will to be weighed down in desire for delights sought for some form of self-satisfaction. Sensually inclined people, for instance, often tend to have a more difficult time with the effort to recollect themselves in prayer and quietly seek the presence of God in solitary silence.

    Saint John of the Cross addresses still another form of

gratification that must be tempered as a joy sought for its own satisfaction. This is the problem of rejoicing in our own exercise of virtue, in making the motivation for the good works in our life the satisfaction that they may give us of living uprightly, nobly, or even heroically. It is again the same effort of self-renunciation heard earlier, but played now in a different chord. We should turn our thought to pleasing God and giving honor to him as the only worthy motive for our actions. Undoubtedly, we want also to do good for others, but this should ultimately mean to do good for the salvation and sanctification of others. It is a basic truth repeated throughout Catholic tradition that the value of works is in the love by which they are performed. Small acts done with great love have value beyond our reckoning; indeed, there is nothing small when the love is great. The following words of Saint John of the Cross certainly have affected countless Carmelites in cloistered convents over the last four centuries. But why not us as well, for they have an equivalent pertinence for lives outside the walls of monasteries:

> Christians should keep in mind that the value of their good works, fasts, alms, penances, and so on, is not based on quantity and quality so much as on the love of God practiced in them; and consequently that these works are of greater excellence in the measure both that the love of God by which they are performed is more pure and entire and that self-interest diminishes with respect to pleasure, comfort, praise, and earthly or heavenly joy. They should not set their heart on the pleasure, comfort, savor, and other elements of self-interest these good works and practices usually entail, but recollect their joy in God and desire to serve him through these means. And through purgation

and darkness as to this joy in moral goods they should desire in secret that only God be pleased and joyful over their
works. (AMC 3.27.5)

What we are hearing, in effect, is that a cultivated tendency
toward hiddenness must accompany every serious spiritual
life. What God sees is only what ultimately matters; the
things no one else sees or knows about is often in saintly
lives the greater truth of their sanctity. The motive out of
love to give delight to God, when this desire animates the
core of a life, leads quite logically to a life of secret gifts
extended to God throughout a day. A self-interest in the satisfaction of praise and recognition for works, by contrast,
is in direct contradiction to this principle. Saint John of the
Cross comments on this harmful tendency: "Since they look
for satisfaction in their works, they usually do not perform
them unless they see that some gratification or praise will
result from them" (AMC 3.28.4). The consequence in such
lives is to limit the good they do, confining their generosity
to what will be visibly seen and appreciated. Is it so different
today from what it was in Saint John of the Cross' time?
"There is so much misery among human beings as regards
this kind of harm that I believe most of the works publicly
achieved are either faulty, worthless, or imperfect in God's
sight. The reason is that people are not detached from these
human respects and interests" (AMC 3.28.5). He comments
on this unfortunate need for receiving praise, recognition,
accolades, and thanks from others for works done. "It can
be said that in these works some adore themselves more
than God. And this is true if they undertake such works for
these reasons and would not do so without them" (AMC
3.28.5). The corrective Saint John of the Cross offers is a
fundamental one, and clearly not just appropriate for life in

a monastery or cloistered convent. It is apt for every life that places itself with regularity before the hidden presence of our Lord in the Eucharist. "These persons must hide their work so that only God might see it, and they should not want anyone to pay attention to it. Not only should they hide it from others, but even from themselves: They should desire neither the complacency of esteeming their work as if it had value, nor the procurement of satisfaction. This is the meaning of our Savior's words: *Let not the left hand know what the right hand is doing* [Mt. 6:3]" (AMC 3.28.6).

Another interesting insight in this treatment is the observation that we are easily deluded into thinking that the works that give us some particular satisfaction have most value in the eyes of God. In fact, the opposite may be true: "Those works that usually require more mortification from a person (who is not advanced in the way of perfection) are more acceptable and precious in God's sight because of the self-denial exercised in them, than are those from which one can derive consolation, which very easily leads to self-seeking" (AMC 3.28.8). Persevering through difficulty and remaining faithful to duty and commitment are not always honored with the respect they deserve. But this steadfast cleaving to moral and spiritual uprightness is a delight to God. When we do not seek our own satisfaction, indeed, when this has been tempered and burned away from our underlying motive in actions, we become more malleable for God. We can be used by him more easily. Diligence in faithfulness to our choices in life is in proportion to our desire to give delight to God by this faithfulness. The contrary is nonetheless often seen. Those who seek their own satisfaction, their own happiness or fulfillment, without regard for faithful commitment, tend to habits of inconstancy. Resolutions, if made, are not kept; works are not completed;

promises are boldly pronounced and then broken. It is common for works to be taken up and then abandoned, including the work of pursuing God or holiness or a particular vocation. The habitual seeking of our own satisfaction has harmful repercussions in spiritual commitments. If the tendency is not corrected, the fruit is perceived in time, sometimes tragically. The following passage should be read as a commentary on the ultimate choices of a commitment to marriage, priesthood, or religious life undertaken in a life.

> As a result people usually become inconstant in their practice of good works and resolutions; they leave these aside and take up others, starting and stopping without ever finishing anything. Since they are motivated by satisfaction, which is changeable—and in some temperaments more so than in others—their work ends when the satisfaction does, and their resolution too, even though it may concern an important endeavor. We can say of those for whom the energy and soul of their work is the joy they find in it that when the joy dies out the good work ceases, and they do not persevere. (AMC 3.29.2)

If we return again for a moment to the will in its three operations, we can see how important are the consequences in what Saint John of the Cross is teaching. The third operation of the will—what we delight in, find satisfaction in—inevitably becomes a motivation for what we pursue. The challenge that Saint John of the Cross poses is to examine the purity of our motives in the spiritual life. If we seek to give delight to God above all other satisfactions, we are on the path to holiness and on the road to likely graces of contemplation in prayer. We are allowing our will to be emptied for a greater love of God, and this always affects our life of prayer. If, however, we withdraw into a pursuit of our own satisfactions, motivated by self-interest, we are bound to suffer a diminished desire for God. Prayer then limps and staggers as well. Satisfactions in things other than God are often repetitively chosen as desires to experience the same satisfactions again, as we have said. What we find delight in comes back to provoke a desire in the will to enjoy the delight once again. The trap in this pattern is never overcome in many lives; the underlying egoism is never released from a life. A serious pursuit of God can be so different. The consuming desire of our soul can be to give delight to God with a pure motive of love. When this desire also fills prayer, repercussions follow and the fruits in time show themselves, including the initial graces of contemplation. In concluding this chapter, we turn to three short aphorisms of singular value from *The Sayings of Light and Love*. For one thing, they are evidence of how much Saint John of the Cross can say in a few short words. The first two aphorisms express the reward in love for detachment and for a great passion of soul for the will of God, which likewise affects then the life of prayer. The third aphorism on love has an even more powerful impact. It can perhaps serve for a lifetime as a piercing examination of conscience.

> If you purify your soul of attachments and desires, you will understand things spiritually. If you deny your appetite for them, you will enjoy their truth, understanding what is certain in them. (SLL 49)

> What does it profit you to give God one thing if he asks of you another? Consider what it is God wants, and then do it. You will as a result satisfy your heart better than with something toward which you yourself are inclined. (SLL 73)

> When evening comes, you will be examined in love. Learn to love as God desires to be loved and abandon your own ways of acting. (SLL 60)

7

BARRICADES ON THE ROAD TO CONTEMPLATION

We can view this next chapter as an argument in defense of the rigors of purification proposed in the many previous instructions. It is a preparatory chapter for taking up a more concentrated examination of the prayer of contemplation in the subsequent chapters. The treatise of *The Dark Night* begins in book 1 with a vivid treatment of certain imperfections commonly seen in those still in the earlier stages of spiritual pursuit. Saint John of the Cross is referring here to people who have already committed themselves to a habit of spiritual exercises and daily prayer, usually in the structured context of religious life, yet among laity as well, but who typically do not understand yet the serious nature of giving themselves fully to God. They are untried in the rigors of dedicated virtue and have not faced yet the arduous interior struggles that must be withstood over some time before a depth of spiritual quality embraces the soul. There can be no tested endurance in a soul that has not had sufficient time to persevere through hard trials.

This demand is not just a need for seasoning and maturing in the experience of the spiritual life. The essential testing is much more fundamental. As an astute spiritual psychologist, Saint John of the Cross plunges underneath the surface of lives and identifies the *motivation* of souls in the early period of spiritual pursuit as often sullied and impure. Almost everyone in this early period of the spiritual life professes to be seeking only God, while at the same time the person shows signs of being excessively preoccupied with self in the spiritual pursuit. Saint John of the Cross comments explicitly: "Since their motivation in their spiritual works and exercises is the consolation and satisfaction they experience in them, and since they have not been conditioned by the arduous struggle of practicing virtue, they possess many faults and imperfections in the discharge of their spiritual activities" (DN 1.1.3). In this incisive section at the beginning of *The Dark Night*, he uses the schema of the seven capital vices to expose seven spiritual vices that generally afflict souls in the early period of a spiritual life. It proves to be an interesting commentary on the factor of underlying self-interest in the pursuit of spiritual life. This tendency to self-preoccupation demands a clear effort of interior mortification if we are to seek God with the selfless spirit that can lead eventually to contemplative graces in prayer.

Saint John of the Cross begins with pride, a pride that is often generated by the uplifted, inflamed feelings for God that are not unusual in the early days of committed prayer. Souls at this time, especially in convents, feel a fervor for doing all things for God with a diligence and an external shine that comes easily. The result is usually a complacency in their works and in the devotion that marks their interior life of prayer. Are these feelings of fervor primarily due to grace? They may be to a certain extent, but the spiritual vice is nonetheless activated by the lack of spiritual maturity at this early time. The signs and symptoms are not hard to see in a person's sense of superior advancement, when really the soul is just getting started. Saint John of the Cross describes a typical symptom: "They develop a somewhat vain —at times very vain—desire to speak of spiritual things in others' presence, and sometime even to instruct rather than be instructed; in their hearts they condemn others who do not seem to have the kind of devotion they would like them to have" (DN 1.2.1).

Interestingly, the devil is observant of such matters and is intent not to see a soul enter more genuinely on the spiritual path of humble self-understanding. Saint John of the Cross says that at times the devil may inspire a person to an increased fervor of devotion and a greater readiness to perform good works precisely to swell and expand the pride of the soul. This is certainly not our usual expectation. In these souls, as well, relations with authority, whether in religious life or in spiritual direction or with the Church herself, begin possibly to show tensions. The persons want approval and esteem for their apparent spiritual quality. They assume that this elevated quality must be seen by others, for it is quite visible to themselves, and so should be acknowledged and respected. And with that respect, writes Saint John of the Cross, should come permissions and encouragement to pursue their own preferential path to God. They have sharp opinions on what they think is best for their own spiritual advancement and, perhaps, strong opinions about areas of spiritual concern in a congregation or in the Church. If this encouragement is not forthcoming to confirm them in their preferences or their opinions, "they quickly search for some other spiritual advisor more to their liking, someone who will congratulate them and be impressed by their deeds; and they flee, as they would death, those who attempt to place them on the safe road by forbidding these things—and sometimes they even become hostile toward such spiritual directors" (DN 1.2.3).

The Sacrament of Confession, writes Saint John of the Cross, can be a symptomatic sign of pride in a soul. Today, when Confession is perhaps not respected enough for its profound impact on a soul humble in seeking mercy, the words are a reminder that the sacrament is meant to be a naked exposure of our soul before God. Saint John of the Cross was a confessor over many years to some hundreds of nuns in Carmelite convents in Spain. These Sisters were clearly intent to give to God a total offering of their lives; yet they apparently could fall into spiritual faults and impediments that were often seen by him. Pride is a particular trap lurking in lives that aspire to make a great gift of themselves to God. The presence of personal fault and imperfection is a goad that either humbles a soul or leads in an opposite direction toward pride, as we will see. Saint John of the Cross will write in this section on the spiritual pride manifested in private conversation and in Confession: "Sometimes they minimize their faults, and at other times they become discouraged by them, since they felt they were already saints, and they become impatient and angry with themselves, which is yet another fault" (DN 1.2.5). And again he returns to the issue of motivation, which is often a self-interested one: "They are often extremely anxious that God remove their faults and imperfections, but their motive is personal peace rather than God" (DN 1.2.5). Human nature is very vulnerable to the wounds of original sin that linger for a lifetime in our soul. The spiritual pride that can leak into the pious Confessions of good souls was transparently evident to Saint John of the Cross. He writes about religious Sisters in the following comment, but the statement is a reminder to all of us of the need to treat this sacrament of mercy with utmost respect as a direct entry into the gaze of God upon our soul.

> Many want to be the favorites of their confessors, and thus they are consumed by a thousand envies and disqui-

etudes. Embarrassment forbids them from relating their sins clearly, lest their reputation diminish in their confessor's eyes. They confess their sins in the most favorable light so as to appear better than they actually are, and thus they approach the confessional to excuse themselves rather than accuse themselves. Sometimes they confess the evil things they do to a different confessor so that their own confessor might think they commit no sins at all. Therefore, in their desire to appear holy, they enjoy relating their good behavior to their confessor, and in such careful terms that these good deeds appear greater than they actually are. It would be more humble of them . . . to make light of the good they do and to wish that no one, neither their confessor nor anybody else, should consider it of any importance at all. (DN 1.2.4)

On the other hand, the value of humility is strongly espoused by Saint John of the Cross in a manner that most people do not recognize as qualities of serious humility. True humility inclines souls to see their deeds as insignificant and to keep them hidden, far removed from praise. Souls of humility "not only place little importance on their deeds, but also take very little self-satisfaction from them" (DN 1.2.6). They do not do things for the satisfaction of being appreciated or acknowledged. Their deeds are not a pretext for self-esteem and self-congratulation. Rather, they are more often conscious of the "inadequacy of their service" to God. "The more they do, the less satisfaction they derive from it" (DN 1.2.6). Because their love for God is great, they think they are doing very little for him. They would wish to do much more to show their love, but they are unable, and this sense of inadequacy is a humbling awareness. "This loving solicitude goads them, preoccupies them, and absorbs them to such an extent that they never notice what others do or do not accomplish" (DN 1.2.6). The following comment, if emulated, points our life in the direction of holiness: "They think they themselves are insignificant, and want others to think this also and to belittle and slight their deeds. Moreover, even though others do praise and value their works, these souls are unable to believe them; such praises seem strange to them" (DN 1.2.6).

The second imperfection often seen in the beginnings of spiritual pursuit is spiritual avarice. The avarice here is not directed toward the accumulation of material things but rather involves a possessive desire for spiritual experiences. Saint John of the Cross thus speaks of people who go to prayer for the sake of what can be received in feeling during prayer, looking always for consoling experiences. "They hardly ever seem content with the spirit God gives them" (DN 1.3.1). The result in time is often disgruntled souls, "unhappy and peevish because they don't find the consolation they want in spiritual things" (DN 1.3.1). They want to feel uplifted and moved in their spiritual lives as though this were the measure of relations with God. Perhaps in reaction to frustration in interior prayer, an obsessive chase after new spiritual stimuli may begin to occupy a life. Certainly, this is not all there is in such a life, and virtue is practiced, but the imperfection bespeaks an insecurity of soul. One symptom of that insecurity may be an excessive concern with acquiring tokens of piety that will placate a lack of spiritual depth. Examples of this weakness are here presented:

> Many never have enough of hearing counsels, or learning spiritual maxims, or keeping them and reading books about them. They spend more time in these than in striving after mortification and the perfection of interior poverty to which they are obliged. Furthermore, they weigh themselves down with overdecorated images and rosaries. They now put these down, now take up others; at one mo-

ment they are exchanging, and at the next re-exchanging. Now they want this kind, now they want another. And they prefer one cross to another because of its elaborateness. (DN 1.3.1)

Saint John of the Cross makes clear that he is not simply criticizing the human foibles of pious sentiment. He is addressing the possessiveness of attachment to secondary things, a more serious impediment to spiritual life. The inability of the soul to direct its attention to the great goal of pursuing God himself can occur because it is taken up with trinkets of cheap worth, as it were, that substitute for giving itself more generously to God. Devotion, writes Saint John of the Cross, does not depend on the external accoutrements and surroundings in which we pray. The beauty or simplicity of the rosary we hold in our hands does not determine the value of the Hail Marys we pray with it. A vivid artistic depiction of Jesus crucified on the cross can on a particular day enhance our wonder at his love. Yet prayer is never dependent on the possession of objects that stimulate our senses for the sake of the interior act of love. The imperfection here of spiritual avarice is to forget that God loves primarily our willingness to embrace poverty and our longing to please him. The latter must be the primary motive in prayer, indeed, the only motive for holding on and keeping anything in our personal possession. As he writes in illustration:

I knew a person who for more than ten years profited by a cross roughly made out of a blessed palm and held together by a pin twisted around it. That person carried it about and never would part with it until I took it—and the person was not someone of poor judgment or little intelligence. I saw someone else who prayed with beads made out of bones from the spine of a fish. Certainly, the

devotion was not for this reason less precious in the sight
of God. . . . They, therefore, who are well guided from
the outset do not become attached to visible instruments
or burden themselves with them. (DN 1.3.2)

Saint John of the Cross next addresses the imperfection
of what he calls spiritual lust. He acknowledges here the
possibility that spiritual persons sometimes suffer involun-
tary temptations against purity at a time one would least
expect, namely, in the midst of spiritual exercises. Impure
feelings can arise, he writes, from three causes outside the
soul's control. The first cause can be that spiritual exercises
at times are a pleasurable activity for the inner spirit. The
person is not seeking to elicit impure thoughts, but the bodily life is not unaffected by the loving spiritual feelings that
sometimes may fill a person. The gratification of the spiritual feelings at times overflows bodily. The result can be
some sensual repercussion experienced, ordinarily with displeasure and as an unwelcome thing. The need is simply to
mortify this by not turning to the bodily aspect, leaving it
outside one's direct attention and letting it fade away. The
second possible cause is the devil, who in order to bring
disturbance to a soul precisely in the time of prayer, will try
to excite impure feelings in the bodily experience of prayer.
Again, the proper response will be to pay no attention to the
bodily agitation. The subtle danger, as well, is that a soul will
give up prayer or reduce it to a more superficial approach
because of this temptation, thinking that the prayer itself
has become the occasion for the temptation. This is a mistake and would play into the hand of the devil, who wants
a soul to diminish or abandon prayer and has provoked the
temptation for that reason. The third cause of impure feelings in prayer, writes Saint John of the Cross, is the fear of

them. A kind of anxious concern for impurity rises up in certain souls when they turn to prayer. Perhaps they have been converted from a more lax time of immoral behavior in life, and a worrisome concern about impurity becomes a recurrent remembrance for them, especially disturbing in their silent time alone with their own thought and imagination during prayer.

As a last item of note in the treatment of spiritual lust, Saint John of the Cross speaks of the issue of attachment. Human beings, even without the temptation of impurity, are inclined to take great satisfaction in the human consolation of friendship. Friendship is always good when it leads to God, but not a good thing when it becomes a barrier to God. The affections we might experience for another person tend to disclose their true nature when we are honest with ourselves. Either God is loved just as much as ever or more, or we end up drifting away from our need and hunger for God because a human satisfaction has begun to replace God as our primary contentment in the experience of love. In the following passage, Saint John of the Cross is using the term lust as an expression, not simply of impure desire, but of an inordinate attachment to another person. Again, the context for these remarks is directed at convent life; yet surely there are general lessons here, including care with friendships in the world that can compete with the fidelity required by our vocations.

> Some spiritually acquire a liking for other individuals which often arises from lust rather than from the spirit. This lustful origin will be recognized if, on recalling that affection, there is remorse of conscience, not an increase in the remembrance and love of God. The affection is purely spiritual if the love of God grows when it grows, or if the love of God is remembered as often as the affection is

remembered, or if the affection gives the soul a desire for
God. . . . But when the love is born of this sensual vice
it has the contrary effects. As the one love grows greater,
the other lessens, and the remembrance of it lessens too.
If the inordinate love increases, then, as will be seen, the
soul grows cold in the love of God and, because of the
recollection of that other love, forgets him—not without
feeling some remorse of conscience. (DN 1.4.7)

The imperfection that parallels the capital vice of anger
has much to do with the desire of souls for spiritual gratification in their spiritual exercises of prayer. When delight
and satisfaction fade or disappear from prayer, and no spiritual savor is tasted, the immature soul plunges often into
a state of indulged frustration. Soon enough the symptom
of anger begins to show. Finding now a distastefulness in
prayer, "they become peevish in the works they do and easily angered by the least thing, and occasionally they are so
unbearable that nobody can put up with them" (DN 1.5.1).
This irritability is indeed often manifested after these souls
have experienced some consolation in prayer. Instead of being strengthened in virtue by what might be considered a
grace, they are upset by the vapid and empty return to life's
daily demands and the need to exercise a hard effort in virtue
and in work. It is ordinary to experience this "letdown" of
sorts after a period of consolation in prayer. But the soul
must not allow that minor dejection to influence its approach to generous self-giving outside the time of prayer.
Saint John of the Cross mentions also the problem of another form of spiritual anger commonly seen. This is to turn
with "a certain indiscreet zeal" of anger at the sins of others,
and to "reprove these others, and sometimes even feel the
impulse to do so angrily, which in fact they occasionally do,
setting themselves up as lords of virtue" (DN 1.5.2). Others

grow angry in "an unhumble impatience" with their own failings and fault. "So impatient are they about these imperfections that they would want to become saints in a day" (DN 1.5.3). The need to accept a long duration of hard effort in the spiritual life is always a salutary awareness. The last sentence in the following passage, from another point of view, is certainly a vintage comment of Saint John of the Cross.

> Many of these beginners make numerous plans and great resolutions, but since they are not humble and have no distrust of themselves, the more resolves they make the more they break, and the greater becomes their anger. They do not have the patience to wait until God gives them what they need, when he so desires. Their attitude is contrary to spiritual meekness. . . . Some, however, are so patient about their desire for advancement that God would prefer to see them a little less so. (DN 1.5.3)

Spiritual gluttony is next on the list of imperfections. As Saint John of the Cross writes: "Many, lured by the delight and satisfaction procured in their religious practices, strive more for spiritual savor than for spiritual purity and discretion; yet it is this purity and discretion that God looks for and finds acceptable throughout a soul's entire spiritual journey" (DN 1.6.1). Once again, we see that the primary motivation in good practices can be a self-centered desire for the experience of some spiritual feeling of delight. Saint John of the Cross comments that the symptom of this imperfection is sometimes to adopt excessive practices of penance or fasting. The action is not purely out of a desire for mortification or to offer the penance for the sake of others, but for some impure motive of satisfaction. These souls lack discretion and moderation; even more, they fail in seeking counsel and advice from another. They prefer to undertake at times extreme, overtaxing penances that result occasionally in some damage to their health.

Nonetheless, their primary fault in this excess is typically not the presumption of their unlimited physical capacity for penance. It is the failure to place themselves in obedience to another in the exercise of penances. The danger is that this unwillingness to submit to some form of obedience extends soon into other areas of spiritual effort. An aversion to submission of any kind takes hold in a life, replaced by a desire to be in command, directing one's own conduct. "Their only yearning and satisfaction is to do what they feel inclined to do" (DN 1.6.2). Saint John of the Cross writes perhaps from his own experience of the difficulty that some souls display in placing themselves in submission to the spiritual direction of another: "Some are very insistent that their spiritual director allow them to do what they themselves want to do, and finally almost force the permission from him" (DN 1.6.3). Refusals elicit strong reactions of distaste for the director as one who opposes God because he disagrees with their desires. "They are under the impression that they do not serve God when they are not allowed to do what they want" (DN 1.6.3). The problem harks back to the desire to indulge what pleases self: "They think that gratifying and satisfying themselves is serving and satisfying God" (DN 1.6.3). The desire to indulge corporal penance in excessive ways serves as an illustration of what is a problem of much deeper implications. The problem of requesting penances does not seem to be our problem today. But pride has its ways to manifest itself in every age. Obedience to the direction of another can be an onerous thing, especially when disapproval is voiced. The following comment on souls who want to practice their own excessive penances, seeking their own ways arbitrarily, rather than submitting to the direction of another, remains a useful instruction with wide application, especially when it makes mention of the necessary practice of a "penance of reason".

> Such individuals are unreasonable and most imperfect. They subordinate submissiveness and obedience (which is a penance of reason and discretion, and consequently a sacrifice more pleasing and acceptable to God) to corporeal penance. But corporeal penance without obedience is no more than a penance of beasts. And like beasts, they are motivated in these penances by an appetite for the pleasure they find in them. Since all extremes are vicious and since by such behavior these persons are doing their own will, they grow in vice rather than in virtue. For through this conduct they at least become spiritually gluttonous and proud, since they do not tread the path of obedience. (DN 1.6.2)

Saint John of the Cross goes on to speak of spiritual gluttony in prayer itself. The first example is in the reception of Holy Communion. It is not uncommon, he writes, for souls to measure their relations with God by the feelings of satisfaction received or not received in the precious time after taking Holy Communion. If feelings are understood to be a sign of closeness to the Heart of God, then naturally a soul places much value on whether any experience of delight takes place. But this is an erroneous view, even as it is so evident in early and even later stages of the spiritual life. The importance of deep faith in our encounter with the ultimate mysteries of our Catholic life is missing in that case. The Eucharist is a sacrament of great mystery in the intimacy of our union with our Lord. The mystery is sometimes not honored sufficiently when souls seek an experience of emotional delight as their primary desire in Holy Communion. Jesus in the Eucharist remains the Lord of utter transcendent mystery even as he gives himself fully to us. Saint John of the Cross is sharp in his criticism of this form of superficial desire when receiving our Lord and God in Holy Communion:

> In receiving Communion they spend all their time trying to get some feeling and satisfaction rather than humbly praising and reverencing God dwelling within them. And they go about this in such a way that, if they do not procure any sensible feeling and satisfaction, they think they have accomplished nothing. As a result they judge very poorly of God and fail to understand that the sensory benefits are the least among those that this most blessed Sacrament bestows, for the invisible grace it gives is a greater blessing. God often withdraws sensory delight and pleasure so that souls might set the eyes of faith on this invisible grace. Not only in receiving Communion, but in other spiritual exercises as well, beginners desire to feel God and taste him as if he were comprehensible and accessible. This desire is a serious imperfection and, because it involves impurity of faith, is opposed to God's way. (DN 1.6.5)

The section on spiritual gluttony concludes with a reiteration of the need to give up a craving for feelings of delight and satisfaction in prayer. These are souls "always hunting for some gratification in the things of God" (DN 1.6.6). It is a path of self-seeking that has little to do with genuine love, which always releases a soul from preoccupation with self and from what is received for self. The mistake is a misinterpretation of the true effects of love upon the soul. These souls do not yet understand deeply enough God's desire to purge the soul of all self-seeking. "They think the whole matter of prayer consists in looking for sensory satisfaction and devotion" (DN 1.6.6). When this is not forthcoming, they are disconsolate and think they have wasted their time. "They lose true devotion and spirit," writes Saint John of the Cross, "which lie in distrust of self and in humble and patient perseverance so as to please God" (DN 1.6.6). The danger is that a soul will lose interest and even give up a serious pursuit of prayer. "Once they do not find delight in prayer, or in any other spiritual exercise, they feel extreme reluctance and repugnance in returning to it and sometimes even give it up" (DN 1.6.6). The lesson is clear enough. A habit of self-denial toward our own craving for satisfaction in prayer is necessary if we are to walk the authentic path to the loss of self out of love for God.

Saint John of the Cross finishes the two last imperfections, spiritual envy and spiritual sloth, with a certain expedience, as though he had tired of the subject. Spiritual envy is what we might expect it to be: the sadness that souls feel in seeing others advancing ahead of them in spiritual practices, at least according to their own measure of this advancement. They experience annoyance and disturbance at hearing others praised for spiritual qualities. "They long for preference in everything" (DN 1.7.1). The competitive spirit can be evident in religious communities as much as in the world. The only difference is the criteria for advancement and superiority to others. But this, too, is a problem. In the spiritual life, the signs of growing closer to God, when they are authentic, are largely hidden from the eyes of others. Once we realize that nothing seen in appearance conveys the full truth of a soul before the gaze of God's eyes, much spiritual envy should dissipate.

Spiritual sloth, the last imperfection treated, is seen at times in the weariness experienced in spiritual exercises and prayer when the soul seems to receive nothing for its efforts. The inclination to flee and avoid what has become arduous leads some souls to diminish their spiritual commitment and perhaps to go through the motions of spiritual exercises without any fervent effort. Boredom is a special problem in this regard once a harder experience in prayer or in spiritual commitment ensues. "Since they are so used to finding delight in spiritual practices, they become bored when they do not find it" (DN 1.7.2). Or they become bored "when told to do something unpleasant" (DN 1.7.4). Those who are accustomed to looking for gratification and delight in their spiritual exercises tend to run from what is unpleasant and what demands hard perseverance. The result is an immature reaction of laxity and a giving up of what has been begun. "If they do not receive in prayer the satisfaction they crave —for after all it is fit that God withdraw this so as to try them—they do not want to return to it, or at times they either give up prayer or go to it begrudgingly" (DN 1.7.2). The question returns once again to what the soul is really seeking in prayer. Some under the guise of seeking God "strive to satisfy their own will rather than God's" (DN 1.7.2). The effort of the soul to be docile and malleable before God, allowing the inner recesses of the soul to be purged and formed under his hand, is an immense need. The discovery of the impulse to willful self-seeking in what has seemed until then a pursuit of God is a valuable insight, if the truth of our own need can be disclosed. As Saint John of the Cross writes: "Many of these beginners want God to desire what they want, and they become sad if they have to desire God's will. They feel an aversion toward adapting their will to God's. Hence they frequently believe that what is not their will, or brings them no satisfaction, is not God's will, and, on the other hand, that if they are satisfied, God is too. They measure God by themselves and not themselves by God" (DN 1.7.3).

What we have been encountering in these portrayals of imperfection is a kind of concrete summary of the demands of love reiterated throughout the writings of Saint John of the Cross. A soul aspiring to union with God must truly allow itself to be emptied and purified in radical ways. The road of purification can take a long time, or it can be relatively short in duration, depending in large part on how serious we are in mortifying our own self-absorbed tendencies. This is the primary lesson of these pages on the spiritual vices at the beginning of *The Dark Night*. The great need of our soul is to refine our desire to please God alone and to leave ourselves empty and unimportant in our own estimation. We have to give ourselves away, strip ourselves of self-preoccupation; it is never sufficient simply to be generous in charitable actions. The Gospel admonition to lose ourselves for love is an effort of interior and exterior demands that allows no compromise and no turning back on self. Such efforts are not without effect. They are the preparation for the purer longing for God and the accessibility to God that are traits of a soul ready to receive the grace of contemplation.

8

THE DAWNING LIGHT OF
THE GIFT OF CONTEMPLATION

We are ready now to take up the teaching of Saint John of
the Cross on contemplation. However, it can be beneficial
to ease a bit into the subject, which is what Saint John of the
Cross does in his writings. On a few occasions, for instance,
he mentions a primary motive for him in taking up his pen.
A matter of critical importance for him—"extremely necessary to so many souls" (AMC Prologue 3)—is the harm
done to souls who do not recognize the initial symptoms
of contemplative graces and do not adjust their approach
to prayer accordingly. The failure to advance into contemplation when the grace is being offered is, for him, a great
misfortune. A lack of understanding is the obvious reason
and an excuse of sorts; nonetheless, this ignorance is consequential and requires remedy. The loss is inestimable, not
just to particular souls, but to the vast fruitfulness that a contemplative soul can bear for the sake of others. Saint John
of the Cross wastes no time in bringing up the issue. The
first pages of the Prologue to *The Ascent of Mount Carmel* express his lament. When he refers to the "dark night" in the
following passage, he is referring to the initial experience
of purification that occurs as the grace of contemplation
commences. What should not be missed in this passage is
also the opening phrase. The initial graces of contemplative
prayer do not presume the rarity of a saintly life, but a life
sincerely engaged in a wholehearted pursuit of virtue.

Even though these souls have begun to walk along the road
of virtue, and our Lord desires to place them in the dark
night that they may move on to the divine union, they do
not advance. The reason for this may be that sometimes
they do not want to enter the dark night or allow themselves to be placed in it, and that sometimes they misun-
derstand themselves and are without suitable and alert directors who will show them the way to the summit. God
gives many souls the talent and grace for advancing, and
should they desire to make the effort they would arrive
at this high state. And so it is sad to see them continue in
their lowly method of communion with God because they
do not want or know how to advance, or because they receive no direction on breaking away from the methods of
beginners. (AMC Prologue 3)

In these preliminary remarks, the metaphor of the "dark
night" is invoked, a term we have already encountered. It
is an image for purifications in the spiritual life of various
kinds. One of the most daunting experiences of a "dark
night" of purification occurs exactly at the onset of contemplative graces, which he has just been referencing in these
words from the Prologue to *The Ascent of Mount Carmel*.
The image of darkness takes on different meanings in the
course of his works. But in the discussion of contemplation, the metaphor of the dark night invokes the confusion
and incomprehension that trouble souls when contemplative graces first begin, leaving them often unable, out of
ignorance, to meet the challenge of advancing in prayer.
This transitional period of entry into contemplation is a
major subject for Saint John of the Cross. Typically, souls
are thrown into an inner turmoil at that time. A painful
experience invades the silence of prayer that is at variance
with their understanding of prayer until that point in time.
For many people, it seems almost as though an injury to the

soul takes place that has no explanation. Yet what is actually occurring is a summons in grace to cross a threshold into a "dark night" of interior purification within the silence of prayer.

The darkness can be viewed in part as a metaphor for the soul's inability to understand what is happening. But it is also a description, as we will see, of the benefits of the experience itself in this graced period of purification in prayer. A deeper entry into the mystery of God's infinite love requires, as we have seen in the chapter on faith, that our soul undergo a certain blinding of the intellect while exercising the certitude of our faith. And, unfortunately, souls almost always resist this effect of deeper grace. They do not surrender to the initiative of God's grace because they do not understand what is taking place. All indications seem to point to something gone wrong in prayer, as though a detour off the road had occurred and the correct path had been lost. The ignorance itself becomes a serious hindrance at this time. The soul refuses to move forward in grace because it does not know what going forward means. For most people, the experience seems initially to be more a collapse in prayer than an invitation to a deeper intimacy with God. The great need at this time, which Saint John of the Cross intends to supply, is a knowledge of what is happening, followed by a proper adjustment in prayer in accord with reliable instructions. Without sound guidance, it is unlikely that our soul will make the necessary choice to alter how it prays in a way that will respond properly to contemplative graces. This adjustment requires forsaking familiar methods of prayer and adopting new approaches. A statement from the Prologue of *The Ascent* is descriptive in this regard:

> In resisting God who is conducting them, they make little progress, and fail in merit because they do not apply their

wills; as a result they must endure greater suffering. Some souls, instead of abandoning themselves to God and cooperating with him, hamper him by their indiscreet activity or their resistance. They resemble children who kick and cry and struggle to walk by themselves when their mothers want to carry them; in walking by themselves they make no headway, or if they do, it is at a child's pace. (AMC Prologue 3)

Another factor can also be stressed. A sensitive ability to engage paradoxical interior experiences is a crucial element in a soul's navigation through this confusing interval in the spiritual life. The difficulty may explain why Saint John of the Cross is so keen to make this transitional period in prayer a major component of his writing. Souls at this stage of the spiritual life require clear advice and encouragement. What can seem discouraging and dark in a subjective manner may be symptomatic of a deeper experience of God. But how is a soul to know? The purifying experience in prayer at this juncture easily invites false interpretations. Cooperation with contemplative graces is all-important, but this presumes a correct interpretation of what is happening. Almost always some guidance is needed. Trying to live this purification alone, with an absence of instruction, tends to confuse and even paralyze souls. Addressing precisely this predicament was a primary motive for Saint John of the Cross, if we take measure of the number of places in his writings that he returns to the teaching on the early stages of contemplation. He is a master of clarity in both his diagnosis of initial contemplative symptoms and his treatment of contemplative prayer itself. In effect, he is offering a necessary guidance for souls who often can find no direction elsewhere.

A further remark is apropos: There have always been naïve

ideas that surround the notion of contemplative prayer. One is that this prayer is completely passive and entirely dependent on the action of God within the soul. But cooperation *is* essential. The perplexing nature of contemplation implies a need for interior choices undertaken with a clear response. The "dark night" must be handled properly, in a receptive manner, or else the soul finds itself as though walking with its head down and banging it into a thick wall. A soul must come to an intuitive sense of the destination to which this purification in prayer is leading. It has to know, clearly, that it is no easy, paved path that leads up the rocky summit of Mount Carmel. In the words of Saint John of the Cross, the soul is being led into a "nakedness of spirit", into that vast emptiness of the "caverns" of the interior faculties. A strong sense of unseen mystery must attract us in seeking God. At the same time, the sight of the narrow path must hold our focus. A determined desire to seek God at all cost is essential, as Saint John of the Cross makes clear to his reader in this short, pointed remark from the Prologue: "We are not writing on moral and pleasing topics addressed to the kind of spiritual people who like to approach God along sweet and satisfying paths. We are presenting a substantial and solid doctrine for all those who desire to reach this *nakedness of spirit*" (AMC Prologue 8; emphasis added).

It can also be said at this preliminary stage that the experience of the "dark night", while sharp and painful in early contemplative prayer, is not simply a trial that descends on the soul like a temporary sickness, only to be endured until it passes. Rather than a trial that disappears with the passage of time, it signifies a critically important shift in relations with God. It is the entry into a kind of naked emptiness of interiority so conducive to deeper "apophatic" relations with a hidden God. With the onset of contemplation, the reality of faith assumes a far more intense role in the spiritual life. The recognition of a need for the will to surrender fully to God likewise becomes more acute. As we will see, there are suitable responses that ease the advancement of a soul in contemplation. Saint John of the Cross is going to provide much instruction and guidance. But the primary need is to step forward into a new experience of prayer that contradicts our prior expectations of prayer. Our soul has to learn a different sense of God's presence of concealment in prayer, one that permits him to draw closer to the soul, but which also brings a painful poverty to a soul in its prayer.

The problem of resisting God in these matters, out of ignorance, is a telling point. Indeed, the temptation to resist God's initiative is at the heart of the paradoxical dilemma in every form of interior purification. The question of resistance to God is especially interesting in the discussion of early contemplation. Resistance at this time is not the ordinary notion of a refusal to God because of indifference or rebellion. Let us remember that these are not the kinds of souls, if they are receiving contemplative graces, who ordinarily set themselves in opposition to God in their conduct of life. But in the realm of prayer, they often do resist the divine lead and initiative, not realizing the harm they are doing to themselves when they fail "to practice abandonment to God's guidance when He wants them to advance" (AMC Prologue 4). The issue at stake can be simply a stubborn preference for one's own way of praying and a refusal to make needed adjustments, despite the signs of a need for change. "They do not willingly adapt themselves to God's work of placing them on the pure and reliable road leading to union" (AMC Prologue 3). What that reliable road of prayer is will be in due time a subject of careful examination.

Still another factor arouses the ire of Saint John of the Cross in this matter of early contemplative graces, which he mentions in the Prologue of *The Ascent* and repeats on further occasions. This is the problem of spiritual directors who in a heavy-handed manner constrain souls and force them to continue praying in meditative ways that are no longer suitable for them. These guides do not understand the symptoms of a soul's advancement in its prayer and offer an uninformed diagnosis. Indeed, according to Saint John of the Cross, they often torment souls with their assertive direction and add to the difficulty of this time of interior trial. They are quick to conclude that the struggles in prayer that accompany early contemplative prayer have some cause in personal infidelity and backtracking. The difficulties, in their view, can be due only to a personal fault or some failure of concentration and focus in prayer. Greater effort and exertion is typically advised. Unfortunately, a frustration for the soul is the fruit of this guidance. The frequency with which such advice was dispensed in Saint John of the Cross' time is impossible to know. But his own indignation at this tendency of spiritual direction is notable. It was a cause for souls not to advance in response to contemplative graces. Apparently, in many cases, it meant a permanent loss of opportunity. He writes strongly on this issue in the following passage:

> It is arduous and difficult for a soul in these periods of the spiritual life when it cannot understand itself or find anyone else who understands it. It will happen to individuals that while they are being conducted by God along a sublime path of dark contemplation and aridity, in which they feel lost and filled with darknesses, trials, conflicts, and temptations, they will meet someone who, in the style of Job's comforters [Jb. 4:8–11], will proclaim that all of

this is due to melancholia, depression, or temperament, or to some hidden wickedness, and that as a result God has forsaken them. Therefore the usual verdict is that these individuals must have lived an evil life since such trials afflict them. (AMC Prologue 4)

These words are a useful reminder, incidentally, that in the delicate realm of spirituality, it is better to be led by God (or by the writings of a saint) than to place one's spiritual life in inferior hands. There are many casualties in the enterprise of spiritual pursuit. It is, indeed, a remarkable thing that the path to sanctity can be waylaid quite easily by foolish ignorance, even among the most intelligent people. An example is certainly present in this question of the initial experience of contemplative graces. The paradox of seemingly negative experiences serving as a sign of serious advancement in the spiritual life is obviously a difficult point of evaluation. Indeed, the trials that can come to souls from poor advice can be a test whether a soul will entrust itself fully to God, not relying on misguided interpretations for measuring relations with God. Abandonment to God, while suffering interior darkness, as we shall see, often unleashes a leap of the soul deeper into the mystery of God. Saint John of the Cross' own comment in the passage that follows is a subtle statement. We are not in control of this journey in prayer to God. Oftentimes we can do nothing but allow the mysterious graces of purification to take hold in our soul secretly and incomprehensibly and have their way. In the realm of the interior life with God, trying to solve problems, or striving to overcome difficulties, is often not a good choice. We have to let God be the master of our soul. Relations with him in prayer are always very personal, calling for a great respect toward the mystery of God's hand at work. These words express the wisdom of Saint John of the Cross in his respect for God and souls: "It is a period for leaving these persons alone in the purgation God is working in them, a time to give comfort and encouragement that they may desire to endure this suffering as long as God wills, for until then no remedy—whatever the soul does, or the confessor says—is adequate" (AMC Prologue 5).

In both *The Ascent of Mount Carmel* and *The Dark Night*, just prior to extended sections treating contemplative prayer, there are notable introductory passages that echo the tone of frustration we have now heard expressed in the Prologue to *The Ascent*. The comments in these two cases serve as an immediate preparation for his teaching on contemplative prayer. But it is striking again to see Saint John of the Cross introduce this subject by mildly bemoaning the harm to souls when they are unaware of the actual workings of contemplative graces. In these remarks, one additional refinement is the explicit reference to the practice of meditative prayer prior to the onset of contemplative graces. A daily exercise of the silent prayer of meditation is assumed as well-known to souls in the context of Saint John of the Cross' teaching on contemplation. In the history of the Church, beginning in the early 1500s, and then under the influence particularly of Saint Ignatius of Loyola (1491–1556) and his important *Spiritual Exercises*, an initial training in the prayer of meditation occurred in almost all settings of religious life. Saint John of the Cross writes with this background already in mind. A brief description of this prayer of meditation can be helpful.

Meditative prayer, as taught in this Catholic context, consists ordinarily in a quiet reflection for a half hour or longer on a section of the Gospel or other portions of Scripture. A primary method is to read daily through some select portion of Scripture, especially from the four Gospels, and then to gaze with the imagination at particular scenes, entering as an observer of sorts into the described event, seeking to draw out meaningful lessons from our Lord's words, finally concluding with resolutions for one's own conduct and pursuit of virtue. A more technical term for this kind of prayer is to call it a discursive meditation. One takes up a reflective thought or a particular view of a Gospel scene and then moves on to the next thought or next scene, and so on, during the course of the set period of time. Underlying the effort is a desire to deepen knowledge of God, and of Jesus in his incarnate humanity as God, and ultimately to know him personally and love him. Prayer is always for the sake of love; it is also to induce clear desires for virtuous living and imitation of saintly lives. An assumption underlying the practice of meditation is that this method of prayer generally produces satisfying experiences, especially when a person has first begun to meditate on the Gospel. The interest that Jesus draws, the profound influence he exerts, the attraction of his words and actions, when a person has real love for him, is usually strong in using this method of prayer. But the method over time, after many months, or some years, tends to yield diminishing returns. The Gospels become familiar and the feelings of the soul tend to plateau as a steady practice of such prayer takes place over a certain length of time.

This dying out of feelings and of tangible satisfaction is the context for the purifying experience in prayer that will be one indication, among others, of the possible onset of contemplative graces. Again, the "dark night of the senses", a phrase Saint John of the Cross adopts for this transitional time, will be invoked as the telling metaphor for this purification, which dries up feeling and closes down fruitful experiences of reflection or of the imagination. Instead of the "light" that for some time shone on the practice of meditative reflection, providing new insights and steady consolation, the soul begins to encounter a sharp dissonance with its prior experience in prayer. A troubling sense of struggle with the exercise of meditation begins to arise. And there is no understandable reason or any evident solution to correct this. It is not simply as though a tool used in prayer had broken for the moment, a tool that could be fixed or replaced with a better tool; nor is it simply a need of finding an improved method of reflection that can cast richer light in meditation; nor is it a matter of manipulating feelings and restoring them to their former warmth. The reality of what seems now to be an ineffective effort in prayer has a source in God's action on the soul. He apparently seeks, for one thing, to expose the soul to a greater awareness of its own inner poverty.

Perhaps it should be said as well that many people who approach prayer seriously enough to commit time to a daily prayer of meditation do not realize how seriously God takes the soul. What begins possibly to happen—the commencement of contemplative graces in prayer—is a sign that God does not seek just a devout form of prayer from a soul, whatever that might mean. He longs for the soul to *give* itself to him, so that he in turn can give to the soul a fuller gift of himself. The discussion of contemplative prayer is never simply to aid a soul in the advancement of prayer. That goal is always subordinated to the more primary purpose of interior prayer in opening a door within our soul to a progressive union of the soul with God. Two substantial passages from *The Ascent* that include preliminary remarks on contemplative prayer can be helpful at this point in exposing the contextual setting of prayer in which a soul will find itself in need of this teaching on contemplation. The inability to practice the prayer of meditation is emphasized in these paragraphs. Nonetheless, the more critical issue is the failure of the soul to understand the need of an adjustment in prayer at this time. The common reaction out of ignorance is to make choices in prayer that undermine grace and work to a soul's detriment.

> Many spiritual persons, after having exercised themselves in approaching God through images, forms, and meditations suitable for beginners, err greatly if they do not determine, dare, or know how to detach themselves from these palpable methods to which they are accustomed. For God then wishes to lead them to more spiritual, interior, and invisible graces by removing the gratification derived from discursive meditation. They still try to hold on to these methods, desiring to travel the road of consideration and meditation, using images as before. They think they must always act in this way. Striving hard to meditate, they draw out little satisfaction or none at all. Rather, aridity, fatigue, and restlessness of soul increase in the measure they strive through meditation for that former sweetness, now unobtainable. (AMC 2.12.6)

Another complementary passage from this same section stresses the problematic zeal that often is displayed as a soul fights to recover former experiences of satisfaction in meditative prayer that are no longer forthcoming.

> Thus in their struggle with considerations and discursive meditations they disturb their quietude. They become filled with aridity and trial because of efforts to get satisfaction by means no longer apt. We can say that the more intense their efforts, the less will be their gain. The more they persist at meditation, the worse their state becomes because they drag the soul further away from spiritual peace. They resemble one who abandons the greater for the lesser, turns back on a road already covered and wants to redo what is already done. (AMC 2.12.7)

If we turn, finally, to some parallel passages in *The Dark Night*, we find a different nuance in the description of the soul's frustration. Saint John of the Cross probes more forcefully here the need for a purification. The satisfaction that meditation had been providing, which is now painfully absent, may have been feeding a certain self-seeking in prayer. God begins to draw the soul away from a "lowly" manner of prayer that was to some degree rife with subtle tendencies of self-absorption. Meditative prayer may have become over time an effort to arrive at pleasing experiences for the self. Now God begins to strip this self-seeking from prayer by leaving the soul in dissatisfaction. In the view of Saint John of the Cross, a direct action of God, while concealed and secret, is implicitly present in the struggles that the soul undergoes at this time. These are not primarily struggles with a personal incapacity for prayer itself or a breakdown in general spiritual life. Rather, God is secretly at work emptying the soul in silent prayer for the sake of a greater encounter in faith with himself. The emphasis in the following passage from *The Dark Night* is on God's watchful, overseeing role in the transitional period into contemplative prayer. The trials of that time are meant, not to impede prayer with insurmountable barriers, but to lead it to a new depth. The words in this passage of Saint John of the Cross begin with a sharp comment on meditative prayer. It is not that he is dismissive of this practice; it has its place in the formative period of spiritual life. But he is insistent that it is a type of prayer that must be forsaken with the advent of contemplative graces.

> Since the conduct of these beginners in the way of God is lowly and not too distant from love of pleasure and of self, as we explained, God desires to withdraw them from this base manner of loving and lead them on to a higher degree of divine love. And he desires to liberate them from

the lowly exercise of the senses and of discursive meditation, by which they go in search of him so inadequately
and with so many difficulties, and lead them into the exercise of spirit, in which they become capable of a communion with God that is more abundant and more free of
imperfections. (DN 1.8.3)

And in an even more descriptive comment from the same
section of the painful struggle in prayer at this time of transition, Saint John of the Cross exposes the disturbance for
a soul in not knowing why prayer now has become a trial
and a reversal of the previous experience in prayer. These
preliminary comments, ample in themselves, are nonetheless simply the preparation for examining what a soul should
do in responding to the unusual character of divine grace at
this time, which we will address in the next chapter:

Consequently, it is at the time they are going about their
spiritual exercises with delight and satisfaction, when in
their opinion the sun of divine favor is shining most brightly
on them, that God darkens all this light and closes the door
and the spring of sweet spiritual water they were tasting
as often and as long as they desired. . . . God now leaves
them in such darkness that they do not know which way to
turn in their discursive imaginings. They cannot advance
a step in meditation, as they used to, now that the interior
sense faculties are engulfed in this night. He leaves them in
such dryness that they not only fail to receive satisfaction
and pleasure from their spiritual exercises and works, as
they formerly did, but also find these exercises distasteful
and bitter. . . . This change is a surprise to them because
everything seems to be functioning in reverse. (DN 1.8.3)

One last note of interest can be the statements that Saint
John of the Cross makes regarding the timeline, so to speak,
for the initiation of the soul into contemplative graces. The

thought for some people might be that this is a rare grace, a privileged state of prayer only for the most holy. The comments of Saint John of the Cross make it clear that contemplative graces are an ordinary progression in the life of a soul that is sincerely generous with God. "God does this after beginners *have exercised themselves for a time* in the way of virtue and have persevered in meditation and prayer" (DN 1.8.3; emphasis added). The primary requirement for crossing this threshold in prayer is the effort to please God in obedience to his will and a reluctance to offend him deliberately. When souls give themselves to God and his will and have acquired to some extent a true sacrificial spirit, it is not surprising that God draws closer. When we take the Gospel to heart, embrace some detachment from the world and its pleasures, and seek to lose ourselves in generous actions for others, it is not remarkable that God is generous with us. The *manner* in which he draws closer to a soul, as we are seeing, will be unexpected, more filled with trial initially than with apparent favor, but that is another matter. It is important to underscore that, in accord with Saint John of the Cross' teaching, the grace of contemplation can await us on the condition that we sincerely love our Lord and prove this love in action. The religious Sister faithful in following her vows; the seminarian for the priesthood serious about prayer, study, and virtue; the married person devout and sacrificial in love to spouse and family: these souls are candidates for the onset of contemplative prayer, if they give themselves to a committed practice of silent prayer. Without some dedication to silent prayer, of course, there will be no contemplative prayer. But it may be a more available possibility than is ordinarily thought. The description that follows from *The Dark Night* makes evident this truth.

When God sees that they have grown a little, he weans them from the sweet breast so that they might be strengthened, lays aside their swaddling bands, and puts them down from his arms that they may grow accustomed to walking by themselves. . . . This usually happens to recollected beginners sooner than to others since they are freer from occasions of backsliding and more quickly reform their appetites for worldly things. A reform of the appetites is the requirement for entering the happy night of the senses [initial contemplative prayer]. Not much time ordinarily passes after the initial stages of their spiritual life before beginners start to enter this night of sense [initial contemplative prayer]. And the majority of them do enter it, because it is common to see them suffer these aridities. . . . We could adduce numerous passages from Sacred Scripture, for since this sensory purgation [initial contemplative prayer] is so customary we find a great many references to it throughout, especially in the Psalms and the Prophets. But I do not want to spend time citing them, because the prevalence of the experience of this night should be enough. (DN 1.8.3, 4, 5)

All the passages we have referenced in this chapter are preparatory statements of Saint John of the Cross before he plunges in a more concentrated manner into the subject of contemplation. It is time now with this next chapter to examine more intently this saint's masterful instructions on contemplation—beginning with the symptoms of initial contemplative graces, then in subsequent chapters addressing the conduct necessary for the soul in contemplative prayer, and finally exposing more deeply the proper understanding of the purification of intellect and will in contemplative prayer.

9

THE INCIPIENT SIGNS OF
THE GRACE OF CONTEMPLATION

We turn our attention now to one of the most important contributions to spirituality in the writings of Saint John of the Cross. This concerns the signs that indicate a need to discontinue the practice of discursive meditation and shift to a prayer of contemplation. Two things might be stressed before providing an extensive treatment of these signs. One is that a soul's practice of meditation as a daily method of prayer is presumed in this teaching. A person has a regular commitment to silent prayer and is employing some method of reflective consideration on the Gospels or other parts of Scripture, as spoken of previously. The signs that Saint John of the Cross will identify make no sense except as a trial and struggle that enter into the prayer of meditation. There is no encouragement here to forgo the preliminary effort of meditation, as though one might simply enter into a more graced and intimate relationship with God by leaping ahead into contemplative prayer as a favored method of prayer. The preliminary stages must be observed. A propaedeutic period of learning to pray reflectively in silence is indispensable. We have to learn to think about our Lord and the mysteries of faith in order to enter into deeper love for our God. This effort in turn must be accompanied by a serious pursuit of virtue and of faithfulness to the will of God. A life without a clear sacrificial dimension should not expect graces of contemplation in the interior life of prayer.

The second important point to stress is the delicacy of discernment and the proper timing of this move from one method of prayer to a different state of prayer. Saint John of the Cross is insistent that a soul not rush prematurely from one to another; nor, on the contrary, to delay and wait hesitantly once the signs are evident. As he writes: "At the proper time one should abandon this imaginative meditation so that the journey to God may not be hindered, but, so that there is no regression, one should not abandon it before the due time" (AMC 2.13.1). A final introductory remark: It is customary to hear that Saint John of the Cross presents three signs indicating the need for this transition to contemplation. In fact, he has two explicit treatments of the matter—in book 2 of *The Ascent of Mount Carmel* and in book 1 of *The Dark Night*—each offering three signs, but not the same in each case. Combining the two sections, we can really speak of five signs, a point never mentioned, it seems, in commentaries on the subject. All of these signs should be "checked off" and present to some degree to ensure that the abandonment of meditative prayer for the sake of contemplation in prayer is being led by grace.

The first sign identified in the treatment of *The Ascent of Mount Carmel* is the inability to do a discursive meditation with any satisfaction, a marked change from the prior experience of meditative reflection in silent prayer. This incapacity to do what has been done with a fair amount of ease and delight up until then is naturally a cause of disturbance to a soul. The frustration that begins to take place in meditation is soon found to be a steady condition in prayer, despite efforts to overcome it. The trial overflows as well into feelings and perhaps becomes most noticeable there: "Dryness is now the outcome of fixing the senses [the imagination] on subjects that formerly provided satisfaction" (AMC 2.13.2).

The sharp, lingering aridity that ensues is a sign that this activity of meditation is no longer profitable. Gratification to some degree ordinarily accompanies graced activity, as Saint John of the Cross comments: "This agrees with what the philosophers hold: *Quod sapit, nutrit* (What is savory nourishes and fattens)" (AMC 2.14.1). It is an interesting observation that might raise an objection. Can one not say at times the opposite? It is also the case that what poses difficulty is often a means used by God to advance a soul in grace. But in this context, with the loss of any satisfying fruitfulness from meditation and without any change over time, the principle holds true as a sign that an adjustment in prayer is indicated. With no satisfaction obtained from meditation, the grace of prayer would seem to lie elsewhere. A passage from *The Dark Night* describes vividly the experience of meditation as a frustrating and futile effort at this time:

> They then grow weary and strive, as was their custom, to concentrate their faculties with some satisfaction on a subject of meditation, and they think that if they do not do this and do not feel that they are at work, they are doing nothing. This effort of theirs is accompanied by an interior reluctance and repugnance on the part of the soul, for it would be pleased to dwell in that quietude and idleness without working with the faculties. They consequently impair God's work and do not profit by their own. In searching for spirit, they lose the spirit that was the source of their tranquility and peace. They are like someone who turns from what has already been done in order to do it again, or like one who leaves a city only to re-enter it, or they are like a hunter who abandons the prey in order to go hunting again. It is useless, then, for the soul to try to meditate because it will no longer profit by this exercise. (DN 1.10.1)

In *The Dark Night*, this sign of the inability to meditate is the third in the series; it is the one sign that overlaps in both treatises. In the treatment of *The Dark Night*, the sign is described as a "powerlessness, in spite of one's efforts, to meditate and make use of the imagination, the interior sense, as was one's previous custom" (DN 1.9.8). Saint John of the Cross explains that a different form of communication from God is beginning to take place in prayer. Thus, the incapacity to meditate is not a symptom of turning backward or losing a proper focus in prayer, which the frustration might seem to demonstrate. Formerly, God used meditation as a means to teach *about* himself, but he did so in a manner somewhat detached from a more personal contact with himself. Imaginative reenactment of Gospel scenes, while at times vivid and arousing to the feelings, is not equivalent to the immediacy of actual personal contact with God. Discursive reflection, while capable of insightful thought, is likewise not equivalent to meeting God himself in his infinitude of love. Instead, at this time of a transition into the grace of contemplation, a kind of negative experience in the incapacity for discursive reflection begins to be constant in meditative prayer. The following words from *The Dark Night* convey some aspect of this initial symptom in words that will need further comment in due time: "[God] begins to communicate himself through pure spirit by an act of simple contemplation in which there is no discursive succession of thought. The exterior and interior senses of the lower part of the soul cannot attain to this contemplation. As a result the imaginative power and phantasy can no longer rest in any consideration or find support in it" (DN 1.9.8).

The second sign listed in *The Ascent of Mount Carmel* is mentioned only in this work, not in *The Dark Night*. This sign might best be understood as connected to the painful inability to meditate in silent prayer. Here Saint John of the Cross writes of an awareness of aversion or disinclination to turn the imagination with fixed concentration upon particular subjects for spiritual consideration. However, that is not all that is taking place. Equally so, the imagination shows no desire to dwell on temporal concerns that might substitute in a distracted way for the inability to focus on a spiritual subject. The imagination seems to undergo a general stiffening of its ordinary operation, at least in the time of prayer. It is noticeably unable in prayer to take up spiritual interests as it previously did. At the same time there can be a flow of distractions *disturbing* the mind, but none of these draws the attention as a desirable interest. These distractions are irritations to the mind. Saint John of the Cross stresses in *The Ascent of Mount Carmel* that the second sign of the inability to fix the imagination on subjects is important for confirming the reliability of the first sign, the inability to meditate. One might be unable to meditate because of "melancholia" or because a lax approach has entered into one's general life and has led to a certain loss of interest in prayer. In that case, distractions might be an escape from the effort of prayer. The mind then chases after them as an attractive pursuit. A realistic understanding of human nature is present in the following comment: "It could be that the inability to imagine and meditate derives from one's dissipation and lack of diligence. The second sign, the disinclination and absence of desire to think about extraneous things, must be present. When this inability to concentrate the imagination and sense faculties on the things of God proceeds from dissipation and tepidity, there is yearning to dwell on other things and an inclination to give up meditation" (AMC 2.13.6).

We turn now to *The Dark Night* for a third sign of initial

contemplative graces. In this treatise, it is the first in the series of three signs. Here Saint John of the Cross focuses on the important symptom of a sharp aridity of feelings in prayer and outside of prayer. An immediate description from the text can be helpful: "Since these souls do not get satisfaction or consolation from the things of God, they do not get any from creatures either. Since God puts a soul in this dark night in order to dry up and purge its sensory appetite, he does not allow it to find sweetness or delight in anything" (DN 1.9.2). It is a significant sign, not simply because it brings a serious trial to prayer. In that case, it might only require an effort of perseverance. Rather, more importantly, the fading of feelings as a support in prayer is symptomatic of a work of grace leading to a greater loss of self in prayer and in the whole of life. With no satisfaction or delight felt tangibly in prayer, the soul ought to turn in its emptiness more intently to seeking God alone. Our Lord is beginning to show a soul in a deeper manner that it belongs exclusively to him. Unfortunately, it usually takes time for this insight to gather strength and provoke a recognition. The more common early reaction is a preoccupied focus on the pain of inner aridity. Saint John of the Cross makes clear as well that the lack of satisfaction in the things of God extends also to a dry absence of consolation in things outside of prayer. Now it seems that in work and in human relations nothing draws the soul so strongly in attraction; the emotional life feels dry and deadened in a general way.

The constancy and prevalence of aridity in this general sense is a first taste of what can eventually become a graced detachment from all that is not God. But some graces take more time to bear their fruit. This sign is not a matter of a person being torn between conflicting desires, both of which have their attractive appeal. Rather, the soul is simply oppressed by a general emptiness of feeling. A psychological diagnosis of this condition of affective emptiness is likely to mistake it as some form of mild depression. But, in fact, the energies of the person for God and for doing good are not diminished at all, which in itself is a striking indication of grace at work. The dry emptiness of feeling does not translate into a lack of virtuous self-giving, and this is of course important to remember. The problem is simply a painful absence of feeling in all the things that are pursued for the sake of God. In *The Dark Night*, Saint John of the Cross provides a helpful explanation of why the feelings become so dry and empty in prayer at this time. The grace of contemplation is a movement into a greater depth of encounter with God, beneath the surface experience of feeling. In the following passage, the term "sense" or "sensory", in contrast to "spirit", is referring to feelings in prayer.

> The reason for this dryness is that God transfers his goods and strength from sense to spirit. Since the sensory part of the soul is incapable of the goods of spirit, it remains deprived, dry, and empty. Thus, while the spirit is tasting, the flesh tastes nothing at all and becomes weak in its work. But through this nourishment the spirit grows stronger and more alert, and becomes more solicitous than before about not failing God. If in the beginning the soul does not experience this spiritual savor and delight, but dryness and distaste, the reason is the novelty involved in this exchange. (DN 1.9.4)

A fourth sign, which is the second of the three treated in *The Dark Night*, is a painful self-questioning in a person due to the experience of losing satisfaction in the things of God. The soul thinks it must be in reversal and declining spiritually: "The soul thinks it is not serving God but turning back, because it is aware of this distaste for the things of

God" (DN 1.9.3). In other words, a soul is convinced that it must be at fault for the condition in which it now finds itself. The aversion felt for its customary practices in prayer seems to confirm the existence of some personal fault and infidelity as a cause for this state. The only possible reason for the painful experience in prayer must be some moral failure or lack of fidelity. It is necessary, the soul thinks, to discover it and root it out. The more ignorant the soul is of what is happening in grace, the greater likelihood of suffering this sign with some intensity.

This sign is of interest in part because in many souls it leads to a scrupulosity for a time. The turning inward in self-questioning, distrustful of self and the genuineness of personal motives, is a common affliction at this time. Let us remember that these are people of serious virtue if they are experiencing these contemplative symptoms. Now they begin to narrow their self-examination, trying to root out everything in their lives that might exhibit imperfection, causing themselves grief with this self-preoccupied attention. We might comment also that whereas the three previous signs manifest their symptoms strongly in all cases, this fourth sign would seem to exhibit a strength in proportion to a person's sensitivity. If a person is ignorant of what is happening in grace, and at the same time very sensitive to its aridity, the tendency to blame self for what seems to be a downturn in relations with God in prayer is magnified. In discussing this sign, Saint John of the Cross clarifies also the clear distinction between a tepid laxity that empties consolation from a soul and the quite different loss of affectivity that is one sign of entering into the grace of contemplation. These are very different states of soul, although the symptoms of aridity and aversion in prayer can seem to resemble each other. As Saint John of the Cross writes:

It is obvious that this aversion and dryness is not the fruit of laxity and tepidity, for lukewarm people do not care much for the things of God nor are they inwardly solicitous about them. There is, consequently, a notable difference between dryness and lukewarmness. The lukewarm are very lax and remiss in their will and spirit, and have no solicitude about serving God. Those suffering from the purgative dryness are ordinarily solicitous, concerned, and pained about not serving God. (DN 1.9.3)

The last or fifth sign, identified only in _The Ascent of Mount Carmel_ and the third sign in that series, is the most significant and will enter into the longer discussion of Saint John of the Cross on contemplation. It is unique among these signs in lacking a painful dimension. The other four signs give evidence of the prayer of meditation no longer functioning properly, and they do so with some painful frustration or disturbance to the soul. When discerned as present together, these four signs demonstrate a need to move beyond what is not working any longer in prayer. They need to be discerned before responding to the fifth sign, which will point the soul in the direction of a new state of prayer. This fifth sign indicates, without the soul at first ordinarily realizing it, a desire and inclination to enter into the grace of contemplation. For that reason, it is appropriate for the fifth sign to belong at the end of this series and is confirmed only after the soul has suffered the previous signs to some extent.

Before examining this sign, a comment might be helpful. A deliberate shift into a different manner of praying should not take place, according to Saint John of the Cross, simply because an inclination is felt to enjoy a more quiet prayer. The possibility of a premature move is the reason why a series of signs must be adduced. Saint John of the Cross, as we have said already, understands the grace of contemplation to be a transitional step after a committed period of time making use of meditative prayer, usually at least for a year in the best of souls. Nonetheless, this last sign is critically important in itself when it is evident along with the four other signs. God uses the symptoms present in this fifth sign to draw a soul to himself in a more direct and personal manner in prayer. At the same time, a further comment is also appropriate. The teaching of Saint John of the Cross regarding this sign is not primarily to propose a new method of prayer. Rather, he intends in his extended treatment to draw out the deeper repercussions for prayer that are first indicated by a delicate inclination felt in the silence of prayer, as described below in this sign. Hardly noticed at first, this inclination to a greater quiet in prayer can lead in time to relations of a much more profound depth with God. Responding to this inclination is as such of fundamental importance in the early stages of contemplation. A proper response also paves the road for later advancement in the grace of contemplation. What follows is the brief statement by which Saint John of the Cross introduces this sign in *The Ascent of Mount Carmel*. In the course of our examination, this initial description will have to be expanded and amplified at length. But even here, Saint John of the Cross is already speaking of the door of entry into contemplation, which implies a necessary surrender of the inner spirit to a new experience in prayer.

> The third and surest sign is that a person likes to remain alone in loving awareness of God, without particular considerations, in interior peace and quiet and repose, and without the acts and exercises (at least discursive, those in which one progresses from point to point) of the intellect, memory and will. Such a one prefers to remain only in the general loving awareness and knowledge we men-

tioned, without any particular knowledge or understanding. (AMC 2.13.4)

In the last chapter, in an earlier reference from *The Ascent* (AMC 2.12.6–7) to the transition from meditation to
a state of contemplation, the uncertainty that accompanies
this sign was already mentioned. It may be difficult for people to respond to the grace present in this sign because it
seems to indicate a need to give up a particular practice
of prayer without a person knowing very well what to do
next. It is easier to comment from the vantage of a knowl-
edgeable practitioner of prayer, as Saint John of the Cross
is, than for a neophyte contemplative to discern correctly a
new approach to take in silent prayer without some clear
direction. Even when given sound advice to do so, the soul
has to discover for itself that following the inclination it
feels to remain quiet, without the pursuit of meditative effort, is a threshold it should cross without anxiety. It has to
come to know for itself that reducing its mental activity,
indeed, letting it fade from a conscientious effort in prayer
and, instead, allowing itself to remain alone and silent with
the Lord is not a betrayal of prayer.

As we will see, the implicit instruction that Saint John of
the Cross repeats in various ways is the need for the soul to
go where deep down in desire it wants to go. Resisting the
inclination to remain quiet and alone with God only frus-
trates the soul. And yet reluctance to go forward in grace
at this time is common. These are souls who are virtuous
and thus desirous to do things in a right way, in accord with
directions, training, and obedience. In the context of Saint
John of the Cross' time, they have been taught a method
of meditative prayer to practice and, indeed, to strive to get
better in the practice of it. And their thought is often that it

is not correct to forgo meditation, despite their inclination to do so. They are ordinarily hesitant to enter into what can seem an inward state of non-activity. The following passage from that earlier section of *The Ascent* captures something of the dilemma and something of the new experience that is beginning to manifest itself. The soul so often does not know what to do with what it "feels" in this delicate and deeper inclination. A partial answer to the dilemma is also introduced in the passage:

> They will no longer taste that sensible food, as we said, but rather will enjoy another food, more delicate, interior, and spiritual. Not by working with the imagination will they acquire this spiritual nourishment but by pacifying the soul, by leaving it to its more spiritual quiet and repose. The more spiritual they are, the more they discontinue trying to make particular acts with their faculties, for they become more engrossed in one general, pure act. Once the faculties reach the end of their journey, they cease to work, just as we cease to walk when we reach the end of our journey. If everything consisted in going, one would never arrive; and if everywhere we found means, when and where could we enjoy the end and goal? (AMC 2.12.6)

The great challenge, ironically, is to fight off an initial resistance to the graced *attraction* of contemplation. The reluctance of souls to follow a delicate inclination felt obscurely within them can be quite strong. They hesitate, perhaps scrupulously, to enter into an inward quiet unlike any silence previously experienced in prayer. The hesitation is understandable, because this entry into a kind of inactive quiet would seem to be contrary to the activity that ostensibly obliges them if a period of meditation is scheduled in the life of prayer. So much depends on a soul being free and open to a subtle invitation of grace. It is being drawn to a deeper quiet, not just of external silence and the absence of noise, but to a purity of inner quietude in which God is drawing to himself the inner spirit of the soul. This inner quiet is a place of rest to which the soul is drawn and which it wants to enter, but the person may not yet recognize such a "place" as a true destination for prayer. As Saint John of the Cross writes: "Since these individuals do not understand the mystery of this new experience, they imagine themselves to be idle and doing nothing" (AMC 2.12.7).

And so the reaction is often initially to think that a temptation to idleness is taking place. As a result, it is common to see in souls a forced attempt to exert some strenuous effort in meditative reflection, which only agitates the soul. It is not God's will for them to do meditative activity now, but they strive to do it anyway. In Saint John of the Cross' description, these souls have arrived at a goal without realizing their arrival. By trying to meditate or reflect in prayer, they act in a manner that works against their own interest. The clinging to meditative activity is counterproductive, most often resulting in a distracted mind. What they ought to do instead is give way to the delicate desire they do feel to remain quiet and alone in God's presence. They should remain without a labor of thought, enjoying a subtle peace and a longing for God. The effort to force active reflection brings frustration; it is a hindrance to their prayer. Yet it happens often that souls do not recognize the actual graces working upon their desires and attractions at this time. They put their heads to the grindstone, as it were, and try to continue doing what has been familiar in their conduct of prayer. As Saint John of the Cross writes:

It is sad to see many disturb their soul when it desires to abide in this calm and repose of interior quietude, where it is filled with God's peace and refreshment. Desiring to make it retrace its steps and turn back from the goal in which it now reposes, they draw their soul out to more exterior activity, to considerations, which are the means. They do this with strong repugnance and reluctance in the soul. The soul wants to remain in that peace, which it does not understand, as in its rightful place. People suffer if, after laboring to reach their place of rest, they are forced to return to their labors. (AMC 2.12.7)

If contemplative graces are to be received fruitfully, the attraction to remain in this empty condition of interior quietude must come to be perceived as an invitation of God rising up from a deeper region of the inner spirit. The soul must come to perceive that an entry into that inactive quiet is not a temptation to an unfaithful choice that somehow threatens prayer. Indeed, the primary effect of the contemplative grace is not to incapacitate reflections. Rather, much more significantly, it makes possible a different encounter with God. The interior quiet invites us to enter an ambiance of depth in the soul for a new contact with our Lord's presence. The soul must step across this boundary with a certain blind trust in God. A conscientious effort of activity in prayer must give way to a deeper receptivity drawing the soul toward a subtle divine action within the recesses of the soul. Crossing that threshold toward God takes place by surrendering to the peaceful quiet and by a simple desire to love within the soul. And, importantly, this does not happen without some cooperation from a soul. A definite choice is necessary to refrain from mental activity. Likewise, a choice is necessary *not to resist* the inclination to remain in a wordless quiet without thought, if that grace is given. The realization that God invites this choice, that he is mysteriously at work, can of course help a soul. As Saint John of the Cross writes in a striking passage from *The Living Flame of Love*, a soul's hesitation may collapse precisely by turning its thought to God's apparent intention in all this.

> It cost God a great deal to bring these souls to this stage, and he highly values his work of having introduced them into this solitude and emptiness regarding their faculties and activity so that he might speak to their hearts, which is what he always desires. Since it is he who now reigns in the soul with an abundance of peace and calm, he takes the initiative himself by making the natural acts of the faculties fail, by which the soul laboring the whole night accomplished nothing [Lk. 5:5]; and he feeds the spirit without the activity of the senses because neither the sense nor its function is capable of spirit. (LF 3.54)

The whole matter is nonetheless very delicate in description. The beginning of contemplation is not just a passive drifting with an interior current of grace that carries the soul away easily into the presence of God. A soul must learn to give itself to a quiet, loving attentiveness and discover that in the silence itself the mystery of God is hidden. There is a need to learn that nothing is lost in relinquishing active, reflective thought, as long as one's attentiveness remains turned toward the mystery of the divine presence. Letting go in this way, so that God himself permeates the inner "activity" of prayer, requires a gradual adjustment to a new attraction felt inwardly in the soul. Receptivity is certainly the key word of advice. The soul must receive the inclination of quiet and respond to it with surrender, without seeking to grasp at an experience that it can claim as its own. It has to trust that God is mysteriously near and strive to be receptive to his hidden, drawing action. Saint John of the Cross offers this description:

> The proper advice for these individuals is that they must learn to abide in that quietude with a loving attentiveness to God and pay no heed to the imagination and its work. At this stage, as was said, the faculties are at rest and do not work actively but passively, by receiving what God is effecting in them. If at times the soul puts the faculties to work, it should not use excessive efforts or studied reasonings, but it should proceed with gentleness of love, moved more by God than by its own abilities. (AMC 2.12.8)

The essential adjustment into this new stage of prayer is thus twofold in nature. The four earlier signs demonstrate a need to relinquish meditative prayer because it no longer works. If a soul perceives itself at fault for the inability to meditate, it tends to impede and block the desire it feels delicately for a silence alone with God. It has to fight off, if necessary, an anxious concern that it is failing in diligence if it no longer pursues meditative prayer. The advice to trust one's heart and its deeper desire at this time is apt. The choice to leave behind meditation happens more easily to the degree a person is more docile to the deeper inclination. Nonetheless, there remains the dilemma what to do now in a quiet and solitary state, without giving thought and imagination to any subject. This is the second aspect of a necessary adjustment. A soul almost always finds itself initially in a transitional state of some confusion. It needs to cross a bridge not knowing what it means to be on the other side of a silence without thought. The recommendation to embrace a "loving knowledge" of God is not refined sufficiently in most lives to be identified clearly as a target

of desire. The soul may be subject to gentle waves of intermittent desire and feel an inclination drawing it. When it
abandons meditation and gives way to the desire "to remain
alone in loving awareness of God" (AMC 2.13.4), forsaking considerations, it is possible that it may soon find a new
satisfaction. "Interior peace and quiet and repose" (AMC
2.13.4) may now gradually permeate it, without any need to
respond with acts and exercises. A preference to stay in that
quiet and peace may be gently felt, without realizing so well
that it is being drawn to a deeper love for God. At the same
time, a lack of perception is often experienced because a
painful aridity is also felt. The aridity can be strong despite
the obscure desire to enter into a greater love for God. A
passage from *The Dark Night* exposes some of the difficulty
of this moment of adjustment. It also identifies benefits that
accrue precisely from the difficulty.

> Individuals generally do not perceive this love in the begin-
> ning, but they experience rather the dryness and void we
> are speaking of. Then, instead of this love which is enkin-
> dled afterward, they harbor, in the midst of the dryness
> and emptiness of their faculties, a habitual care and solici-
> tude for God accompanied by grief or fear about not serv-
> ing him. It is a sacrifice most pleasing to God—that of a
> spirit in distress and solicitude for his love [Ps. 51:17]. Se-
> cret contemplation produces this solicitude and concern in
> the soul until, after having somewhat purged the sensory
> part of its natural propensities by means of this aridity,
> it begins to enkindle in the spirit this divine love. Mean-
> while, however, as in one who is undergoing a cure, all is
> suffering in this dark and dry purgation of the appetite,
> and the soul being relieved of numerous imperfections
> acquires many virtues, thereby becoming capable of this
> love. (DN 1.11.2)

The delicate attraction to remaining in this quiet and simply loving God, despite the strong aridity, is a notable thing. The attraction for this love may be hardly perceived because it is not felt so strongly. But what the soul does clearly experience is a reluctance to reflect actively with the mind. As Saint John of the Cross writes in *The Ascent*, the soul "prefers to remain only in the general loving awareness and knowledge . . . without any particular knowledge or understanding" (AMC 2.13.4). The combination of a painful absence of feeling and an aversion to reflective meditation is a reason why people often do not discern the grace of contemplation in their lives. The new experience is so strangely different and incomparable to prior experiences of strong feelings of delight found in meditative satisfaction, which was able to touch the emotions unmistakably. The difficult aspects of contemplation in its initial period may seem to indicate nothing of a new grace at all. Becoming sensitively aware of the delicate quiet and calm as an inner ambiance of grace is highlighted in the following passage from *The Ascent*. Again, a choice is necessary: first a letting go, and then a giving in to the interior inclination felt in the soul:

> Actually, at the beginning of this state the loving knowledge is almost unnoticeable. There are two reasons for this: First, the loving knowledge initially is likely to be extremely subtle and delicate, almost imperceptible; second, a person who is habituated to the exercise of meditation, which is wholly sensible, hardly perceives or feels this new insensible, purely spiritual experience. This is especially so when through failure to understand it one does not permit oneself to rest in it but strives after the other, more sensory experience. Although the interior peace is more abundant, the individual allows no room to experience and enjoy it. (AMC 2.13.7)

The more a soul in responding to contemplative grace becomes "habituated" to the calm that is drawing it from within, the more likely that a "general, loving knowledge of God" rises up from within the recesses of the soul. In time, it can be expected that this loving knowledge will pervade the soul's awareness more distinctly and more appealingly. Nonetheless, it would seem clear that this last sign is in a certain way the most difficult to discern. The previous four signs exhibit strong negative reactions. This last sign is subtle always in its beginnings and delicate in its attraction, and to answer to it means to respond to a grace that may not seem so assured. In many cases, it may be that a soul gives itself to this inclination quite unknowingly. It is led by God and surrenders to the calm and loving knowledge without thinking much about what it is doing. This may certainly be true in the lives of simple souls who are not so analytical and intellectual. As Saint John of the Cross comments: "It is noteworthy that this general knowledge is at times so recondite and delicate (especially when purer, simpler, and more perfect), spiritual and interior that the soul does not perceive or feel it even though the soul is employed with it" (AMC 2.14.8). The last phrase seems to make clear that souls often initially enter into the graces of contemplation without realizing that they are doing so. The general loving knowledge that descends on the soul is accompanied by a deep interior calm and draws the soul like the fragrance of newly baked bread for a hungry man. The man in hunger simply moves in the direction of that bread, not thinking so much what he is doing. And this is precisely what can happen in prayer. The more a soul finds itself following the deeper inclination to enter this inward calm and quiet peace, the more likely it is that the soul begins to be attracted to the simple desire to love that it is receiving in grace. The movement forward to contemplation is a response to this grace: "The more habituated persons become to this calm, the more their experience of this general loving knowledge of God will increase. This knowledge is more enjoyable than all other things because without the soul's labor it affords peace, rest, savor, and delight" (AMC 2.13.7).

Lastly, in this chapter on the signs of early contemplation, we should hear the interpretation Saint John of the Cross provides on the shift taking place from the knowledge of God ordinarily received in meditation to the very different "loving knowledge" of God that is the gift of contemplation. This difference also casts light on the discernment necessary in recognizing the important fifth sign. If we step back a moment, certainly we can say that a logic of love is at work in the practice of meditation. The repeated practice of gazing on our Lord while listening intently to his words in the Gospel can bring the soul to a habitual love for him. But when the soul becomes more seized by love for God, the isolated and separate acts of love that may occur inconsistently at various times in meditative prayer are likely, with the onset of contemplative graces, to fuse together into a more continual longing of love. What has just been said has a parallel truth in the life of charity toward others, and this, too, is a symptom of crossing the threshold into contemplation. Over time, the soul itself, and not just the particular acts it performs, can become full of a steady quality of love. It is as though the flame of loving desire for God now burns almost without ceasing. This more continual state of a longing for God and for his will is an essential condition for contemplation. Saint John of the Cross teaches that sometimes God favors a soul and draws it into the loving knowledge of contemplation without a great need for prior acts of knowledge and insight gained through meditation. The reason for this, we can assume, is because the love of the soul is continuously and generously in act. If so, meditation in itself, then, is not always the stepping-stone into contemplation. Many souls open themselves to contemplation because they are simply in love with God and generous and sacrificial in all ways with him. It is always love that leads to the grace of contemplation. The following passage implies that this "placing" of a soul by God in contemplation can occur precisely because a soul is distinguished by its love. As he writes:

> It should be known that the purpose of discursive meditation on divine subjects is the acquisition of some knowledge and love of God. Each time individuals procure through meditation some of this knowledge and love they do so by an act. Many acts, in no matter what area, will engender a habit. Similarly, through many particular acts of this loving knowledge a person reaches the point at which a habit is formed in the soul. God, too, is wont to effect this habit in many souls, placing them in contemplation without these acts as means, or at least without many of them. (AMC 2.14.2; emphasis added)

The teaching in this passage casts further light on the discernment of shifting away from the activity of meditation to the calm receptivity of a quiet, loving knowledge of God, as described in the fifth sign. The knowledge gained from meditation was a loving knowledge of God received intermittently at first, in isolated moments, and increasingly a steady feature in prayer. Somehow, without the soul being aware, this loving knowledge of God can become a more general habitual state of love within the soul. Presumably, it is also carried outside prayer into actions of sacrifice and generosity as a way of expressing love for God. When the soul turns now to prayer, this love for God, a direct and personal love for him, is available to be embraced and fostered with a certain immediacy. Often the soul does not yet realize this change in its own interior condition, and it continues to follow a familiar method of meditation. But in turning to the silence of prayer, the drawing power of a desire to love God alone is more intensely present. More often now, as prayer begins, a soul can sense, if it is receptive, that an immediate response to the presence of God can replace the need to search for a thought or image that might lead it to a focus on God. As Saint John of the Cross writes:

> What the soul, therefore, was gradually acquiring through the labor of meditation on particular ideas has now, as we said, been converted into habitual and substantial, general loving knowledge. This knowledge is neither distinct nor particular, as was the previous knowledge. Accordingly the moment prayer begins, the soul, as one with a store of water, drinks peaceably without the labor and the need to fetch the water through the channels of past considerations, forms, and figures. The moment it recollects itself in the presence of God it enters into an act of general, loving, peaceful, and tranquil knowledge, drinking wisdom and love and delight. (AMC 2.14.2)

The ease with which contemplation can take place when a soul is accustomed to approach God with a deeper surrender of itself is evident in this passage. The great obstacle to the soul at this time, on the other hand, as mentioned already, lies in an excessively conscientious approach to prayer that resists adaptation. And in a real sense, this involves a lack of surrender to God. The conscientiousness to "do prayer" as taught in one's training is not necessarily a virtue; it actually can be a fault that makes a soul reluctant to alter its ways. The person may have become accustomed for many months, sometimes for years, to fill a silent time of prayer with an imaginative gaze on the Gospel or in searching for spiritual insights. The familiarity of the method has trained the person to seek satisfaction in the acquisition of new thoughts or in the enjoyment of some felt sense of loving God. The virtuous resolutions that may conclude such prayer give the time of prayer a sense of a purposefulness. For many souls, it becomes very hard to accept that a prayer less active, less searching, a prayer more inconclusive, more open-ended, can be an advancement in prayer. The suggestion to remain quiet seems to invite the laziness of non-activity into prayer and to yield fruitless results. As we have mentioned, these souls, if they are receiving contemplative graces, are the fervent and dedicated people of the spiritual life. They are people who do give themselves generously in charity and to the will of God. They work hard and spend themselves. Otherwise, the grace of contemplation would not be occurring. But it is precisely this conscientiousness that can work against them at this time. They are not acclimated to a more receptive acceptance of subtle graces from God. If the person can trust inwardly and allow the soul to follow its deeper instinct of love, as described in the fifth sign, then the door opens to the graced inner desire to seek nothing but to love God in prayer. Unfortunately, an active mentality may tend for a time to resist the "apparent" abandonment of concrete fruits from its prayer. Such a soul may prefer, as Saint John of the Cross comments, to do over and over again what has been done and completed already. The aversion can be strong to doing what is thought to be doing nothing. Yet how mistaken this may be. Saint John of the Cross employs a striking image: removing the rind from a piece of fruit, so that it is ready to eat, and then trying to peel it once again:

> Many behave similarly at the beginning of this state. They think that the whole matter [of prayer] consists in understanding particular ideas and in reasoning through images and forms (the rind of the spirit). Since they do not encounter these images in that loving, substantial quietude

where nothing is understood particularly and in which they like to rest, they believe they are wasting time and straying from the right road; and they turn back to search for the rind of images and reasoning. They are unsuccessful in their search because the rind has already been removed. (AMC 2.14.4)

And what happens as a result? The dissatisfaction described in the earlier four signs continues for a soul and a failure to move forward toward the graced encounter with God in contemplation that the fifth sign indicates. The passage continues:

There is no enjoyment of the substance nor ability to meditate, and they become disturbed with the thought of backsliding and going astray. They are indeed getting lost, but not in the way they imagine, for they are losing the exercise of their own senses and first mode of experience. This loss indicates that they are approaching the spirit being imparted to them, in which the less they understand the further they penetrate into the night of the spirit—the subject of this book. They must pass through this night to a union with God beyond all knowing. (AMC 2.14.4)

Clearly, there is a great need to respond with surrender to God when the grace of contemplation begins to manifest itself. The willingness of the soul to pass beyond the familiar experience of prayer into a more obscure prayer, where the "God beyond all knowing" is encountered, requires careful commentary and analysis in accord with the exact teaching of Saint John of the Cross. This discussion on the soul's conduct in the prayer of contemplation will continue as the subject of the next chapter.

10

THE CONDUCT OF THE
SOUL IN CONTEMPLATIVE PRAYER

The proper approach to silent prayer for a soul experiencing the initial signs of contemplation is the important next topic. This is not a matter of adopting a particular method of prayer, but rather of growing accustomed to a different inner *ambiance* of soul in prayer. Greater depth in relations with God will bring a new mysterious sense of his personal reality. As highlighted in the last chapter in the fifth sign, there is a subtle inclination of grace drawing the soul in contemplation to enter its own quiet inner depths. This attraction has a source in God, and our soul must allow itself to be allured toward that inner quiet, a place of mystery. A receptive disposition of soul is especially required at this time. With the onset of contemplative graces, a flame of love burns secretly within the recesses of the soul. Our soul must remain near that flame, not disturbing it, not letting this fire die out, which we might do by seeking to occupy ourselves in some active manner in prayer. Instead, by remaining in a receptive state of quiet desire, in a loving attention toward our Lord, without trying to think reflectively or to conjure any image before our inner eyes, our soul disposes itself to the grace of contemplation.

By remaining in this receptive state of quiet, without a labor of interior mental activity, the soul does not get in the way, as it were, and thereby obstruct the grace of contemplation. This effort is not a matter of practicing a method or technique in prayer. The great need is simply to remain in the presence of our Lord's love without thinking so consciously about what we are doing. The pursuit of thought and activity is unnecessary; rather, the receptive attitude of a quiet longing for God is what is needed. The following passage from *The Dark Night* is perhaps the clearest, most basic instruction on how our soul should conduct itself when the symptoms of contemplation make themselves evident. It can serve well in introducing this chapter. The combination of a withdrawal from a previous method of activity in prayer and of a necessary surrender to a delicate inward inclination is quite explicit in the passage. In effect, it affirms the need to accept a new form of contentment in prayer.

> The attitude necessary in the night of sense [incipient contemplation] is to pay no attention to discursive meditation since this is not the time for it. They should allow the soul to remain in rest and quietude even though it may seem obvious to them that they are doing nothing and wasting time, and even though they think this disinclination to think about anything is due to their laxity. Through patience and perseverance in prayer, they will be doing a great deal without activity on their part. All that is required of them here is freedom of soul, that they liberate themselves from the impediment and fatigue of ideas and thoughts, and care not about thinking and meditating. They must be content simply with a loving and peaceful attentiveness to God, and live without the concern, without the effort, and without the desire to taste or feel him. All these desires disquiet the soul and distract it from the peaceful, quiet, and sweet idleness of the contemplation which is being communicated to it. (DN 1.10.4)

In *The Ascent of Mount Carmel*, Saint John of the Cross instructs us that souls in the early period of acclimation to contemplative graces may "find themselves in this loving or peaceful awareness without having first engaged in any active work (regarding particular acts) with their faculties; they will not be working actively but only receiving" (AMC 2.15.2). The comment suggests that at times, once contemplation commences as a grace, we can enter prayer expecting a kind of release within our inner spirit into a silent desire for our Lord. Other days may differ; indeed, variation and unpredictability may be a more frequent experience. When there is no release of desire, as just mentioned, we can take up gentle efforts that dispose us to the encounter with our Lord's loving presence. Saint John of the Cross writes, for instance: "On the other hand they will frequently find it necessary to aid themselves gently and moderately with meditation in order to enter this state" (AMC 2.15.2). The key phrase of interest here is ". . . in order to enter this state". The early experience of contemplation often requires that we try to "place" ourselves in an inner ambiance by which the grace of contemplation can ignite more readily. There are ways in which this entry into an inner quiet conducive to contemplation can possibly take place. These choices do not become the direct cause of contemplation, which is a gratuitous grace. Rather, they dispose the soul for a receptivity to a quiet inner longing for God that opens the way to responding to contemplative graces. For instance, the repetition of a short sacred phrase, such as the Jesus Prayer ("Lord Jesus Christ, Son of God, have mercy on me, a sinner."), or of a single verse from a psalm; looking in silence at a holy image or at a crucifix or a statue of Mary; or gazing with love toward the tabernacle in silence—these are possible examples that allow the mind to be quiet and the inner spirit to enter into a longing for God. The choice in each case is to give oneself to an inner quiet without active thought.

And then a delicate desire to love may be encountered that is drawing the soul from within its own depths. This desire to love is the crucial condition for contemplation. In the following passage, Saint John of the Cross concentrates on the essential attraction of love in this early period of contemplation:

> The fire of love is not commonly felt at the outset, either because it does not have a chance to take hold, owing to the impurity of the sensory part, or because the soul for want of understanding has not made within itself a peaceful place for it; although at times with or without these conditions a person will begin to feel a certain longing for God. In the measure that the fire increases, the soul becomes aware of being attracted by the love of God and enkindled in it, without knowing how or where this attraction and love originates. At times this flame and enkindling increase to such an extent that the soul desires God with urgent longings of love. (DN 1.11.1)

Saint John of the Cross asks the question whether, with the onset of contemplation, a person needs at times to return to meditation as a form of prayer. Is a threshold crossed in contemplation once and for all, eliminating the need for reflective thought in prayer? Does a person ever gain by meditating as before if that person now enjoys the grace of contemplation? His answer displays spiritual common sense: "As long as one can make discursive meditation and draw out satisfaction, one must not abandon this method. Meditation must be discontinued only when the soul is placed in that peace and quietude" (AMC 2.13.2). One truth is certainly clear: The transition into the delicate nature of contemplative prayer is never so definitive and complete at the time of its beginnings. The soul needs to acquire a taste for the inward inclination to a calm, loving turn toward the presence of our Lord. It would be an improper notion to imagine this taking place like a leap into a lake that keeps us afloat without any effort on our part. A better image of the early experience of contemplation is to think of allowing a boat tethered to the shore to be released from what ties it so that it can drift into the deeper water. The oarsman may have to exercise himself a bit at first to get the boat moving. Meditation can prove an aid in that untying and release, if the activity is done gently, in a simpler manner, without strain and force, drawing our soul to a loving awareness of our Lord. Certainly the practice of a quiet repetition of a phrase or a gentle receptive focus on a single statement of Jesus in the Gospel or from a psalm can serve this purpose. These are ways, if done with simplicity and no strain of effort, to facilitate and encourage a quiet release into the deeper waters. Then, on certain days, the inner calm of contemplation may incline our soul to enter into the deeper resting in God that marks the inward grace of contemplation. As Saint John of the Cross describes this early adjustment period:

> We did not mean that those beginning to have this general loving knowledge should never again try to meditate. In the beginning of this state the habit of contemplation is not so perfect that one can at will enter into this act, neither is one so remote from discursive meditation as to be always incapable of it. One can at times in a natural way meditate discursively as before and discover something new in this. Indeed, at the outset, on judging through the signs mentioned above that the soul is not occupied in repose and knowledge, individuals will need to make use of meditation. This need will continue until they acquire the habit of contemplation to a certain perfect degree. The indication of this will be that every time they intend to meditate they immediately notice this

knowledge and peace as well as their own lack of power
or desire to meditate, as we said. Until reaching this stage
(of those already proficient in contemplation), people will
sometimes meditate and sometimes be in contemplation.
(AMC 2.15.1)

With these preliminary comments as a foundation, it
would be good to highlight more specific instructions about
what to do in prayer when the signs of contemplation have
shown themselves. How should we respond in the silence of
prayer to the delicate inclination to remain alone and quiet
in a loving awareness of God? For Saint John of the Cross,
an important component in that answer is always what not
to do. We should make every effort to hold back from laboring actively with the faculties of intellect, memory, and will.
What is meant by not working actively in this sense is not to
propose an exaggerated passivity but, rather, to encourage a
withdrawal from the ordinary activity by which these faculties have been accustomed to occupy themselves in prayer.
This could be the intellect's reflective searching for religious
insights, the memory's recovery of spiritual thoughts or images, or the will making interior acts to speak words to God
to fill what seems to be a vacant space in prayer. The affective dimension of feelings likewise calls for restraint. We
should not seek to feel anything but, rather, try to forget
about feelings. Any effort to take hold of some experience
of God in order to "feel his presence" will sidetrack the
soul. The great need in prayer now is to surrender and let
go, so that our soul finds itself drawn into a deeper inclination to long for our Lord while remaining in his presence.
This must take place without watching or examining what
is happening.

There is a knowledge given in contemplation, as Saint
John of the Cross teaches, but given in an obscure, secret

manner, as we will see. It is not a knowledge that is carried back outside prayer for the sake of a journal entry. The knowledge in contemplation is bestowed by the inclination of love. Indeed, it is precisely a knowledge *by* love and *through* love. It does not come by thinking about love, but in the simple awareness of a longing to love. It is a knowledge of wanting God, of wanting to love God. Saint John of the Cross writes in *The Dark Night*: "For contemplation is nothing else than a secret and peaceful and loving inflow of God, which, if not hampered, fires the soul in the spirit of love" (DN 1.10.6). The "inflow of God" is the love drawing the soul to love in return. In the early period of contemplation, the soul must respond as best it can to that "secret and peaceful and loving inflow of God". It does so when it keeps a loving attentiveness toward God, without thinking of self. It does this, not as a method or technique, but simply by giving way to its own deepest desire and inclination, which is to turn its love toward the Beloved. The following passage from *The Ascent* is revealing; the combined aspects of grace and of a necessary receptivity of soul are strongly underscored.

> But once they have been placed in it [contemplation], as we already pointed out, they do not work with the faculties. It is more exact to say that then the work is done in the soul and the knowledge and delight are already produced, than that the soul does anything besides attentively loving God and refraining from the desire to feel or see anything. In this loving awareness the soul receives God's self-communication passively, just as people receive light passively without doing anything else but keeping their eyes open. (AMC 2.15.2)

The nature of the passivity in contemplation ought to be further clarified, for misconceptions and false interpretations

are possible. The soul is not plunging into a state of qui-
etistic oblivion. It is not disappearing into an inward state
of nothingness, with a loss of identity and all awareness.
The passivity stressed by Saint John of the Cross has to do
with the withdrawal from any active pursuit of a knowledge
or an experience. The passivity is in the refusal to direct or
control what is taking place. The soul allows God to take the
lead. On the other hand, there *is* a certain active receptivity
necessary in such prayer, at least in its beginnings. Our soul
must accept the inclination that it delicately experiences of
being drawn to an inner "cavern" of loving quiet where a
desire for God is present deeply within it. The effort, mildly
and gently undertaken, is to remain open, receptive, free to
being drawn, but refusing as well to grasp at an experience
or at any kind of knowledge. As Saint John of the Cross
just affirmed in the last passage, one is not entirely passive in
keeping one's eyes open to receive light. The surrender to
that light occurs passively but cannot take place except that
our soul is *willing* to be receptive and does not obstruct this
receptive disposition. The result is a knowledge bestowed
on the soul by a love to which it surrenders itself. As Saint
John of the Cross writes: "This reception of the light infused supernaturally into the soul is passive knowing. It is
affirmed that these individuals do nothing, not because they
fail to understand but because they understand with no effort other than receiving what is bestowed. This is what
happens when God bestows illuminations and inspirations,
although here the person freely receives this general obscure
knowledge" (AMC 2.15.2).

It is important also to reaffirm that the inclination to remain alone and quiet with God, in a peaceful desire and loving awareness, without making acts or pursuing discursive
exercises, must be a real state of grace granted to a soul. The

danger in the realm of deeper prayer is to seek possessively after a "state of prayer" that is not being given by grace. There are people who might choose by way of preference to cultivate a state of "induced quietude" in prayer. The practice, for instance, of slowly repeating a single word or a mantra, as so-called "centering prayer" teaches, can be an example of this. The method may bring a "quietude" to the psyche, emptying thoughts from the mind and conveying a noticeable tranquility to the inner feelings. But these effects have their likely source in the rhythmic repetition of the mantra. It is a serious misrepresentation to identify this practice and its effects with genuine contemplative prayer. The symptoms induced by the method are quite capable of coexisting with an indifference in some lives to grave personal immorality. That in itself should raise questions. No method of prayer advertised as a contemplative practice of prayer can dispense with the need to pursue virtuous and sacrificial living. Even for a person in a state of grace, however, the inward quiet and tranquilizing peace experienced in pseudo-contemplative approaches pose a dubious and deluding feature. These effects are generally sought as a goal in themselves as part of a self-oriented pursuit, rather than coming as an inclination moved by a grace drawing the soul to God. In that case, the real focus is not directed toward God. And the passivity of inner emptiness, with the mind doing nothing, becomes over time a harmful condition for a soul. The person would not be turning with loving attentiveness to God, but descending into a progressive exercise in self-absorption. The fruits, as always, are seen in time. Without addressing, of course, contemporary practices, Saint John of the Cross is nonetheless clear on the importance of a careful discernment. The fifth sign, as outlined earlier, is delicate, but it needs to be felt a bit, and perhaps undeniably acknowledged as present, to ensure its genuineness. The deceptive enticement for those who discover a new interest in prayer is to plunge prematurely, without the divine bestowal of grace, into what seems to be a higher state of prayer, but that only ends up turning the soul inward on itself. These are Saint John of the Cross' words of warning:

> Were individuals not to have this knowledge or attentiveness to God, they would, as a consequence, be neither doing anything nor receiving anything. Having left the discursive meditation of the sensitive faculties and still lacking contemplation (the general knowledge in which the spiritual faculties—memory, intellect, and will—are actuated and united in this passive, prepared knowledge), *they would have no activity whatsoever relative to God.* (AMC 2.14.6; emphasis added)

The genuineness of a true contemplative grace makes itself evident precisely by the act of surrender to the inward inclination to remain quietly in a longing for God. The surrender to this longing to love conveys an awareness in itself. The soul is drawn mysteriously to lean to inner depths, and it comes in time to know and recognize this desire as a longing for God himself. A pacification of the inner spirit takes place, becoming more noticeable and desirable. The emptying of thought occurs on some days easily, not by a methodic expulsion of thoughts, but because thoughts have faded from importance. Loving attentiveness to the presence of Another replaces thinking or imagining. We may seem to be doing nothing, with nothing apparently achieved and nothing so concrete being pursued. But as Saint John of the Cross insists, our soul is accomplishing a great deal if it allows itself to be drawn into the inner loving quiet. It is there in the "inner caverns" that an encounter of love with our Lord takes place, but often unawares. This is a vastly superior encounter to any previous prayer, despite the common experience of a poverty felt in the soul itself. The poverty deepens to the degree that we embrace a "pure nakedness" and simplicity in prayer, seeking nothing for ourselves. The effort to seek nothing but God alone coincides with a need to desire no other satisfaction in prayer. The result is greater nakedness, poverty, purity, and simplicity in the time of silent prayer. The following passage concretely addresses the conduct of the soul in contemplation in its earliest stage.

> When spiritual persons cannot meditate, they should learn to remain in God's presence with a loving attention and a tranquil intellect, even though they seem to themselves to be idle. For little by little and very soon the divine calm and peace with a wondrous, sublime knowledge of God, enveloped in divine love, will be infused into their souls. They should not interfere with forms or discursive meditations and imaginings. Otherwise the soul will be disquieted and drawn out of its peaceful contentment to distaste and repugnance. And if, as we said, scruples about their inactivity arise, they should remember that pacification of soul (making it calm and peaceful, inactive and desireless) is no small accomplishment. This, indeed, is what our Lord asks of us through David: *Vacate et videte quoniam ego sum Deus* [Ps. 46:10]. This would be like saying: Learn to be empty of all things—interiorly and exteriorly—and you will behold that I am God. (AMC 2.15.5)

The insistence on being poor and empty, averse to self-seeking, is crucial especially in these earliest stages of contemplation. The "tying up" of the faculties, as though they are unable to function well, is a true taste of poverty for the soul. Any conscious effort to take hold of experiences in prayer at this time will cause frustration and hinder graces.

The need is simply to let go and allow God to lead. Remaining quiet in response to a deeper desire for this quiet attentiveness is perhaps not so difficult. A grace is being given precisely for this attraction to be silently attentive to the presence of God. The greater challenge may be to refrain from trying to grasp possessively for some experience in such prayer. Any self-conscious act proves to be debilitating to contemplative prayer. We are no longer "in control" of our prayer and may need at times to remember this. The lack of control must be accepted on two levels. The binding of the faculties—the so-called "ligature" of these faculties —so that they are unable to exercise discursive efforts of reflection or imaginative activity with any profit is one form of losing control over prayer. The other is the much more delicate need to give way to a desire that often seems a step ahead of the soul. It can be difficult to identify a feeling of desire in the heart, but this is unimportant. The grace of contemplation is present as our soul, so to speak, looks the other way, that is, looks in the direction of the invisible face of God. If we examine this experience of contemplation, analyze it, or try to hold on to it in some manner, it disappears. The last sentence in this passage conveys the point; it can remind us of the need to hide ourselves if we are to find the God who hides in our prayer:

> If those in whom this occurs know how to remain quiet, without care or solicitude about any interior or exterior work, they will soon in that unconcern and idleness delicately experience the interior nourishment. This refection is so delicate that usually if the soul desires or tries to experience it, it cannot do so. For, as I say, this contemplation is active while the soul is in idleness and unconcern. It is like air that escapes when one tries to grasp it in one's hand. (DN 1.9.6)

In later spiritual theology, the word "ligature" recently mentioned became useful for describing the binding or tightening effect on the faculties in their incapacity to exercise themselves in discursive meditation or to find satisfaction in it. This tying down of the faculties extends into the early period of contemplation. Everything now in prayer becomes at times very dim and imperceptible to the soul. Grace is at work in drawing the soul to the deeper quiet where God hides his presence in the inner recesses and caverns of the soul. But for the moment, the soul is unable to appreciate what is happening. It is conscious more of the tightness it feels and the inability to move freely in any internal activity. The inclination gently stirring within the soul from infused grace is not so noticeable. What our soul does know, if it is attentive to its inner inclination, is a desire to be alone with God in silence, which compensates for the tightening of the faculties and their incapacity: "Ordinarily this contemplation, which is secret and hidden from the very one who receives it, imparts to the soul, together with the dryness and emptiness it produces in the senses, an inclination to remain alone and in quietude" (DN 1.9.6). And yet it is often the case that souls do not surrender to this inclination to remain quietly alone with God. The reason is usually the confused state of the experience in the early period of contemplation. The following passage from *The Dark Night* insists on the importance, in effect, of an exercise of spiritual intelligence in allowing God to do *his* work of sanctification in this new experience of contemplation. Receptive surrender to God is always the key disposition that a soul should cultivate in contemplation.

> And even though more scruples come to the fore concerning the loss of time and the advantages of doing something

else, since it cannot do anything or think of anything in
prayer, the soul should endure them peacefully, as though
going to prayer means remaining in ease and freedom of
spirit. If individuals were to desire to do something themselves with their interior faculties, they would hinder and
lose the goods that God engraves on their souls through
that peace and idleness. If a model for the painting or re-
touching of a portrait should move because of a desire to
do something, the artist would be unable to finish and the
work would be spoiled. Similarly, any operation, affection,
or thought a soul might cling to when it wants to abide
in interior peace and idleness would cause distraction and
disquietude, and make it feel sensory dryness and emptiness. The more a person seeks some support in knowledge
and affection the more the soul will feel the lack of these,
for this support cannot be supplied through these sensory
means. (DN 1.10.5)

Indeed, nothing so evident may be understood at first
about the manner in which God is working in secret within
the soul at this time. And so the first reaction of a soul is
often to strive to exercise itself more strenuously in prayer
and to seek an insight or a satisfaction of some sort. This
is not surprising, given the fact, as we have commented before, that a soul who has been serious in its practice of virtue
is the likely candidate for undergoing these initial graces of
contemplation. A person accustomed to a dedicated pursuit
of virtue generally accepts that there is a need periodically
to work harder for the sake of holiness. A parallel response
is often adopted in reacting to the difficulty experienced in
silent prayer when contemplative graces begin. That type
of diligent person thinks quite reasonably that a more con-
certed effort must be made in prayer and that this will resolve
the "problem". But this reaction proves to be counterpro-

ductive when the grace of contemplation is present: "God conducts the soul along so different a path, and so puts it in this state, that a desire to work with the faculties would hinder rather than help his work; whereas in the beginning of the spiritual life everything was quite the contrary" (DN 1.9.7). Moreover, the faculties, in undergoing contemplative graces, do not recover at a certain point a proficiency for doing what has become no longer suitable for the soul in prayer. The stage of meditative reflection has now been completed. The binding effect on the faculties, their inability to function as previously, is a clear sign of the need to move beyond an active working with the intellect, memory, and will in prayer. Saint John of the Cross comments in this manner:

> The reason is that now in this state of contemplation, when the soul leaves discursive meditation and enters the state of proficients [i.e., contemplative prayer], it is God who works in it. He therefore binds the interior faculties and leaves no support in the intellect, nor satisfaction in the will, nor remembrance in the memory. At this time a person's own efforts are of no avail, but are an obstacle to the interior peace and work God is producing in the spirit through that dryness of sense. Since this peace is something spiritual and delicate, its fruit is quiet, delicate, solitary, satisfying, and peaceful, and far removed from all the other gratifications of beginners, which are very palpable and sensory. (DN 1.9.7)

It may be helpful to return a moment to the notion of a knowledge by love in contemplation. The binding of the faculties in ligature is not incompatible with the soul being drawn in love and the soul knowing this. The supernatural knowledge given in contemplation is certainly a new taste in prayer, though not immediately appealing and not easily digested. The shift from meditation to contemplation entails, in effect, a different manner of knowing God. Saint John of the Cross writes in *The Ascent* of a "loving knowledge", a "general loving knowledge" (AMC 2.14.2), a knowledge "where nothing is understood particularly and in which they like to rest" (AMC 2.14.4), "an act of general, loving, peaceful, and tranquil knowledge" (AMC 2.14.2). The stress is on a *loving* knowledge. The more spiritual and penetrating this loving knowledge, and the more interior it is to the soul, the more the soul does not perceive it in any clear manner, even as it is a loving knowledge. "The purer, simpler, and more perfect the general knowledge is, the darker it seems to be and the less the intellect perceives" (AMC 2.14.8). Perhaps we may question how it can be a knowledge if it is unperceived. The reply would be that it is a knowledge *by love*, a knowledge by means of an inclination drawing the soul. If it is not perceived or felt initially, the reason is the delicacy of this inclination *and* the strong sense of incapacity due to the ligature of the faculties. But in time this knowledge *is* felt, as it were, if a soul is receptive. It is felt as a simple inclination to love in the inner quiet of prayer. The desire to love is what is given to the soul in this knowledge, the awareness of a longing within the hidden depths of the soul to love God.

In order to be receptive to this inclination of love, the intellect needs, then, to forgo pursuit of other forms of thinking and of any search for particular knowledge. In other words, it must cooperate with the "binding" of the faculties, which no longer provide their former satisfactions. Only in this way does the inner longing to love become known to our awareness. What can seem to be the absence of an object of knowledge is replaced by a simple, pure *awareness* of a longing to love in the soul. The lack of a direct focus in an act of intellect gives way to an inclination to love at a deeper level of awareness in the soul: "This supernatural general knowledge and light shines so purely and simply in the intellect and is so divested and freed of all intelligible forms (the objects of the intellect) that it is imperceptible to the soul" (AMC 2.14.10). Saint John of the Cross expands further on this knowledge given in contemplation. While often imperceptible to the intellect, it nonetheless touches the will more noticeably. Since it is a knowledge *by* love, it should not be surprising that contemplation affects the will more strongly than the intellect. The latter usually remains in a condition of obscure darkness. This difference of experience for the intellect and will in contemplation is notable, and we will see this teaching again in the next chapter. The absence of a direct object of knowledge for the intellect is often accompanied by a vague, indistinct, yet perceptible experience of the will being drawn in love. Saint John of the Cross comments on this difference:

> When, however, there is also a communication to the will, as there almost always is, people will not fail to understand more or less their being occupied with this knowledge if they want to discern the matter. For they will be aware of the delight of love, without particular knowledge of what they love. As a result they will call it a general loving knowledge. This communication, consequently, is called a general loving knowledge, for just as it is imparted obscurely to the intellect, so too a vague delight and love are given to the will without any distinct knowing of what is loved. (AMC 2.14.12)

In treating the conduct of the soul in the early period of contemplation, a consideration that should be addressed concerns the four earlier signs identified of incipient contemplation. Do these signs and symptoms pass away entirely once a person responds to the grace of contemplation? Are they no longer present once a soul begins to remain quiet and alone with God, withdrawing from active thinking, in order to give itself to a loving attentiveness toward God? Clearly, discursive or imaginative meditation will cease to the extent that contemplation becomes more prominent as a grace in prayer. The one replaces the other. We mentioned already Saint John of the Cross' comment that in the period of transition, which could be at least for some months, there is usually a need to return at times to meditation before contemplation is more firmly established as a consistent grace in prayer. But an advancement in contemplation will make discursive meditation more unnecessary over time. The second sign of a disinclination to make use of the imagination will follow the same pattern. The fourth sign of a concern and solicitude for personal fault as a cause of the difficulty in prayer at this time likewise fades as meditation discontinues and contemplation becomes more steadily an accepted grace in prayer.

On the other hand, the third sign of aridity, a painful emptiness of feeling in prayer, is quite different in the treatment of Saint John of the Cross. It is not a transient feature and extends well along into the new state of contemplation. It tends to remain a purifying aspect of prayer, even for long years, and plays its own role in the advancement of contemplation in a soul. A remark might be made in that regard. In spiritual theology, the entry into contemplation is a crossing from the purgative way into the illuminative way. The latter phrase as a new stage of spiritual advancement seems to imply a time of increased light and consolation for the soul. But the actual reality is certainly in part a lingering experience of seeking God in a painful absence of feeling and in the darkness of faith's obscurity. The presence of a hidden God who must be sought with greater love becomes a dominant experience now in prayer, often for long years. Despite these features, which are hardly consistent at first glance with the idea of an "illuminative" stage, it is important that a soul does not draw back from the path it has undertaken, lest it ruin the good work God has begun. The acclimation of the soul to a greater depth of encounter with God is crucial in this time and, indeed, for a lifetime. This does not signify necessarily a more satisfying experience in prayer. It does mean for the most part that a soul must surrender itself in love to a new sense of intimacy with the presence of God.

A perseverance undergirds all of the spiritual life, but it has special pertinence in the early period of contemplation. The so-called "dark night of senses" is the term Saint John of the Cross employs for the transitional period from meditation to contemplation. As a metaphor, it refers to the emptying out of satisfaction in meditative prayer. The phrase is speaking especially of the acute dryness of feeling that afflicts silent prayer, often without respite. But this emptiness of feeling, even painfully so, is more than a transitional feature affecting prayer for a passing period of time, as we have said. It is an aspect of purification that continues usually for a long time after a soul has crossed the threshold of contemplation in prayer. It summons a need for steady perseverance. And yet the aridity is one of the ways in which contemplation—contrary to expectation—begins to bestow fruitful benefits upon a soul. It is notable that Saint John of the Cross, in identifying the early fruits of contemplative prayer, perceives them all as linked to the suffering of aridity that continues in the prayer of contemplation. The benefits of aridity accrue as the suffering of this experience in prayer continues. The first of these benefits is a more refined knowledge of self and of the true misery of self—due to the dryness and emptiness of satisfaction in prayer. "The aridities and voids of the faculties in relation to the abundance previously experienced and the difficulty encountered in the practice of virtue make the soul recognize its own lowliness and misery, which was not apparent in the time of its prosperity" (DN 1.12.2). The emphasis is on a new knowledge of self taking place in the midst of the aridity. When all is relatively consoling and productive in prayer, with insights and easy satisfactions, a soul is likely inclined to take a certain pleasure in its own achievement. By contrast, new gains in grace take place in a paradoxical manner, namely, in the suffering of the interior life:

> Now that the soul is clothed in these other garments of labor, dryness, and desolation, and its former lights have been darkened, it possesses more authentic lights in this most excellent and necessary virtue of self-knowledge. It considers itself to be nothing and finds no satisfaction in self because it is aware that of itself it neither does nor can do anything. God esteems this lack of self-satisfaction and the dejection persons have about not serving him more than all their former deeds and gratifications, however notable they may have been, since they were the occasion of many imperfections and a great deal of ignorance. (DN 1.12.2)

Saint John of the Cross includes other benefits that come from a more lowly sense of self, which again is a fruit of the aridity undergone in contemplation. One benefit is a more respectful approach to the majesty of God. The soul is no longer inclined to treat God as someone with whom it can be "discourteous and inconsiderate" (DN 1.12.3). More fully aware of its own misery and need, the soul's tone of approach to God gains in respect and discretion.

Saint John of the Cross points to the example of Moses, who after facing God and speaking directly with him, "was fully aware of his misery in the sight of God, for this was the manner in which it was fitting for him to hear God's word" (DN 1.12.3). At the same time, in its anguish and aridities, the soul realizes much more the grandeur of God: "The dark night with its aridities and voids is the means to the knowledge of both God and self" (DN 1.12.6). We cannot grow in a true knowledge of the greatness of God except by advancing in knowledge of our own need before God. A spiritual humility thus begins to deepen: "Aware of their own dryness and wretchedness, the thought of their being more advanced than others does not even occur in its first movements, as it did before; on the contrary, they realize that others are better" (DN 1.12.7).

Saint John of the Cross writes as well of the benefit from aridity in a more habitual remembrance of God, a dread of going backward on the spiritual path. A concern for personal fault is an expression of the soul's desire to please God. Temptations, perhaps at times severe and demonically induced, can be prevalent. Yet in resisting them, a soul advances in its love for God. They serve a definite purpose: "For if a soul is not tempted, tried, and proved through temptations and trials, its senses will not be strengthened in preparation for wisdom" (DN 1.14.4). Now a deeper quality of a holy fear of offending God and of misusing his great gifts takes hold. The virtues tend to operate in a newfound harmony: patience and forbearance in facing aridity, perseverance in the dissatisfaction of spiritual exercises, single-mindedness for God alone growing as motive in a life. Nothing else appeals to the soul as much as the chance to serve God and love him. Saint John of the Cross writes on this point:

> These aridities, then, make people walk with purity in the love of God. No longer are they moved to act by the delight and satisfaction they find in a work, as perhaps they were when they derived this from their deeds, but by the desire of pleasing God. They are neither presumptuous nor self-satisfied, as was their custom in the time of their prosperity, but fearful and disquieted about themselves and lacking in any self-satisfaction. (DN 1.13.12)

A final comment in this chapter might be offered about the length of time in which the purifying experience of a dark, arid contemplation continues. The soul, even in this aridity and darkness, is tasting the grace of contemplation. Depending on its response to the inclination to remain quiet and withdraw from thought, it opens itself to the grace of contemplation. Nonetheless, aridity and an absence of satisfaction are bound to accompany this advancement in contemplation through the years ahead. The benefits just mentioned as fruits of this experience are likewise bound to deepen. There is no way of knowing how God treats one soul differently from another. But a long experience of regular aridity should be expected as a normal course in contemplative prayer. Saint John of the Cross acknowledges that one factor that may play a part will be the courage or weakness that a soul displays in bearing with purification. God does not force too much on a soul unwilling to face suffering; but such a soul takes much longer to walk the path to the divine encounter. Courage takes on a key role in contemplation, and especially in regard to aridity and an incapacity for satisfaction in prayer. A soul must turn its eyes away from its own struggles and enter more purely into the graced path that leads to God. Saint John of the Cross offers a striking passage on the question of the duration of the purification taking place in contemplation.

We cannot say certainly how long a soul will be kept in this fast and penance of the senses. Not everyone undergoes this in the same way, neither are the temptations identical. All is meted out according to God's will and the greater or lesser amount of imperfection that must be purged from each one. In the measure of the degree of love to which God wishes to raise a soul, he humbles it with greater or less intensity, or for a longer or shorter period of time. Those who have more considerable capacity and strength for suffering, God purges more intensely and quickly. But those who are very weak he keeps in this night for a long time. . . . God acts with other weaker souls as though he were showing himself and then hiding; he does this to exercise them in his love, for without these withdrawals they would not learn to reach him. Yet, as is evident through experience, souls who will pass on to so happy and lofty a state as is the union of love must usually remain in these aridities and temptations for a long while no matter how quickly God leads them. (DN 1.14.5, 6)

One thing is certain in all cases when a soul is introduced into contemplation. God is desirous to lead that soul to union with his love. We can assume that we respond better to his love to the degree we surrender entirely to everything he asks us to embrace in the interior life of prayer. And, of equal importance, to the degree that we strive to give ourselves generously to all he asks of us in events and in daily opportunities for charity and sacrifice. Nonetheless, the manner in which contemplation affects a life remains a unique question of utterly personal relations between each soul and God in a long lifetime of prayer.

II

A PURE RECEPTIVITY
TO GOD IN CONTEMPLATION

Saint John of the Cross has one other important treatment
about the initial period of contemplation, this time within
a sizable portion of his commentary on the third stanza of
his poem "The Living Flame of Love" in the treatise of
the same name. It is a rich section with a more extended
commentary on the adjustment from meditation to contemplation. It addresses in particular how the intellect ought to
respond to the silencing of the mind that accompanies the
grace of contemplation. Before examining the commentary,
it is worthwhile to see how this section is introduced. Saint
John of the Cross affirms once again that it is often during a
fairly early time in a serious spiritual life that contemplation
is granted as a grace. This does not mean that the practice
of contemplative prayer is deliberately chosen as a method
of prayer. Rather, if a soul is faithful in pursuing virtue and
the will of God, it is not uncommon to experience after
a reasonably short time the initial signs of incipient contemplation. A necessary adjustment must then take place in
prayer, as we have seen already. But this can happen not so
long after the spiritual life takes on a determined dedication.
One year of faithful observance and generosity in a stricter
religious congregation can suffice, according to Saint John
of the Cross, depending on God's grace. It is a significant
point worth stressing, because many people do not realize

that contemplation is a grace God wants to bestow on souls who approach prayer and virtue seriously. It is not a grace reserved for so-called elite souls or for those alone who inhabit the cloisters and monasteries. If we are fervent in responding generously to God, with all the requirements our vocations entail, we can expect that he is generous eventually in granting this grace. As Saint John of the Cross writes in *The Living Flame of Love*:

> It should be known that the practice of beginners is to meditate and make acts and discursive reflection with the imagination. Individuals in this state should be given matter for meditation and discursive reflection, and they should by themselves make interior acts and profit in spiritual things from the delight and satisfaction of the senses. For by being fed with the relish of spiritual things, the appetite is torn away from sensual things and weakened in regard to the things of the world. But when the appetite has been fed somewhat, and has become in a certain fashion accustomed to spiritual things, and acquired some fortitude and constancy, God begins to wean the soul, as they say, and place it in the state of contemplation. *This occurs in some persons after a very short time*, especially with religious; in denying the things of the world more quickly, they accommodate their senses and appetites to God and pass on to the spirit in their activity, God thus working in them. This happens when the soul's discursive acts and meditations cease, as well as its initial sensible satisfaction and fervor, and it is unable to practice discursive meditation as before or find any support for the senses. The sensory part is left in dryness because its riches are transferred to the spirit, which does not pertain to the senses. (LF 3.32; emphasis added)

As might be expected, Saint John of the Cross stresses that with the symptoms and signs already identified in the earlier chapter, a soul must learn to exercise itself in prayer "in a manner entirely contrary to the former" (LF 3.33). He is explicit and unambiguous in his instruction that at this time "they should not meditate" (LF 3.33). An effort to meditate or reflect on a subject in prayer would inevitably lead to distraction. Even with some exertion of mind a soul would suffer in prayer an inability to focus thought in any spiritually profitable manner. Likewise, there should be no seeking of satisfaction in feelings. This, too, does harm and opposes the grace of contemplation given delicately at this time. A letting go of any active pursuit in prayer is necessary. Indeed, there ought to be a relinquishment of personal autonomy in directing one's own prayer. This requirement will need further explanation, but the following statement is quite direct in warning against a labored use of the faculties in the silence of prayer with the onset of contemplative graces: "Individuals can with the greatest ease disturb and hinder these anointings by no more than the least act they may desire of their memory, intellect, or will; or by making use of their senses, appetite, and knowledge, or their own satisfaction and pleasure. This is all seriously harmful and a great sorrow and pity" (LF 3.41).

Instead of prayer being an activity we direct or pursue for our satisfaction, we must allow prayer in this transitional period to pass into the hands of God. He is secretly present within the soul and working through contemplative graces. Our own activity must be surrendered in order that our inner spirit may be drawn to a peaceful tranquility that inclines our soul. If we do not surrender the activity of meditation or reflective thought, or the desire to feel satisfaction, we impede the more concealed action of God. In short, the active work we have been accustomed to undertake in the time of prayer—and there can be other examples besides discursive reflection on Scripture, such as excessive reading or the recitation of nonobligatory formal prayers—is now at odds with God's action and ought to be halted in exchange for a more receptive silence. In the midst of prayer itself, the soul may find this a difficult teaching to embrace. The surrender of a routine of activity in prayer is quite contrary to the prior experience of prayer. Yet it is this choice to let go of an active approach in prayer that can determine whether the grace of contemplation finds an open doorway into the greater depths of the soul. As Saint John of the Cross teaches:

> If previously they sought satisfaction, love, and devotion, and found it, now they should neither desire nor seek it; for not only do they fail to procure it through their own diligence but, on the contrary, they procure dryness. Through the activity they desire to carry on with the senses, they divert themselves from the peaceful and quiet good secretly being given to their spirit. . . . Such activity would place an obstacle in the path of the principal agent who, as I say, is God, who secretly and quietly inserts in the soul loving wisdom and knowledge, without specified acts. (LF 3.33)

Here, in the treatment of *The Living Flame of Love*, Saint John of the Cross repeats a number of times the need to exercise a "loving attention" to God. This is his primary recommendation for what a soul can do itself at this time as it adjusts to the grace of contemplation. Our soul ought to release itself from active reflection and thought, but at the same time it should make an effort to remain attentive in a silent, loving desire directed toward God. A loving attention, in Saint John of the Cross' view, does not require a labor of concentration. It can come at times easily because the soul is drawn precisely by contemplative graces to gaze, as it were, on the mysterious presence of God. A graced inclination usually underneath any feeling of emotion takes place in contemplation. The soul feels a desire simply to turn with its inner being toward God. It is perhaps not felt so strongly at first, not by any emotion, but the desire is nonetheless real and gradually makes itself known in the silence of prayer. This inclination has to be delicately sensed at this time if the grace is to have a fruitful effect on the soul. Indeed, the ability to respond to a delicate feeling of the soul is critically important when these subtle graces are operating. We surrender to God perhaps more fully in prayer when we do what comes most easily. The surrender to God is precisely what we want to do, under the effect of grace. At this time, the soul, in its longing, simply wants to remain in a loving inclination of desire toward God. No activity is needed for that, no deliberate acts need be undertaken, with the exception perhaps of a short phrase slowly repeated in silence to anchor the soul for a time. A single verse from a psalm or the Jesus Prayer can serve this purpose. Ideally, a steady undercurrent of inner desire for God occupies the soul and can hold the soul's attention. Pulling back to some activity of thought or trying to exercise particular acts would only intrude on the deeper inclination of the soul. The hidden recesses of the soul desire simply to be carried toward God in grace, and that is enough. Saint John of the Cross emphasizes especially the receptive quality of the soul at this time. The "inactivity" he recommends in the following passage refers to the lack of an exercise of *deliberate* acts on our part. But, in fact, the soul must be active to some extent in its receptivity to God when the grace of contemplation is still at a delicate stage. A loving attention to God has now become its response to this grace and a form of silent activity in prayer: "Thus individuals also should proceed only with a loving attention to God, without making specific acts. They should conduct themselves passively, as we have said, without efforts of their own but with the simple, loving awareness, as when opening one's eyes with loving attention" (LF 3.33).

The attentiveness a soul directs to God does not need as such a method of controlling mental activity, but comes "naturally" to the soul as a desirable thing to do. At first, this experience has an element of purgation; the soul ordinarily feels nothing and may seem to be at a loss about what it is doing. The purgation is a sign of the disparity between God communicating himself and the soul receiving a communication that it cannot assimilate in an adequate manner. Nonetheless, our soul has to learn to be the receiver, even if it does not understand initially what is happening. The primary need is to learn *how* to receive from God the gift he bestows of himself. Indeed, a proper receptivity to the presence of God conditions an advancement in contemplation: "Pure contemplation lies in receiving" (LF 3.36). God becomes the great giver now in prayer. And what he is giving is himself in an immediate, mysterious manner. He communicates, not novel insights or particular messages to the soul, not lofty experiences of a mystical nature, but simply himself in the mystery of his presence. That is quite enough, even as the experience is typically obscure and dark initially.

The soul in turn can receive God's presence only in the silence of a "passive loving attention" (LF 3.34). A simple awareness of desiring God with any other thought becomes a mode of receptivity to the secret action of God. The awareness of wanting God is the soul's own silent way of communing with God. A mutual loving exchange in silence takes place then mysteriously between the soul and God. It is as though a sacred spring, in which love is flowing, has opened between God and the soul by means of this loving awareness. The flow of "living water" (Jn 4:10) continues inasmuch as the soul receives the hidden communication of God's presence by means of its own desire for God. This desire extends beyond any natural capacity of the soul. It flows as a deep undercurrent within the soul drawing the soul to God. The experience of God for a soul in these beginnings of contemplation, described as a "simple, loving knowledge" of God, may sound nondescript, even bland. But for Saint John of the Cross, it is a quite real loving awareness for the soul, a new experience of God. It is a knowledge by an inner inclination to love, a knowledge of being drawn in the inner depths of one's soul to a love for God. As Saint John of the Cross explains: "Since God, then, as the giver communes with individuals through a simple, loving knowledge, they also, as the receivers, commune with God through a simple and loving knowledge or attention, so knowledge is thus joined with knowledge and love with love. The receiver should act according to the mode of what is received, and not otherwise, in order to receive and keep it in the way it is given" (LF 3.34).

Saint John of the Cross insists, then, on the soul maintaining this interior attitude of passive loving attention as a kind of disposition for contemplation. The word passive in this context can be helped by comments that extend farther what was said in the last chapter. What Saint John of the Cross teaches now is the need to remain in an interior disposition of receptivity and surrender to God—"very passive and tranquil without making any act" (LF 3.34). The passivity is understood by noting its opposite. Acts deliberately undertaken, even under the semblance of some good intention, hinder the divine communication of loving knowledge

being given to the soul. The loving knowledge, a knowledge by inclination, a knowledge of being drawn to love,
is a grace received from God. But it can be deflected and
blocked by taking up acts of our own initiative. A surrender
of self in a receptivity to God is all that is now necessary,
and not any other pursuit on our own part. The key requirement for the soul is to be empty, vacant of internal activity
—"unhampered, idle, quiet, peaceful, and serene, according to the mode of God" (LF 3.34)—allowing itself to be
drawn in a deep, silent inclination toward God himself. At
this point, prayer is really no longer a pursuit, a search, a
quest for God. A veil has been lifted, and the soul has passed
inside, so to speak, into an inner room. There is no need to
chase after anything or to overcome a barrier. A soul needs
only to receive the deeper undercurrent of desire drawing it
toward a love for God. In a telling phrase, Saint John of the
Cross comments: "For God's speech is the effect he produces in the soul" (LF 1.7). A delicate listening, an attentive loving, a silence in the solitude of a mysterious presence, these interior dispositions are all that is needed. "God
alone is the agent who then speaks secretly to the solitary
and silent soul" (LF 3.44). The following longer passage is
striking in regard to the ease with which the soul must enter
into a reverence for God's communication of his presence
in contemplation. The notion of a passive reception is clarified here:

> If as I say—and it is true—this loving knowledge is re-
> ceived passively in the soul according to the supernatural
> mode of God, and not according to the natural mode of
> the soul, individuals, if they want to receive it, should be
> very annihilated in their natural operations, unhampered,
> idle, quiet, peaceful, and serene, according to the mode
> of God. The more the air is cleansed of vapors and the

quieter and more simple it is, the more the sun illumines and warms it. A person should not bear attachment to anything, neither to the practice of meditation nor to any savor, whether sensory or spiritual, nor to any other apprehensions. Individuals should be very free and annihilated regarding all things, because any thought or discursive reflection or satisfaction on which they may want to lean would impede and disquiet them and make noise in the profound silence of their senses and their spirit, which they possess for the sake of this deep and delicate listening. God speaks to the heart in this solitude . . . in supreme peace and tranquility while the soul listens, like David, to what the Lord God speaks to it [Ps. 85:8], for he speaks this peace in this solitude. (LF 3.34)

The last phrases in this passage are moving and provocative. God speaks to the solitude of the heart in contemplation. We can say that he speaks *his* peace in this solitude. When our soul "senses" that it is being drawn inside itself to this solitude of peace, into a listening state of inclination, it should let go and let itself be carried inward toward this inclination of love. This letting go aligns us with the passive receptivity conducive to contemplation. If, on the other hand, there is not a particular sense of the inner peace drawing the soul inwardly, we should then maintain a loving attentiveness as best as we can, trying not to interfere with God by taking up reflective activity. The simplicity of a watchfulness for the One sought in love is the special effort needed at this time when our soul feels little and yet has no inclination for discursive reflection. Perhaps unknown to itself, the soul does have a deeper desire to give itself in love toward God. If this inclination then begins to be felt, it is necessary only to release and let go. The soul simply responds to the undercurrent of being drawn into God's communication of himself through a silent desire for him. In other words, the "practice" of a loving attentiveness is at times necessary because nothing may be felt of a deeper inclination. The loving attentiveness disposes the soul to remain alone with God, in a silence of listening and of inward absorption in peace. The calm, loving desire for God is a preparatory disposition for leading our soul through silence and solitude to the presence of God. If, by grace, God then bestows some contemplative communication of his presence, it comes through the soul's loving desire for God. In the following passage, Saint John of the Cross describes how the grace of contemplation operates upon a person. This takes place in a manner clearly different from self-directed activity, and yet also requiring a cooperation on our part:

> When it happens, therefore, that souls are conscious in this manner of being placed in solitude and in the state of listening, they should even forget the practice of loving attentiveness I mentioned so as to remain free for what the Lord then desires of them. They should make use of that loving awareness only when they do not feel themselves placed in this solitude or inner idleness or oblivion or spiritual listening. So they may recognize it, it always comes to pass with a certain peace and calm and inward absorption. (LF 3.35)

Saint John of the Cross insists in various ways, in a phrase worth repeating, that "pure contemplation lies in receiving" (LF 3.36). And so the need in contemplation is to remain strictly detached from pursuing any type of knowledge in prayer or any particular gratification. The soul is increasingly stripped in the silence of contemplation and comes to a deeper loss of itself, not simply as a purifying factor that accompanies spiritual advancement, but as an essential reality of this prayer of contemplation. The need to mortify the impulse to seek previous satisfactions in prayer is a serious demand. That temptation can be more common than thought, especially with the first beginnings of contemplative graces. The soul does not feel much perhaps at the outset of contemplative graces and, perhaps, would like some comfort or some sense of accomplishing a worthwhile endeavor in prayer. But the best approach is to move forward in what has now begun. The desire for inner solitude and the inclination to an inner quiet in prayer, the symptoms of the fifth sign of contemplation, indicate the "place" where grace resides, waiting for our silent encounter with God's presence. The soul should accept the pain of what may seem an idleness of mental inactivity and simply strive to maintain a loving turn of its attention toward God. And it should avoid drifting off in distraction away from its attentiveness to the presence of God. In time, the realization becomes evident that God's action is greater in its loving impact than our own mental activity. Saint John of the Cross addresses the following passage to spiritual directors guiding these souls, but it can be read as a recommendation for the conduct of the soul itself.

> When a soul approaches this state, strive that it become detached from all satisfaction, relish, pleasure, and spiritual meditations, and do not disquiet it with cares and solicitude about heavenly things or, still less, earthly things. Bring it to as complete a withdrawal and solitude as possible, for the more solitude it obtains and the nearer it approaches this idle tranquility the more abundantly will the spirit of divine wisdom be infused into its soul. This wisdom is loving, tranquil, solitary, peaceful, mild, and an inebriator of the spirit, by which the soul feels tenderly and

gently wounded and carried away, without knowing by
whom or from where or how. The reason is that this wisdom is communicated without the soul's own activity. (LF
3.38)

It is good to repeat, after hearing these instructions, that
our soul must do its part. All is not passivity in contemplation. While contemplation is primarily a work of God
received by the soul, we ourselves have to be careful not to
choose activities that impede this work of grace, which we
can easily do out of ignorance. Our soul should strive to
accept the quiet recollection toward which we are drawn,
at the same time guarding against distraction. The more we
enter into a solitude of apparent "inactivity", of doing nothing in our inner spirit, and embrace the tranquility that accompanies it, the more the grace of contemplation is given
a chance to draw our soul at deeper layers of inclination in
the soul. The solitude, interestingly, consists in being alone
and empty without reflections and knowledge or felt satisfactions; a solitude, in other words, without the companionship of these reflections and satisfactions. It is a solitude of
empty detachment that can seem idle and fruitless, achieving
nothing. And yet the effect of this solitary emptiness is to
detach the soul ever more from a desire for anything other
than God himself. Saint John of the Cross insists on the need
to quiet anxiety in this regard if it is felt. The inactivity of
the soul relative to former pursuits in prayer can cause an
anxious thought of backtracking or wasting time. But the
emptiness of "inactivity" actually carves a great gift of an
interior detachment into the soul. This detachment from
pursuing anything in prayer other than God himself will
have significant spiritual fruits. As Saint John of the Cross
insists:

And a little of this that God works in the soul in this holy idleness and solitude is an inestimable good. . . . The least that a person can manage to feel is a withdrawal and an estrangement as to all things, sometimes more than at other times, accompanied by an inclination toward solitude and a weariness with all creatures and with the world, in the gentle breathing of love and life in the spirit. Everything not included in this estrangement becomes distasteful, for, as they say, once the spirit has tasted, all flesh becomes bitter. (LF 3.39)

Despite what may seem, then, in this interior quiet, to be mental inactivity in prayer, there is, on the contrary, a serious activity taking place in response to grace. The activity is the receptivity to an action of God that we must choose to accept from God. Clearly, it is not an easy thing to respond to the contemplative demand of quiet receptivity. It surely does not mean receiving exalted experiences in prayer. On the contrary, the soul's great initial need in a receptive disposition is to accept becoming poor and dispossessed in itself, so that God may be free to act secretly within it. But, again, this does not happen except with a spirit of courageous cooperation in the inner attitude of our soul. It would be incorrect, of course, to claim that contemplation is "caused" or induced by anything we do. But most definitely it does require cultivation of interior dispositions that are chosen to a certain degree. Our soul must dispose itself to become a suitable setting for God to act and then respond properly to an immense gift of God himself. The receptivity to the inner poverty that can accompany the naked emptying of the soul makes it possible for God to act in communicating himself. Ideally, he finds no interference from us. Saint John of the Cross describes the inner disposition of receptivity in this manner:

Even though the soul is not then doing anything, God is doing something in it. Directors should strive to disencumber the soul and bring it into solitude and idleness so it may not be tied to any particular knowledge, earthly or heavenly, or to any covetousness for some satisfaction or pleasure, or to any other apprehension; and in such a way that it may be empty through the pure negation of every creature, and placed in spiritual poverty. This is what the soul must do of itself, as the Son of God counsels: *Whoever does not renounce all possessions cannot be my disciple* [Lk. 14:33]. . . . When the soul frees itself of all things and attains to emptiness and dispossession concerning them, which is equivalent to what it can do of itself, it is impossible that God fail to do his part by communicating himself to it, at least silently and secretly. It is more impossible than it would be for the sun not to shine on clear and uncluttered ground. (LF 3.46)

Perhaps the hardest adjustment for many people is to interpret the seeming mental idleness of the initial experience of contemplation in a positive manner. It is a testing moment. As we have said, these are souls who would not have arrived at this juncture of contemplative graces in their lives if they had not been devout, hardworking people. It can seem entirely incongruous to everything they know of the spiritual life for grace to be permeating a time of prayer in which they are not actively directing their heart, mind, and will to achieving something with some dedication and effort. *Doing* good works in life may seem to require in a parallel manner *doing* good things in prayer. The recommendation, by contrast, of an absence of activity, the need to remain quiet and empty of thought, attentive to a very delicate inclination to remain alone with God, can seem so very contrary to their spiritual sense. Perhaps because it is so hard to accept for some people, Saint John of the Cross is quite strong at this point in insisting that the emptying of the mind will be a necessity for the direct encounter with God in contemplation. The absence of reflective thought can appear for some souls to be an entry into an absence of all understanding, almost an invitation to plunge into a state of inner oblivion. But that description is not at all what happens in the attentiveness to love that distinguishes a preparation for the grace of contemplation. A withdrawal from understanding—by not pursuing particular thoughts—becomes the initial entry into the truth that God cannot be understood or grasped in thought. Instead of understanding something about God, or even seeking to understand, the soul simply *believes*. Ideally, it embraces in a continual single act the great "yes" of believing in the presence of God without taking up any particular thought. It believes with an unassailable certitude that God simply *is*, and is present in love at that moment and hour of prayer. The truth of his presence in love is all the intellect needs to be occupied with. As Saint John of the Cross writes:

> "Or," you will say, "it doesn't understand anything in particular, and thus will be unable to make progress." I reply that, quite the contrary, if it would have particular knowledge it would not advance. The reason is that God transcends the intellect and is incomprehensible and inaccessible to it. Hence while the intellect is understanding, it is not approaching God but withdrawing from him. It must withdraw from itself and from its knowledge so as to journey to God in faith, by believing and not understanding. In this way it reaches perfection, because it is joined to God by faith and not by any other means, and it reaches God more by not understanding than by understanding. (LF 3.48)

We can observe with this passage that the emptiness of particular thoughts is offset by the intellect embracing a deeper encounter with God in the certitude of a purer faith. It would be wrong to say that emptiness of mind is cultivated for its own sake in contemplation, as some of the mind-emptying methods of contemporary spirituality propose. In true contemplative graces, there is no notion of a mental inactivity meant to tranquilize the soul in a condition of inward oblivion. In genuine contemplation, other significant factors are at stake. The withdrawal from the pursuit of particular thoughts is in part an admission that particular thoughts do not approach the deeper truth of God available in the quiet of contemplation. Particular thoughts must be surrendered in exchange for a simple intense belief in God as an immediate personal presence in prayer. In effect, an encounter with God present personally in mystery replaces thinking about God. The incomprehensibility of God in that personal encounter becomes the great contemplative truth known in the certitude of faith. It is a knowledge far superior to any thought about God. A darkness is likely to envelop the mind precisely in embracing this knowledge. The darkness that accompanies the contemplative encounter with God in faith must be "understood" then as the deeper truth of a genuine personal encounter with God. The soul needs simply to rest in what can seem to be an absence of knowledge and an experience lacking any personal achievement. A darkness of incomprehension permeates the soul, while at the same time, let us recall, a deep longing for God confirms his immediate presence. The incomprehension experienced by the soul does not prevent the soul from longing for One whose reality is impossible to hold in any direct grasp of understanding. This awareness in contemplation of a presence loved, despite the darkness, is a salutary state of soul, leading it into the mystery of God's real contact with the soul. In the following passage, Saint John of the Cross describes the effect on the intellect of the deeper submission of faith in contemplative prayer:

> Do not be disturbed on this account; if the intellect does not turn back (which it would do if it were to desire to be occupied with particular knowledge and other discursive reflections), but desires to remain in idleness, it advances. It thereby empties itself of everything comprehensible to it, because none of that is God; as we have said, *God does not fit in an occupied heart.* In this matter of striving for perfection, not to turn back is to go forward; and the intellect goes forward by establishing itself more in faith. Thus it advances by darkening itself, for faith is darkness to the intellect. Since the intellect cannot understand the nature of God, it must journey in surrender to him rather than by understanding, and thus it advances by not understanding. . . . It should avoid busying itself with particular knowledge, for it cannot reach God through this knowledge, which would rather hinder it in its advance toward him. (LF 3.48; emphasis added)

Saint John of the Cross poses at this point in the treatise a possible objection: If the intellect is understanding nothing and holds nothing in its mind that can attract the will to desire, then the will has nothing to draw it in longing. The result would seem to be a vapid emptiness without value. An intellect empty and idle would seem to result in a will unanchored and idle, with nothing to draw or direct it, which at face value would seem to have no good purpose in prayer. In general, the will is unable to love when the intellect gives it nothing to love. Saint John of the Cross uses this objection to remind us that in contemplation God himself is at work infusing light into the intellect and love into the will.

It is a "loving supernatural knowledge" that God grants to the soul in contemplation. The knowledge is thus aptly described as an awareness of love, an awareness of wanting God and deeply needing God. Even without the intellect's usual aid to attract it to a specific object of desire, the will is receiving infused grace to be drawn toward God himself in strong inclinations. The intellect in faith is already full of certitude of the evident mystery of God's presence. Contemplation becomes for the soul a knowing state, a knowledge of loving a God who is beyond understanding, and yet present in the immediate encounter of loving him in this hour of prayer. In a striking statement, Saint John of the Cross writes: "We can assert that this knowledge is like light that transmits heat, for that light also enkindles love" (LF 3.49). Perhaps the best way to describe this grace is to speak of our soul knowing that it is being drawn in love, but incapable of seeing how this is occurring. It remains blind to the encounter, and yet it knows undeniably that it is drawn in love. The intellect and will, under the effects of faith and charity, work in tandem in contemplation. But the effects of faith and charity can be quite different. It is more often the case that the intellect remains in darkness, while the will is drawn in a longing of love to God. These are Saint John of the Cross' words to describe this dual action in grace:

> Love is therefore present in the will in the manner that knowledge is present in the intellect. Just as this knowledge infused by God in the intellect is general and dark, devoid of particular understanding, the love in the will is also general, without any clarity arising from particular understanding. Since God is divine light and love in his communication of himself to the soul, he equally informs these two faculties (intellect and will) with knowledge and love. Since God is unintelligible in this life, knowledge of

him is dark, as I say, and the love present in the will is fashioned after this knowledge. (LF 3.49)

Because the point is significant for contemplation, it is worthwhile to reference two other incisive passages in which Saint John of the Cross teaches that it is generally the case that the will is more affected in love as the notable experience in contemplation than that the intellect should undergo any unusual advancement in knowledge. The contrast between the will's experience in contemplation and the intellect's experience is important to distinguish. Contemplation is primarily a knowledge by love, and so the will's experience becomes the dominant experiential factor in most instances of contemplation. The first of the following passages is taken from *The Dark Night*, the second from *The Spiritual Canticle*. The repeated allusion to this point indicates its importance also for Saint John of the Cross:

> When God infuses these spiritual goods [contemplation] the will can very easily love without the intellect understanding, just as the intellect can know without the will loving. Since this dark night of contemplation consists of divine light and love—just as fire gives off both light and heat—it is not incongruous that this loving light, when communicated, sometimes acts more upon the will through the fire of love. Then the intellect is left in darkness, not being wounded by the light. At other times, this loving light illumines the intellect with understanding and leaves the will in dryness. All of this is similar to feeling the warmth of fire without seeing its light or seeing the light without feeling the fire's heat. The Lord works in this way because he infuses contemplation as he wills. (DN 2.12.7)

In the passage from *The Spiritual Canticle*, the insistence is more on the profound experience of love in the prayer of contemplation:

It should be known that the teaching of some about the will's inability to love what the intellect does not first know ought to be understood naturally. Naturally, it is impossible to love without first understanding what is loved, but, supernaturally, God can easily infuse and increase love without the infusion or increase of particular knowledge. This is the experience of many spiritual persons; they frequently feel they are burning in love of God, with no more particular knowledge than before. They understand little but love a great deal, or understand a great deal but love little. As a matter of fact those spiritual persons whose understanding of God is not very advanced usually make progress according to their wills, while infused faith suffices for their knowledge. By means of this faith God infuses charity in them and augments this charity and its act, which means greater love, although, as we said, their knowledge is not increased. Thus the will can drink love without the intellect drinking knowledge. (SC 26.8)

These are profound statements, certainly, about the experiential nature of contemplation. In *The Living Flame of Love*, Saint John of the Cross goes on to say that prayer can vary, so that sometimes God communicates more to the intellect, namely, the deeper sense of his incomprehensibility or perhaps a deeper certitude of how real is his presence in mystery at that particular hour. Other times, more often, he communicates more significantly to the will, so that the inner feeling of a longing for God is the much stronger reality experienced in prayer. The image of a fire emitting warmth and light, as we just encountered in the passage from *The Dark Night*, is indeed useful in this regard. Sometimes one or the other phenomenon affects the experience of prayer more intensely. Likewise, in contemplation, the will or the intellect are affected in distinct ways that may have much to do with the uniqueness of a soul. God leads different people in different ways, always for the sake of a greater surrender in love to himself.

> Yet sometimes in this delicate communication God wounds and communicates himself to one faculty more than to the other; sometimes more knowledge is experienced than love, and at other times more love than knowledge; and likewise at times all knowledge is felt without any love, or all love without any knowledge. . . . He can inflame the will with a touch of the warmth of his love even though the intellect does not understand, just as a person can feel warmth from a fire without seeing it. (LF 3.49)

On the basis of these passages, we can affirm that the obscurity with which the intellect knows God as incomprehensible in the darkness of contemplation finds its parallel in the will's experience of God in contemplation. There is a drawing of the will in a way it cannot assimilate with satisfaction. It may not be felt in any clear manner, and yet the will experiences that it is mysteriously drawn by a deeper inclination toward God as One who is unknown. The will, we might say, is *blindly* inflamed in its desire for God in contemplation. It desires without knowing clearly how it undergoes this desire. This is a primary reason why there is no need to be anxious in contemplation about inactivity. The will and intellect need only to be receptive to the action of God that is taking place secretly, often at deeper layers of the soul. Saint John of the Cross writes in this manner of the experience:

> The will often feels enkindled or tenderly moved or captivated without knowing how or understanding anything more particularly than before, since God is ordaining love in it. . . . There is no reason to fear idleness of the will in this situation. If the will stops making acts of love on its own and, in regard to particular knowledge, God makes

them in it, inebriating it secretly with infused love either by means of the knowledge of contemplation or without it, as we just said, these acts are much more delightful and meritorious than the acts the soul makes on its own, just as God, who moves it and infuses this love, is much better. (LF 3.50)

It is also important to acknowledge that the will can receive this action of God drawing its desire only when the will is empty and detached. In the same way that the intellect must step back from the activity of thought and reflection, the will must release itself from any appetitive drive to take possession of particular satisfactions or feelings. Like the intellect, it must be utterly receptive in its interior disposition. The will, too, must enter into a kind of solitude of emptiness, alone and vacant of secondary desires, not wanting anything but God himself. This emptiness is the interior setting for God to draw the will in love. A "solitary quietude" in the will—much like the quiet recollection of the intellect—may often be sufficient to allow contemplative graces to act secretly within the inner layers of the will. The need, as with the intellect, is for the will not to go in a search of particular gratifications of some felt closeness to God. Again we hear the need for some aspect of cooperation and of interior mortification, which involves the refusal to interfere with or intrude upon God's action. A nakedness and emptiness of the will dispose it for the possibility of God to enkindle the will in love. But this state of receptive longing for God must be cultivated by the soul in prayer.

> God infuses this love in the will when it is empty and detached from other particular, earthly or heavenly pleasures and affections. Take care, then, to empty the will of its affections and detach it from them. If it does not retrogress through the desire for some satisfaction or pleasure, it ad-

vances, even though it experiences nothing particular in God, by ascending above all things to him. Although it does not enjoy God very particularly and distinctly, nor love him in so clear an act, it does enjoy him obscurely and secretly in that general infusion more than it does all particular things, for it then sees clearly that nothing satisfies it as much as that solitary quietude. And it loves him above all lovable things. (LF 3.51)

Saint John of the Cross acknowledges the difficulty that this receptivity may pose initially to the soul. It may often have to love without being able to take delight in its love. It must incline itself in desire toward what remains often obscure to the soul. The need to refrain from particular acts, even acts of love taken up in some deliberate way, is a requirement. The will must allow itself to remain passive and receptive before the drawing impulse of love that takes place from within deeper undercurrents in the caverns of the soul. It has to detach itself from seeking a definite pleasure or satisfaction in love and let itself be carried in love like a fragile object swept by a current of wind. And often it must accept that it cannot feel this effect in any tangible manner. Remaining at peace, not restless or agitated, the will must simply do what it can do on its own part, which is to remain in a longing for God. The essential requirement is not to interfere in any intrusive manner with God's action, an action that is quite real on God's part even without our awareness.

One, therefore, should not be disturbed, for the will makes progress if it cannot dwell on the satisfactions and pleasures of particular acts. For by not turning back in the embrace of something sensible, it goes forward to the inaccessible, which is God; and so it is no wonder if it does not feel him. To journey to God, the will must walk in detachment from every pleasant thing, rather than in attachment to it. It thus carries out well the commandment of love, which is to love God above all things; this cannot be done without nakedness and emptiness concerning them all. (LF 3.51)

In concluding this chapter, we can note in these last passages the strong insistence on a detached quality of soul if we are to love God with intensity. Indeed, a pure receptivity to God in prayer is inseparable from a purity of detachment toward secondary desires that can occupy us. The ruling principle of contemplation is that God is known *only* through love. But love for God in the deeper prayer of contemplation depends on this detached quality of "nakedness and emptiness" within the soul toward all things other than God. Contemplation flourishes when the soul is inflamed with a *pure* desire for God, receptive to a deeply interior longing to love him. It advances when a naked desire of soul "goes forward to the inaccessible, which is God" (LF 3.51). Going forward toward the inaccessible naturally implies experiential uncertainties. The road of contemplation lived in daily prayer is not mapped out with clear signals and exact marks of progress. There is a secrecy of love in contemplation often unperceived by the soul, and rarely is there any form of expansive or exceptional knowledge. The knowledge of God by love alone generally predominates in contemplation. For most people, an advancement in contemplation simply intensifies a pure, naked, receptive intent of soul toward the mysterious presence of God himself. But this is a great grace. When a pure desire for God burns within a soul in the silence of prayer, it purifies the soul's engagement with the presence of God, opening it to the greater mystery of his infinite love permeating all of life. And in prayer itself, this pure desire empties a tendency to self-interest. It is the nature of pure love of this sort to instill detachment from self and to replace concern for self with an attachment to God in the naked purity of the soul's inmost desire. Our next chapter will address the dilemma of inner darkness that ordinarily accompanies the deeper experience of a naked self-emptying in contemplation. The inner darkness, too, calls for a calm disposition of detachment. A receptivity to love while in the midst of interior darkness is the secure road to a greater love for God.

12

THE INTERIOR CHALLENGE
OF PARADOXICAL DARKNESS

After these last chapters on contemplation, we pause now to explore more deeply the notion of darkness in contemplative prayer. There are, in particular, some sections in *The Dark Night* that offer material of much interest and benefit. Finding a security in the experience of darkness is one of the paradoxes we encounter in Saint John of the Cross' treatment of contemplation. The idea of security in darkness might sound at first like protective measures to ward off danger; or the need for safeguards and stratagems to prevent darkness from infiltrating and harming one's interior life. But of course this is not what Saint John of the Cross means. Rather, the soul walks securely in contemplative prayer only by a blind surrender to a condition of interior darkness, while animated at the same time by an intense certitude of faith. An essential spiritual principle must be assimilated for progress in contemplation: "*In darkness* [the soul] walks securely" (DN 2.16.1; emphasis added).

If we are growing in contemplative prayer, we must learn to accept, despite a possible repugnance and distaste, the recurring experience of obscure darkness that will permeate in varying degrees the inner life of our prayer. Fighting directly against it, or struggling to overcome it and make it disappear, will impede our advancement in contemplative prayer. The darkness of not knowing God in a satisfying manner is a trial of the mind and spirit, requiring the exercise of a greater certitude in faith. Yet it leads to the fruitfulness of knowing God more intensely in love as the Beloved who in mystery is beyond the limitations of human knowledge. The darkness of "unknowing" lights up with a different quality of knowing when the divine presence of our Lord is encountered by the soul with a more intense love and surrender. At the start of this chapter, a verse from one of the minor poems of Saint John of the Cross entitled "Stanzas concerning an ecstasy experienced in high contemplation" can serve as a suitable introduction.

> The higher he ascends
> the less he understands,
> because the cloud is dark
> which lit up the night;
> whoever knows this
> remains always in unknowing
> *transcending all knowledge.* (stanza 5)

To anyone first experiencing it, the obscure sense in prayer of losing a hold on God, and even, strangely, of not knowing him, may appear to be a sign almost of a spiritual illness. But the experience is not an unhealthy state, and it is important that this is realized without much delay. A painful sense of incomprehension toward God is an aspect of deeper interior prayer. There are clear reasons for this experience of darkness, even as it causes confusion in prayer. The disproportion between the nature of God and our own limited human nature becomes an *experience* in prayer to the degree that our soul draws nearer to God. Even as God loves us in great tenderness and mercy, there remains a measureless chasm between God and our soul. Once the grace of contemplation commences, this truth of divine transcendence is no longer simply a doctrinal claim believed in faith. It now becomes experienced in prayer itself; and not, of course, by any exalted glance into the mysterious depths of the divine presence. Rather, the reality of God's infinite transcendence may seem to sweep into the experience of prayer like a fog from the ocean, closing in and surrounding the mind. It is not, strictly speaking, an absence of knowledge that takes place, but rather an awareness of being stretched uncomfortably and even overwhelmed by the reality of God. The encounter with God in prayer, more direct and immediate in contemplation, brings a sharp sense of blindness into prayer, and often painfully so.

This contemplative effect on the soul has theological reasons, as Saint John of the Cross remarks: "The clearer and more obvious divine things are in themselves, the darker and more hidden they are to the soul naturally" (DN 2.5.3). We can recall from earlier chapters the hidden concealment of God within the soul and the effects of deeper faith on the intellect. Hovering always in the background of Saint John of the Cross' understanding of contemplation is the truth of God's ultimate incomprehensibility and the soul's need to prostrate itself in faith before his infinite mystery. For example, as calm in tone as the following statement may be, the words imply how difficult it is for a soul in love with God to experience the darkness of contemplation. God is known in love, but only by a knowledge that exceeds the bounds of all familiar notions of knowledge. It is a "knowing by unknowing". As Saint John of the Cross writes in a passage from *The Spiritual Canticle*:

> Because of its obscurity, she calls contemplation night. On this account contemplation is also termed mystical theology, meaning the secret or hidden knowledge of God. In contemplation God teaches the soul very quietly and

secretly, without its knowing how, without the sound of words, and without the help of any bodily or spiritual faculty, in silence and quietude, in darkness to all sensory and natural things. Some spiritual persons call this contemplation knowing by unknowing. (SC 39.12)

To provide some explanation for this paradoxical notion of a knowledge by a way of unknowing, we need to ponder more deeply the effect of contemplative graces on the faculties and appetites of the soul. Because of its overpowering effect upon the natural operations of the human faculties, the grace of contemplation causes a kind of disruption in both the appetitive life and in the faculties of the soul. With the onset of contemplative graces, these faculties and appetites are unable to conduct themselves in their usual activity, as we have mentioned earlier. They are unable to arrive at their natural satisfactions as appetites and faculties. This frustration on the natural level is metaphorically identified as a darkness. But it is a real experiential darkness as well, and not just a metaphor. The faculties and appetites experience an incapacity to operate in accord with their customary dispositions and natural inclinations, which means in effect that they can draw little or no satisfaction in the endeavor of prayer. What they have been previously seeking of God has been accompanied by natural appetites and desires. This needs now a radical shift to a purely supernatural receptivity that responds to the divine action within the soul. As Saint John of the Cross writes in *The Living Flame of Love*:

The soul's desire for God is not always supernatural, but only when God infuses it and himself gives the strength for it. This is far different from the natural desire, and until God infuses the desire there is very little or no merit. Thus when you of your own power have the desire for

God, your desire amounts to no more than a natural appetite; neither will it be anything more until God informs it supernaturally. When you of yourself become attached to spiritual things and bound to their savoriness, you exercise your natural appetite and thus you put cataracts before your eyes. (LF 3.75)

This is a significant comment for a better understanding of contemplation. A movement from natural activity to a receptive experience of a supernatural action is necessary. A transition within the soul, in other words, must take place with the onset of contemplative graces. Supernaturally, a dislocation occurs, like a doctor breaking a bone in order to reset it again for healing. The transformation to a contemplative disposition within the faculties and appetites is not readily embraced by any soul, any more than a person is happy to have a bone broken by a doctor. The primary difficulty is usually that the soul has no reference for interpreting what is happening in this transition. It experiences this disruption within its inner life as a condition unlike any previous experience in the interior life of prayer. Yet it has only one safe recourse, as Saint John of the Cross insists. The soul walks securely only by allowing these faculties and interior appetites to remain in darkness or, even better, to be embraced by darkness. They must surrender themselves to this inner experience without trying to resolve it or mitigate its effects. The following passage from *The Dark Night* conveys this need for an acceptance of an entirely new experience in prayer:

Oh, then, spiritual soul, when you see your appetites darkened, your inclinations dry and constrained, your faculties incapacitated for any interior exercise, do not be afflicted; think of this as a grace, since God is freeing you from yourself and taking from you your own activity. However well

your actions may have succeeded, you did not work so
completely, perfectly, and securely—because of their impurity and awkwardness—as you do now that God takes
you by the hand and guides you in darkness, as though
you were blind, along a way and to a place you know not.
You would never have succeeded in reaching this place no
matter how good your eyes and your feet. (DN 2.16.7)

This experience of darkness is precisely the "night of contemplation". Paraphrasing Saint John of the Cross' words
on the effects of contemplation on the inner life, we can
say that it deadens, puts to sleep, deprives of the ability to
find pleasure. It binds the imagination and memory, makes
the intellect unable to understand, causes the will to feel
constrained and arid, without felt desire. All the faculties
may seem to be empty and useless, tied up and shackled.
"And over all this hangs a dense and burdensome cloud that
afflicts the soul *and keeps it withdrawn from God*" (DN 2.16.1;
emphasis added). The last phrase is the most telling. A suffering is indeed taking place, the suffering, it seems, of losing contact with God. The incapacity of the interior life
for normal functioning corresponds to an inability to encounter God in any satisfying way. And yet, contrary to any
impression of a troubled state of soul, the next statement
clarifies the actual truth underneath these symptoms as a
healthy condition of soul: "As a result the soul asserts that
in darkness it walks securely" (DN 2.16.1). The soul can
press on and move forward in responding to contemplative
graces by accepting darkness and emptiness in its natural operations: "In the measure that the soul walks in darkness and
emptiness in its natural operations, it walks securely" (DN
2.16.3). This attitude in prayer is no easy thing, and it is
not learned so quickly by any soul. Saint John of the Cross
acknowledges the difficulty and raises an objection that he

in turn will answer: "Since the things of God in themselves produce good in the soul, are beneficial, and give assurance, why does God in this night darken the appetites and faculties so that these derive no satisfaction in such good things and find it difficult to be occupied with them—in some ways even more difficult than to be occupied with other things?" (DN 2.16.4).

His answer is to reiterate the lowly and impure capacity of the natural appetites and faculties for the things of God. They need to be recast in a radical manner if, as vast inner "caverns of feeling", they can be filled by God. Only by a purging and emptying of their natural activity, in which they ordinarily seek *natural* satisfactions even in the spiritual exercises of prayer, can they become suitable for the reception of a deeper spiritual satisfaction that has a source in God himself. But this requires especially an alert and attentive response in prayer. A disciplined approach not to seek for the easier satisfactions of the past is crucial for the advancement of a soul in contemplative prayer. As Saint John of the Cross writes: "At this time there should be no activity or satisfaction relative to spiritual objects, because the soul's faculties and appetites are impure, lowly, and very natural. And even were God to give these faculties the activity and delight of supernatural, divine things, they would be unable to receive them except in their own way, very basely and naturally" (DN 2.16.4).

The fundamental point here is a subtle one easily ignored in spiritual lives. One can find familiar satisfactions in the things of God that will actually be to a great extent simply natural satisfactions, similar to what we can enjoy in things that are not spiritual. The assumption of religious people is that satisfactions found in spiritual things and in prayer must be due to divine favor and grace. These satisfactions are often thought to signal supernatural advancement. But this is not necessarily so. As Saint John of the Cross writes: "How many persons have numerous inclinations toward God and spiritual things, employ their faculties in them, derive great satisfaction by so doing, and think their actions and appetites are supernatural and spiritual when perhaps they are no more than natural and human" (DN 2.16.5).

The words are a reproof, perhaps, to all who would identify the depth of their relations with God by the satisfaction they derive from their practices of piety, for instance, in a comforting sense of interior peace. A more profound understanding of our relations with God is needed. The description that Saint John of the Cross is going to encourage for our pursuit is not an exaggerated one of an interior paralysis. Rather, it is to accept the basic inability of our faculties to function in the ordinary ways of natural inclination once God grants the grace of contemplation. In the "night of contemplation", the mind is unable to generate insights; the will can arouse no spiritual desire; the feelings are often completely arid. These frustrations would seem initially to indicate a downturn in prayer. But the symptoms are secondary to the hidden spiritual action taking place within the deeper recesses of the soul in contemplative prayer. At this deeper level, without a direct choice on our part, an action of God is taking place that requires our cooperation not to interfere with it. We would interfere with God if we sought to resume an active approach in prayer, trying to recover our former satisfactions in prayer. Instead, we cooperate by giving away control of our prayer to God himself. We have to surrender our inclination to direct our own activity in prayer. The surrender of the soul in contemplation is to be receptive especially to the will being drawn in love to God, and perhaps in a way we cannot confirm in experience.

This cannot happen without a preliminary quieting down of "activity" within our faculties in prayer. The condition for this receptivity is clarified by Saint John of the Cross in this short statement: "If the soul in its interior acts is to be moved by God divinely, it must be obscured, put to sleep, and pacified in regard to its natural ability and operations until these lose their strength" (DN 2.16.6).

The experience for the soul may be more uncomfortable than the description implies. Allowing the natural inclination of our faculties to "be obscured, put to sleep, and pacified" may be quite contrary to our natural desire and may provoke strong interior resistance. Many people of active temperament or who are strong-willed in taking up challenges will find it hard to remain simply receptive to a divine action that they cannot measure or "see". To use another image, one might compare this action of God in contemplation to the "breaking" of a young horse when it first takes a rider and begins to be trained and subject to another. The horse loses its autonomy to run in any direction it wants. The soul under the impact of the hidden action of God in contemplation is losing a certain autonomy to direct its own prayer. It is undergoing a profound modification in its interior faculties precisely by losing control of its prayer. In effect, it is entering a new and unfamiliar place of encounter with God. This adjustment to a divine action taking place more prominently in the life of prayer will mean always an experience of interior darkness and of some uncertainty:

> To reach a new and unknown land and journey along unknown roads, travelers cannot be guided by their own knowledge; instead, they have doubts about their own knowledge and seek the guidance of others. Obviously they cannot reach new territory or attain this added knowledge if they do not take these new and unknown roads

and abandon those familiar ones. Similarly, people learning new details about their art or trade must work in darkness and not with what they already know. If they refuse to lay aside their former knowledge, they will never make any further progress. The soul, too, when it advances, walks in darkness and unknowing. (DN 2.16.8)

The obscurity of being led "to a place you know not" (DN 2.16.7) will have benefits that only a spiritual perspective can discern. Paradox again comes to the fore. The soul advances securely inasmuch as it does not perceive the path that it is walking in darkness. It has to walk in blindness; it gains and profits spiritually even though it "ordinarily thinks it is getting lost" (DN 2.16.8). Indeed, the darkness may thicken and become more profound over time as the soul draws closer to God. This harsher experience of interior obscurity is naturally not received as a favorable change, any more than losing a familiar path in a darkening forest at nightfall would be a welcome occurrence. But in this case, the loss of the familiar experience in prayer is fortuitous and profitable. The soul "is getting lost to what it knew and tasted, and going by a way in which it neither tastes nor knows" (DN 2.16.8). The faculties and appetites in prayer are undergoing a shift from natural to supernatural operations. The crucial test for the soul is not to turn backward and reverse direction. It must continue to walk blindly, not looking to return to old familiar ways in prayer. Security is found in holding steady in desire and love despite the experience of interior darkness. As Saint John of the Cross writes in an earlier passage from *The Dark Night*: "Accordingly, such persons should not mind if the operations of their faculties are being lost to them; they should desire rather that this be done quickly so they may be no obstacle to the operation of the infused contemplation God is bestowing" (DN 1.10.6).

Saint John of the Cross discovers another image of dark contemplation in the "dark waters" invoked in Psalm 17 [Ps. 18:11]: "God made darkness his hiding place and covert, and dark waters in the clouds of the air his tabernacle round about him" (DN 2.16.11). The "dark waters", as the verse states, are a tabernacle and dwelling place for God. The image requires some pondering. The tabernacle, as we know it in our Catholic churches, encloses the Real Presence of the divine Lord in the Eucharist. In the image of the psalm, the tabernacle of darkness is an enclosure where the Lord hides. The darkness is the wall of this tabernacle, inside of which the Lord resides in his hidden presence. This is his dwelling, and the soul has to enter inside this wall of darkness if it wishes to draw near to the hidden God. The darkness will then hide the soul as well: "In this darkness the soul is hidden and protected from itself and the harm of creatures" (DN 2.16.13). The idea of a tabernacle where God hides in his bodily Presence in the Eucharist is familiar to us. The image of a *tabernacle of darkness*, however, where God hides within us, may not initially attract us. Perhaps a visit to a church in the dead of night, with all the lights off and only a tabernacle lamp flickering in the thick darkness, can capture the deeper meaning of this image. The profound sense of our Lord's Real Presence in the midst of that darkness can be undeniably evident. In the certitude of intense faith, we can in a parallel manner know the undeniable presence of our Lord in the darkness of contemplation. The following passage in the course of this commentary on the "dark waters" conveys how deeply Saint John of the Cross values the willingness of our soul to walk through darkness on our way to God. In darkness, in the intense certitude of faith, our soul walks securely. This awareness is a serious insight not commonly embraced. We naturally prefer light and satisfaction, but these can often deceive us. The safer path, at least for the contemplative, is the darkness of intense faith.

> Oh, what a miserable lot this life is! We live in the midst of so much danger and find it so hard to arrive at truth. The clearest and truest things are the darkest and most dubious to us, and consequently we flee from what most suits us. We embrace what fills our eyes with the most light and satisfaction and run after what is the very worst thing for us, and we fall at every step. In how much danger and fear do humans live, since the very light of their natural eyes, which ought to be their guide, is the first to deceive them in their journey to God, and since they must keep their eyes shut and tread the path in darkness if they want to be sure of where they are going and be safeguarded against the enemies of their house, their senses and faculties. (DN 2.16.12)

Saint John of the Cross offers a further insight into the necessity of a "dark contemplation" by speaking of an essential "secrecy" in contemplation. There is always a communication by God to the soul in contemplation. The question, however, is what kind of communication takes place? In *The Spiritual Canticle*, Saint John of the Cross writes two short phrases that convey the great secret at work in contemplation: "For God, to gaze at is to love . . . for God to look is for him to love" (SC 31.8; 32.3). The soul in contemplation, even unknown to itself, is under the sway and attraction of this divine gaze of love. The communication of God to the soul occurs through love, by means of a deep longing in the human soul for God, and usually without any notable experience for the intellect other than the darkness of its understanding. By love, a wisdom is imparted secretly to the soul about the incomparable value of love. The knowledge *by* love in contemplation often brings nothing but a knowledge *of* love in its drawing power upon the soul. The drawing of the human will in love to God's will; the desire felt in love to surrender one's soul to him; sometimes, more rarely, a living flame ignited in the soul as though in proximity to an immense unseen fire near at hand: these are the realities of the divine communication of love to the soul in contemplation. Saint John of the Cross comments on the secrecy of this divine communication by love:

> It calls this dark contemplation "secret" since, as we mentioned, contemplation is the mystical theology, which theologians call secret wisdom and which St. Thomas says is communicated and infused into the soul through love. This communication is secret and dark to the work of the intellect and the other faculties. Insofar as these faculties do not acquire it but the Holy Spirit infuses it . . . the soul neither knows nor understands how this comes to pass and thus calls it secret. (DN 2.17.2)

The secrecy is in the inability of the soul to comprehend or understand contemplation in any satisfying way. It is a knowledge by love that offers no clarity for the mind to carry away as a remembrance. The soul simply knows that it is being drawn, at times with intensity, in its love for God. But this is enough; no other knowledge is necessary. The inward infusion of love is received from God and attributed to him, without a need to understand. The secrecy in this description should not be equated, however, with a complete lack of understanding. The experience of love in contemplation has a secret aspect of ineffability, but that does not mean it is entirely unknown. It simply cannot be conveyed in description: "Not only does a person feel unwilling to give expression to this wisdom, but one finds no adequate means or simile to signify so sublime an understanding and delicate a spiritual feeling" (DN 2.17.3). While no image or idea can wrap itself around this experience of love, "yet the soul is clearly aware that it understands and tastes that delightful and wondrous wisdom" (DN 2.17.3). This is the wisdom of love that is given in contemplation. The language of God is spoken in the silence of prayer by means of love. Saint John of the Cross writes quite beautifully of the ineffability of this divine language:

> The language of God has this trait: Since it is very spiritual and intimate to the soul, transcending everything sensory, it immediately silences the entire ability and harmonious composite of the exterior and interior senses. . . . Since the wisdom of this contemplation is the language of God to the soul, of Pure Spirit to pure spirit, all that is less than spirit, such as the sensory, fails to perceive it. Consequently this wisdom is secret to the senses; they have neither the knowledge nor the ability to speak of it, nor do they even desire to do so because it is beyond words. (DN 2.17.3, 4)

Saint John of the Cross proposes another aspect of this secrecy of contemplation: "It has the characteristic of hiding the soul within itself" (DN 2.17.6). The more intense the love in contemplation, the more it hides the soul within the deeper regions of the soul. Love has the effect of drawing the soul to the hidden center of itself, to the inward caverns where God himself hides. The indwelling of God in the soul takes on a new resonance of attraction when we realize that love allows us to yield ourselves to God's presence residing within us. Saint John of the Cross writes strikingly that "the soul's center is God" (LF 1.12). This truth is never comprehended in a final, conclusive manner. Rather, it serves to animate a life of prayer in a progressive gift of the soul to God. There is a profound passage in *The Living Flame of Love* precisely on love as the dynamic path leading the soul to its hidden center in God. Love is not an ideal or an abstract notion here. It requires a fullness of exterior sacrificial generosity and interior surrender and offering to God. These words of Saint John of the Cross are provocative for any soul in love with God, as it realizes that an endless pursuit of love is all that ultimately matters in life:

> Love is the inclination, strength, and power for the soul in making its way to God, for love unites it with God. The more degrees of love it has, the more deeply it enters into God and centers itself in him. We can say that there are as many centers in God possible to the soul, each one deeper than the other, as there are degrees of love of God possible to it. A stronger love is a more unitive love, and we can understand in this manner the many mansions the Son of God declared were in his Father's house [Jn. 14.2]. Hence, for the soul to be in its center—which is God, as we have said—it is sufficient for it to possess one degree of love, for by one degree alone it is united with him through grace. Should it have two degrees, it becomes united and concentrated in God in another, deeper center. Should it reach three, it centers itself in a third. But once it has attained the final degree, God's love has arrived at wounding the soul in its ultimate and deepest center. (LF 1.13)

All this deeper entry into the mystery of love takes place, then, in a great secrecy. There are no marks of progress for the mind to chart and by which to navigate the interior experience of contemplation: "The way to God is as hidden and secret to the senses of the soul as are the footsteps of one

walking on water imperceptible to the senses of the body"
(DN 2.17.8). The experience of love in contemplation simply draws the soul more deeply underneath layers of love
within its own soul. The stress on an unknown and concealed adventure in love is strong: "The traces and footsteps
God leaves in those whom he desires to bring to himself, by
making them great in the union with his wisdom, are un-
recognizable" (DN 2.17.8). Saint John of the Cross writes
that at times the wisdom of contemplation "occasionally
so engulfs souls in its secret abyss that they have the keen
awareness of being brought into a place far removed from
every creature" (DN 2.17.6). The effect of such prayer is
inexpressibly profound, detaching the soul from concern for
worldly matters that are of little importance in the sight of
God. Love in this contemplative experience of the interior
vastness within the soul leads to a secret knowledge of love
as the only worthy pursuit in life. The following description
can be read with a view to its effect on a soul's life after a
time of prayer. The words can remind us again of the earlier
depiction of the faculties as inner caverns of the soul that
God can enter and inhabit. "They accordingly feel that they
have been led into a remarkably deep and vast wilderness
unattainable by any human creature, into an immense, un-
bounded desert, the more delightful, savorous, and loving,
the deeper, vaster, and more solitary it is. They are conscious
of being so much more hidden, the more they are elevated
above every temporal creature" (DN 2.17.6).

One more image used by Saint John of the Cross in describing contemplation is to speak of this secret wisdom as
a ladder. The communications that the secrecy of contemplation brings to the soul have a dual effect: they elevate the
soul in love and humble it even to the point of humiliation
as the soul realizes its meager return of love to God. The

combination is a necessary one, that of being exalted in love and humbled by love. "For on this road, to descend is to ascend and to ascend is to descend" (DN 2.18.2). The most poignant aspect of this dual quality is the apparent inconsistency encountered in the experience of contemplation. God does not allow the soul to experience only an exaltation of uplifted love. He humbles the soul in various ways, leaving it often for long periods in a seeming wasteland of humiliating emptiness within itself. This, too, is an unavoidable feature on the path of contemplation. The soul travels up and down a ladder of shifting experiences in its relations with God. Nothing remains so steady and predictable. The ongoing demand for self-knowledge requires a plunge into experiences of the soul's absolute need for God in every way. Only by being humbled does the soul become emptied for a further entry into the depths of divine love. The result is a healthy elimination of presumption, vainglory, judgment, or condemnation of others; for "such persons think inwardly that they are really worse than all others" (DN 2.19.3). All desire becomes more concentrated on giving delight to God and rendering him service in return for the favors he has bestowed. Saint John of the Cross writes of this contrast of experiences in contemplation in a way that some people will find necessary to ponder and remember. Those who expect a leveling off of interior trials in prayer and the arrival at last of a steady, secure experience of closeness to God, rather than the swerving, winding path described in the following passage, might take note of these words:

> The soul, if it desires to pay close attention, will clearly recognize how on this road it suffers many ups and downs, and how immediately after prosperity some tempest and trial follows, so much so that seemingly the calm was given to forewarn and strengthen it against the future penury. It

sees, too, how abundance and tranquility succeed misery and torment, and in such a way that it thinks it was made to fast before celebrating that feast. This is the ordinary procedure in the state of contemplation until one arrives at the quiet state: The soul never remains in one state, but everything is ascent and descent. (DN 2.18.3)

Diverse and contradictory experiences are a typical pattern, as this passage affirms, on the contemplative road to God. These contrary experiences sometimes occur in combination. We may be perplexed, for instance, how advancement in prayer can involve both a loving wisdom and an absence of understanding. One way to explain this is that in contemplation God prefers that his instruction in love be a concealed lesson for the soul. Love may be often received in prayer without the soul being able to know how this occurs. Is it possible that God can lead the soul to greater love in what may seem an emptiness of encounter with him? The secrecy of what is taking place in a hidden realm of the soul provides the sacred clue to this reality. The secrecy of divine love drawing the soul at inner unseen depths is an essential truth in contemplation. The recognition *in faith* of this secret action of love is a crucial need if the soul is to be taught by love: "Through this contemplation," writes Saint John of the Cross in an earlier passage from *The Dark Night*, "God teaches the soul secretly and instructs it in the perfection of love without its doing anything or understanding how this happens" (DN 2.5.1). A soul can be quite unaware of great desires for God inflaming deeper layers of its soul, but this does not mean that these desires are not burning beneath awareness. God keeps the soul unaware, in darkness, in order to strip and empty it of all self-seeking impulses. He desires a "departure from self" whereby a soul can take no measure of its progress in love, which remains at deeper recesses of concealment. The first stanza of "The Dark Night", as interpreted by Saint John of the Cross, is a poetic allusion to this effect of contemplation. The stanza reads as follows:

> One dark night,
> fired with love's urgent longings
> —ah, the sheer grace!—
> I went out unseen,
> my house being now all stilled.

"I went out unseen": The words convey this need to depart from self in order to enter into the loving wisdom of contemplation. The wisdom discovered in darkness is a wisdom of interior poverty. The soul has to accept that it simply does not understand when it is immersed in darkness. It is made poor by this absence of understanding. "Love's urgent longings" may not be felt at all, even as this love is a deep reality consuming the soul's inner desire. The wisdom is an intense state of knowing that God is acting upon the soul and animating its love even as the soul cannot understand how this occurs. By means of a deep certitude in its faith, the soul is not plunged into a dark confusion of disturbing shadows. It gives way quietly to God, abandoning itself to God, despite the immersion in darkness. The reins of prayer are handed over to God, and nothing is thereby lost. The following statement comes immediately after the stanza just quoted. It stresses the importance of this release from self by accepting in prayer the darkness of interior poverty. The way to contemplative wisdom is always to walk a road of inner poverty:

> Poor, abandoned, and unsupported by any of the apprehensions of my soul (in the darkness of my intellect, the distress of my will, and the affliction and anguish of my

memory), left to darkness in pure faith, which is a dark
night for these natural faculties, and with my will touched
only by the sorrows, afflictions, and longings of love of
God, I went out from myself. That is, I departed from my
low manner of understanding, and my feeble way of loving, and my poor and limited method of finding satisfaction in God. (DN 2.4.1)

The stark incapacity that may be felt by a soul is not
primarily a condition to be endured stoically. It can be an
interior setting for a great surrender to God, if a soul is
docile and receptive. Surrender to God in the shadows of
inner darkness becomes, as it were, the narrow path into
greater contemplative love. What ensues is a wonderful paradox, namely, that a penetrating light is given by means of
the purifying emptiness of inner darkness. Divine light received in the soul, underneath layers of darkness, is a mark
of contemplation. A soul may not experience this light of
wisdom in a clear manner, but the light of love is given
and eventually manifests itself in the purer vision of the
soul toward all matters of life. A soul realizes more wisely,
more securely, that all things are in the hands of God. All
things begin to take on a more startling sense of purpose
in the divine plan. This wisdom of love is inseparable from
the soul's poverty. The poorer the soul becomes in itself,
the more deeply it may penetrate the mystery of God's
actions. Indeed, a deeper penetration into the spiritual meaning in events is more likely to occur outside prayer precisely when the poverty of interior darkness is overwhelming the soul inside prayer. The essential requirement for such
deeper insight is to be empty and poor during the time of
prayer. We must simply cleave to God in the darkness of that
poverty. The soul may become at times a bruised vessel of
painful craving waiting to be filled with God himself. Yet the

fruits are great when darkness is suffered with a persevering certitude of God's loving presence. "The purest suffering produces the purest understanding" (SLL, 127). There is a wonderful promise in that short aphorism. The following passage can serve as a conclusive description for such a state of soul:

> Hence the Apostle says that the spiritual person penetrates all things, even the deep things of God [1 Cor. 2:10]. What the Holy Spirit says through the Wise Man applies to this general and simple wisdom, that is, that it touches everywhere because of its purity [Wis. 7:24], because it is not particularized by any distinct object of affection. And this is characteristic of the spirit purged and annihilated of all particular knowledge and affection: Not finding satisfaction in anything or understanding anything in particular, and remaining in its emptiness and darkness, it embraces all things with great preparedness. And St. Paul's words are verified: *Nihil habentes, et omnia possidentes* (Having nothing, yet possessing all things) [2 Cor. 6:10]. Such poverty of spirit deserves this blessedness. (DN 2.8.5)

We must believe that God loves this poverty in the human soul if we intend to walk the road of contemplation. But let us be aware that poverty has always a quiet companion. Poverty and darkness operate together in bringing contemplative depth to a soul. There is no need to fear them. Darkness is perhaps difficult until we begin to adjust ourselves to a different perception. But the soul must know also its essential poverty, its own natural incapacity in the pursuit of God. This is not just an attitude of forbearance. The need is to remain always a poor beggar of love waiting on God. The realization that God loves our soul more intensely when it is poor and helpless in its longing for him is a threshold in itself to deeper relations with God. Receptivity to God, to the silence of God, and to our own emptiness becomes then the imperative task. The emptying of the soul in contemplation is no small trial. It means to take leave of a self that is meant to pass away. We must give up control and allow God to refashion our soul in his own manner. Our essential effort must be simply to cultivate an accessibility to the divine action of love, often not knowing what God is doing at deeper layers of our soul. We can trust that a graced departure from self thereby occurs, leaving us open to God's act of love alive within the depth of our soul. In a sense, this loss of self is the one thing needful if we are to love as God desires to be loved, namely, to love with his love present within us. A painful progression, perhaps, this losing of self for love of God, and yet on any day of prayer it opens the passage across a border of solitary silence into the eternal encounter with God's infinite presence of love.

13

THE WILL IN PRAYER
INFLAMED BY PURE LOVE

In a letter written to an unknown Carmelite friar on April 14, 1589, two and a half years before his death, Saint John of the Cross set forth in a relatively short space a remarkable minor treatise on the importance of the will in prayer. It is worthy of some attention, especially after the previous chapter on the experience of darkness in contemplation. The theological truth that undergirds the content of this letter is the transcendence of God in his divine infinitude. A primary effect of God's infinite transcendence is his inaccessibility to the immediate experience of our natural faculties. God in his reality as God is always beyond the grasp of our personal experience. This now familiar truth of apophatic theology plays a serious role in prayer. While it is more common to speak of the apophatic truth of God's incomprehensibility to our intellect, this has a complementary truth in God's inaccessibility to our will in prayer, despite what can seem to be direct experiences of him.

But what exactly is meant by such a strong term as inaccessibility? It is easier to accept that the mind cannot comprehend the divine nature than to submit to a teaching on prayer that might seem to suggest a barrier to the Heart of God. Saint John of the Cross is quite careful and precise in his choice of words. He does not say that God is unknowable or that a door is closed to a real encounter with him.

In fact, as we have already seen, he identifies contemplation as a loving knowledge of God, or a knowledge by love. The inaccessibility of God that he stresses, here in this letter and elsewhere, has to do with the soul's experience of the human will in union with God's will that takes place to some degree in contemplation. An explanation of the apophatic experience in this union of wills is at the heart of this letter.

It can be useful initially to recall the operation of inclination in the will, the first operation of the will, as described in chapter 5. The will by its natural inclination, in or out of prayer, seeks the satisfaction of taking possession of what it desires. This natural inclination plays a crucial role in prayer. The possibility in prayer is that on certain days the delight of consolation can be received in the course of prayer. This satisfaction, which may be graced, nonetheless can detour the soul from a pure pursuit of God if it becomes the primary desire sought in prayer. The desire for a spiritual taste or feeling, as Saint John of the Cross repeats often in his writings, may replace the far greater need to turn our desire fully and exclusively toward God himself in a great surrender to him. In a letter to a Carmelite nun in Córdoba written at almost this same time in July of that same year, he writes: "To possess God in all, you should possess nothing in all. For how can the heart that belongs to one belong completely to the other?" (L17). The pure desire for God himself has to be a consuming need for a soul that would love God with intensity. Secondary desires for experiences of satisfaction in prayer must be understood as an inferior pursuit.

This teaching entails further insights and challenges. Nothing that can be enjoyed as a satisfaction in prayer should be interpreted as taking hold of God, just as no knowledge of God received in prayer is equivalent to comprehending the actual truth of God. No taste of the presence of God in prayer removes the inaccessibility of God in his divine nature to the human soul's immediate experience. To think otherwise is to be deceived. It is necessary, then, not to halt at any experience of satisfaction in prayer as though a possession of God had been enjoyed in this delight. On the contrary, the soul must accept that the deeper truth of prayer extends always beyond any experience in prayer. The inclination of the will in prayer should remain ever desirous for God himself without arriving, as it were, at a destination in some satisfaction. In truth, a pure desire for God never arrives at a final satiation in this life, but rather is inflamed increasingly over time with an intensifying desire for God. If we enjoy some delight in prayer on any day, this experience does not convey the deeper truth of prayer, which is often concealed within unseen layers of the soul. Moreover, we ought not to make the recovery of a delight experienced on any day in prayer the motivation for the next time of prayer. Any excessive resting in prayer in an enjoyment of satiation, without a release from that satisfaction, is to risk in subsequent prayer that we will set out in pursuit of something less than God. This tendency to seek pleasant experiences is to stop prematurely in the quest for God himself. The letter begins by clarifying the nature of the will as a faculty of desire, but also by affirming that nothing particular that the will can experience in satisfaction is an experience of God himself. God is simply beyond all delight that we can enjoy in prayer. "Note that every particular thing in which the will can rejoice is sweet and delightful, since it is in one's opinion satisfying; and nothing delightful and sweet in which one can rejoice is God. For, since God is not apprehensible to the faculties, he cannot be the object of the appetites and satisfactions of the will. Since the soul cannot enjoy God

essentially in this life, all the sweetness and delight it tastes,
however sublime, cannot be God" (L13).

The initial point of instruction is to expose a deceptive
illusion quite common in souls: namely, to divert the pursuit of God in prayer into a search for personal experiences
in prayer. A delightful satisfaction in prayer, if received, can
easily be thought to be a confirmation of greater closeness
to God and, for that reason, worthy of pursuit. Human nature, by its natural inclination, can become enamored of
the consoling delight that may be experienced in prayer.
The real problem in this tendency is the identification of
an experience in prayer with an experience of God himself.
The pure path to God in prayer lies in not stopping at any
passing experience in prayer. God in his transcendent reality extends beyond any experience received in prayer. Whatever satisfaction may be tasted in prayer, even what seems
a taste of the presence of God in some immediate manner,
is *not* an experience of God himself in his infinite mystery.
If the search for subjective experiences becomes the quest
motivating interior prayer, a subtle self-seeking takes root in
the practice of prayer. To avoid that tendency, a clear coun-
termeasure should be adopted. If a gratifying experience in
prayer does occur, it ought to be dropped from attention or
concern afterward. In short, a great detachment is necessary
in prayer, which leaves the will empty and perhaps often
unsatisfied in its desire. The strong advice of Saint John of
the Cross is not to halt at any passing delight but, rather, to
leave it and move on. Again, the principle underlying this
understanding is that the reality of God cannot be grasped in
any particular experience. The soul, in effect, must protect
itself from any illusion that it has somehow taken hold of
God in an experience within prayer.

Since the will has never tasted God as he is or known him through some gratification of the appetite, and consequently does not know what God is like, it cannot know what the pleasure of God is; nor can its being, appetite, and satisfaction know how to desire God, for he transcends all its capacity. Thus it is obvious that none of all those particular things in which it can rejoice is God. In order to be united with him, the will must consequently be emptied of and detached from all disordered appetite and satisfaction with respect to every particular thing in which it can rejoice, whether earthly or heavenly, temporal or spiritual, so that purged and cleansed of all inordinate satisfactions, joys, and appetites it might be wholly occupied in loving God with its affections. (L13)

What is Saint John of the Cross teaching here in this apophatic perspective of God's inaccessibility to our experience? We can return to an essential instruction about contemplation. Contemplation is a knowledge by love, as we have seen, an awareness in prayer of the will longing inwardly for God. When God is loved in contemplation, the experience can on occasion provide enjoyment, because love *is* gratifying. But this gratification, however strong, does not signify in itself an experiential *possession* of God himself. And this is what Saint John of the Cross in this letter is identifying as a problem for souls, who often do identify an experience of feelings in prayer with a presence of God as the immediate source of those feelings. The need is to treat *feelings* of gratification in love as a very secondary reality in prayer. The eyes of the soul ought to remain turned toward God himself, who remains always still inaccessible to the soul and beyond a grasp of experience, despite the most gratifying exaltation of feelings that a soul might enjoy in prayer. The soul knows God through love, not through an experiential gratification. And it knows him in the truth of love as One who remains a Being of mystery. The hidden God of infinite love is the God who must be engaged and sought in prayer. It may be worthwhile to recall the striking phrases we encountered at the beginning of the book from the first stanza commentary of *The Spiritual Canticle*, which also stressed the inaccessibility of God to our direct experience.

> You do very well, O soul, to seek him ever as one hidden, for you exalt God and approach very near him when you consider him higher and deeper than anything you can reach. Hence pay no attention, neither partially nor entirely, to anything your faculties can grasp. . . . Never pause to love and delight in your understanding and experience of God, but love and delight in what you cannot understand or experience of him. Such is the way . . . of seeking him in faith. However surely it may seem that you find, experience, and understand God, because he is inaccessible and concealed you must always regard him as hidden, and serve him who is hidden in a secret way. (SC 1.12)

Another truth equally important to acknowledge is implied in this passage from *The Spiritual Canticle* and then amplified further in the letter. Love in contemplation, when it grows deeper and does not halt, *necessarily* sweeps the soul by grace into the incomprehensible reality of God. It is as though a much deeper undercurrent of inflamed desire is taking place in contemplation than the will can realize in any experience of a particular gratification. The deeper undercurrent of love flowing through the will may often be drawing it to God without a person's full awareness of this fact. What is felt in some tangible manner is a partial and even superficial component of the deeper reality at work in contemplation. The will is united to God by love in contemplation, but in a manner impossible for the will to savor in its full truth. The union of the human will with God's will takes place precisely as an inaccessible truth in contemplation. The important stress in the following passage of this letter is to contrast the distinction between love and gratification as the path to the truth of God in prayer. Saint John of the Cross makes an astute observation that the operation of the will in love is not the same as the gratification of the will's feelings in love. Love in the operation of the will is always the richer reality, superseding any experience of felt gratification that the soul might temporarily enjoy. It is the operation of love, often unseen, that must be the essential pursuit of prayer.

> For if in any way the will can comprehend God and be united with him, it is through love and not through any gratification of the appetite. And since the delight, sweetness, and satisfaction that can come to the will is not love, none of the delightful feelings can be an adequate means for union of the will with God; it is the operation of the will that is the proportionate means for this union. The will's operation is quite distinct from the will's feeling: By its operation, which is love, the will is united with God and terminates in him, and not by the feeling and gratification of its appetite that remains in the soul and goes no further. (L13)

What, then, of the feelings of love that may be experienced in prayer? Are they to be denied or mortified? Ignored or renounced? Saint John of the Cross writes that they should be treated simply as secondary factors in prayer, incidental in importance. The awareness of an inflamed undercurrent of love in the will is far more significant, because it is the deeper truth. Yet it may not be encountered in an experiential manner for its deeper truth. Nonetheless, in a receptive response to a longing for God deep within the soul, this reality of love is fostered. The mistaken approach, on the other hand, is to allow a search for feelings in prayer to dominate the exercise of prayer. For many people, feelings can become a coveted item in prayer as well as a source of continual frustration and instability—a possessive need for a satisfaction that is somehow felt and then becomes the measure of prayer, a habit hard to relinquish. Feelings of love, delightful as they may be, ought to be only a means to recognizing the more inaccessible reality of love operating at hidden layers of depth in the will and in the soul. The greater truth takes place in the unseen "cavern" of the will as it undergoes a profound "soul desire" for God. There is in every contemplative life a need, at least for a time, to release the soul from the pursuit of feelings in order to embrace this deeper recognition. Love in the will, rather than any feeling, is the much deeper truth in prayer and in contemplation. As Saint John of the Cross writes:

> The feelings only serve as stimulants to love, if the will desires to pass beyond them; and they serve for no more. Thus the delightful feelings do not of themselves lead the soul to God, but rather cause it to become attached to delightful feelings. But the operation of the will, which is the love of God, concentrates the affection, joy, pleasure, satisfaction, and love of the soul only on God, leaving aside all things and loving him above them all. Hence if persons are moved to the love of God without dependence on the sweetness they feel, they leave aside this sweetness and center their love on God whom they cannot feel. Were they to love the sweetness and satisfaction, pausing and being

detained in it, making an end and goal of the means, the work of the will would consequently be faulty. (L13)

Again, the essential truth that warrants this teaching is the transcendence of God to human experience. The effort of the soul in contemplation must be to turn its desire exclusively toward God himself, leaning in the direction of the inaccessible mystery of God. Love demands this fixation of our desire on God himself, not yielding to secondary satisfactions as targets of pursuit. The logic of contemplation rests upon the mutual effect of faith and love in prayer. In faith, the soul knows God as incomprehensible. This God, who is both personal and incomprehensible, is the God who must be loved with *all* the soul's desire of will. The will can only love God in truth within the light of faith. Love in the will turns toward a God who is unknown in the fullness of his transcendent reality. Yet in faith he can be known as One who is intensely loved. Our soul has to love precisely what is incomprehensible and inaccessible in God if we are to love in truth. For incomprehensibility and inaccessibility are the truth of our immediate experience of him. We have to love, in a telling phrase, ''according to the demands of faith''. The stress here is the exact opposite of what might be supposed. The seeming darkness of faith standing blindly before the incomprehensibility of God's transcendence might seem to invite a vague quality of love. Quite the contrary is the case, according to Saint John of the Cross. The immense magnitude of God's transcendence, when he is utterly personal in his love for us, yields an essential insight for prayer. This dual awareness awakens a great desire to love him in his ultimate mystery of concealment. When the soul loves intensely what it cannot ultimately know, this does not diminish the

intensity of our love for God as the Beloved. Saint John of
the Cross clarifies this important teaching for contemplative
prayer in this passage:

> Since God is incomprehensible and inaccessible, the will,
> if it is to center its activity of love on him, must not set
> itself on what it can touch and apprehend with the ap-
> petite, but on what is incomprehensible and inaccessible to
> the appetite. Loving in this way, a soul loves truly and cer-
> tainly according to the demands of faith; also in emptiness
> and darkness concerning its feelings, going beyond all the
> feelings it may experience in understanding its concepts.
> Thus it believes and loves above everything it can under-
> stand. (L13)

In this letter, Saint John of the Cross proceeds to address
some mistaken perceptions that measure prayer by what is
experienced in the feelings of the will. Lack of feeling does
not indicate a failure to encounter God in prayer. Nor does
great delight felt in prayer confirm a deeper possession of
God in prayer. Given these truths, which are now familiar
to us, it is foolish to search for such delight and wrong-
headed to lament the absence of such experiences in prayer.
These are superficial understandings of prayer that deflect
us from our goal of seeking God in a pure, naked manner of
soul. The inescapable truth in prayer is a type of crossroad:
either we seek God in a pure desire for him, or we seek
something for ourselves. The purity of our soul in prayer
is in direct proportion to our pure, naked quest for God
alone. This task is an essential demand in contemplation,
inasmuch as the soul can at times experience consolation
and delight and, conversely, can undergo great frustration
in its love when no satisfaction is received for long periods.
It can be as though the first words of Jesus in the Gospel
of Saint John to Andrew and presumably to John himself

hover as a question within prayer at all times—"What do you seek?" (Jn 1:38). When a soul is answering in some manner: "Only you, Lord, nothing but you", then it is entering into a naked longing for God. This pure desire leads in turn to a deeper union of our will with God's will, which is precisely a spiritual fruit that all contemplative prayer fosters and deepens. Saint John of the Cross writes in summary fashion on this point:

> Hence they would be very foolish who would think that God is failing them because of their lack of spiritual sweetness and delight, or would rejoice, thinking that they possess God because of the presence of this sweetness. And they would be more foolish if they were to go in search of this sweetness in God and rejoice and be detained in it. With such an attitude they would no longer be seeking God with their wills grounded in the emptiness of faith and charity, but they would be seeking spiritual satisfaction and sweetness, which are creatures, by following after their own pleasure and appetite. And thus they would no longer be loving God purely, above all things, which means centering all the strength of one's will on him. In being bound and attached to that creature by means of the appetite, the will does not rise above it to God, who is inaccessible. It is impossible for the will to reach the sweetness and delight of the divine union and receive and feel the sweet and loving embraces of God without the nakedness and void of its appetite with respect to every particular satisfaction, earthly and heavenly. (L13)

The conclusion of this remarkable letter returns to a stress on emptying our appetitive desire for all that is not God himself. The road to union with God is a path of radical purification of our will in its desires and delights. Nothing less than God must consume our desire in prayer. Saint

John of the Cross clearly perceives the will as an appetite of immense capacity. So many created things can capture the will's desire and make it long for a possession. As we have seen by now quite strongly, the stripping of the will's appetite out of love for God is never an exercise only of self-denial in bodily asceticism or in virtuous acts of self-giving. There is continual need as well to purge the will in the pure refinement of its desire in prayer. The soul must concentrate its desire toward God in an aspiration of total surrender. Otherwise, it awaits always further purification. The emptying of our desire for anything but God is the exclusive path to a union in love with God. As Saint John of the Cross concludes:

> When the appetite is centered on something, it becomes narrow by this very fact, since outside of God everything is narrow. That the soul have success in journeying to God and being joined to him, it must have the mouth of its will opened only to God himself, empty and dispossessed of every morsel of appetite, so God may fill it with his love and sweetness; and it must remain with this hunger and thirst for God alone, without desiring to be satisfied by any other thing, since here below it cannot enjoy God as he is in himself. And what is enjoyable—if there is a desire for it, as I say—impedes this union. Isaiah taught this when he said: All you who thirst, come to the waters [Is. 55:1]. He invites to the abundance of the divine waters of union with God only those who thirst for God alone and who have no money, that is, appetites. (L13)

~

After examining this letter, it can be beneficial to return to a pair of poignant chapters in book 2 of *The Ascent of Mount Carmel*. These chapters expose the stark challenge of sanctity and enrich what has just been taught regarding the will's operation in love and the need of the will to be emptied for the sake of union with God. For Saint John of the Cross, the degree to which our will is united with God's will determines the depth of love in our soul. The human will seeking union with the will of God is likewise an essential condition for any advancement in prayer. In one sense, contemplative prayer depends *entirely* on this effort to give our will generously to the will of God. This is the one condition without which contemplation will collapse as a grace. A short phrase captures this requirement for every soul seeking the contemplative encounter with God in prayer: "To the soul that is more advanced in love, more conformed to the divine will, God communicates himself more" (AMC 2.5.4). By contrast, resistance to the will of God halts progress in prayer. This does not mean necessarily choosing sin. Resistance to any clear indication of God's will arrests contemplative graces and brings them to an end unless this opposition on our part is overcome. In the interior realm of prayer, a stripping away of our desire for anything less than God and his will is a steady need for prayer to advance. It must be a cultivated interior disposition and must affect our choices outside prayer. There is a conscious need to choose this disposition and respect its importance.

The desire to be united to God's will does not involve only actions of submission to the will of God outside of prayer, although these responses are critically important. As taught strongly in the letter just examined, it entails as well a readiness to cast aside satisfactions as a goal of love within prayer itself. God alone must be sought in love—the God who despite what might be our own intense love remains the inaccessible Beloved beyond an experiential satisfaction of love. The strain of purification can become as such an inevitable and long-lasting ambiance experienced in prayer. All we can do at times, it may seem, is to cooperate in the self-emptying disposition of love. The following short statement may be useful for encouraging mortification of our will outside prayer, but it is perhaps even more pertinent to the need for a spirit of mortification within the interior life of prayer: "A soul makes room for God by wiping away all the smudges and smears of creatures, by uniting its will perfectly to God's; for to love is to labor to divest and deprive oneself for God of all that is not God. When this is done the soul will be illumined by and transformed in God. And God will so communicate his supernatural being to the soul that it will appear to be God himself and will possess what God himself possesses" (AMC 2.5.7).

What does this divestment and deprivation essentially demand in the interior life of prayer? Seeking after experiences in prayer of any sort will always conflict with the pure path of seeking God alone. Contemplation, as a gift of God to our prayer, is not for the sake of an experience to be enjoyed; rather, it fosters in our soul a self-emptying union with God. "The preparation for this union", as Saint John of the Cross writes, "is not an understanding by the soul, nor the taste, feeling, or imagining of God or any other object, but purity and love, the stripping off and perfect renunciation of all such experiences for God alone" (AMC 2.5.8). In other words, a naked void in the desire of the will opens the way to a true encounter with God in contemplation. The God of infinite love is known in the will's pure longing for the One who is always vastly beyond our meager capacity.

Many people who practice prayer adopt a contrary approach. They seek their own gratification and satisfaction, rather than what is pleasing to God. To our surprise, perhaps, what is pleasing to God in our prayer may often contradict our own preference. What God desires especially is that we empty ourselves for love of him; nothing less and nothing more. Yet how difficult to accept this idea of prayer as a progress in self-emptying rather than a path of advancement in knowledge and experience of God. As Saint John of the Cross writes in this section, "I think it is possible to affirm that the more necessary the doctrine the less it is practiced by spiritual persons" (AMC 2.7.4). This "doctrine", as it were, is the reality of the cross encountered, not just in trials in life, but in the purifying interior experiences of the life of prayer. If we forget that the cross is met not only in the exterior trials of life but in prayer itself, then we erect a barrier on the path to greater love for God. The identification with the Beloved who is the crucified Lord must be fully embraced in prayer itself if prayer is to advance in a genuine manner. The seeking of consolation is not just a fault and an indulgent weakness, but essentially a refusal to embrace the crucified Lord as the Beloved. The following words are a sharp rebuke to this tendency: "From my observations Christ is little known by those who consider themselves his friends. For we see them going about seeking in him their own consolations and satisfactions, loving themselves very much, but not loving him very much by seeking his bitter trials and deaths. I am referring to those who believe themselves his friends, not to those who live withdrawn and far away from him" (AMC 2.7.12).

Saint John of the Cross insists strongly on the "narrowness" of the way of sanctity and of deeper prayer. A divestment and stripping away of everything gratifying in prayer must be pursued in order to conquer self-love and so to seek God alone. It is a narrow doorway through which our soul must walk if it is to answer to the precious grace of contemplation. The soul must be light and trim, dispossessed and empty of desire except for God himself and for all that he will ask from our lives. Self-love in all its possible disguises must be increasingly exposed and, then, eradicated. The indulgent tendency to pursue our own consolation in prayer has to be ruthlessly mortified. The most common form of spiritual indulgence is precisely to seek our own satisfaction in any manner, instead of accepting the painful emptiness of an arid purification in prayer. All desire of the soul in prayer for anything other than God himself—that is, for consolation and emotional satisfaction—is a damaging obstacle on this path of deeper prayer. It is indeed rare, according to Saint John of the Cross, that God finds souls who seek him with this kind of consuming and exclusive desire for himself alone, come what may. Yet perhaps some of us are meant to be among these souls. If so, there is need of a radical spiritual insight moved by love, as these words testify: "Few there are with the knowledge and desire to enter into this supreme nakedness and emptiness of spirit. . . . This is a venture in which God alone is sought and gained; thus only God ought to be sought and gained" (AMC 2.7.3).

What we hear in these challenging words is that the self-abnegation demanded by contemplation is a discipline of the spiritual realm, a type of spiritual asceticism directed primarily at the desires we cultivate in prayer. The will in its operation of love must shed every encumbrance that hinders it from a pure desire for God. The primary encumbrance is the great bane of a desire for satisfactions in love. Instead, our soul must seek more deeply what Jesus himself teaches as the true path to union with him, namely, to lose our-

selves in love for him. Deep poverty of spirit is an essential
requirement in prayer and the spiritual life. In prayer, this
poverty comes about as our soul embraces an annihilation of
all desires other than a pure longing for God himself. Saint
John of the Cross offers a striking passage in this section of
The Ascent of Mount Carmel on the true significance of Jesus'
demand for the soul to lose itself for him if it is to gain
its true life (Mk 8:34–35). Few people realize the deeper
implications of this denial and loss of self as it is lived out
in the interior life of prayer. Saint John of the Cross notes
the difference between a lesser form of renunciation and the
great abnegation of the soul that must take place in prayer.

> Oh, who can make this counsel of our Savior on self-
> denial understandable, and practicable, and attractive, that
> spiritual persons might become aware of the difference be-
> tween the method many of them think is good and the one
> that ought to be used in traveling this road! They are of
> the opinion that any kind of withdrawal from the world,
> or reformation of life, suffices. Some are content with a
> certain degree of virtue, perseverance in prayer, and mor-
> tification, but never achieve the nakedness, poverty, self-
> lessness, or spiritual purity (which are all the same) about
> which the Lord counsels us here. For they still feed and
> clothe their natural selves with spiritual feelings and con-
> solations instead of divesting and denying themselves of
> these for God sake. (AMC 2.7.5)

He goes on to stress the difference between self-denial
toward worldly indulgence and the greater effort of self-
abnegation that must confront tendencies to spiritual indulgence in prayer. Many good people do not leap ahead in the
spiritual life and never embrace the grace of contemplation
into their lives because they refuse to accept the demand
to mortify their spiritual desires for consoling delights in

prayer. Yet this detachment from our own preference is essential if we are to receive the grace of contemplation and cooperate with it over time. Before we enter this path of a more serious desire for God, we are unlikely to think of deeper prayer as a test in perseverance and interior mortification. But this testing is a serious and unavoidable aspect of the contemplative path. The purifications of interior prayer are an arena of martyrdom for some souls, especially those who are more sensitive. But if we move forward over time, not halting despite the interior sufferings, we are capable of receiving the great graces God desires to bestow in contemplation. In one of his more incisive comments for those who would desire to love God, Saint John of the Cross writes:

> They think denial of self in worldly matters is sufficient without annihilation and purification in the spiritual domain. It happens that, when some of this solid, perfect food (the annihilation of all sweetness in God—the pure spiritual cross and nakedness of Christ's poverty of spirit) is offered them in dryness, distaste, and trial, they run from it as from death and wander about in search only of sweetness and delightful communications from God. Such an attitude is not the hallmark of self-denial and nakedness of spirit, but the indication of a spiritual sweet tooth. Through this kind of conduct they become, spiritually speaking, enemies of the cross of Christ. (AMC 2.7.5)

Saint John of the Cross continues to propose even more radical challenges in this demanding section of *The Ascent of Mount Carmel*. He insists that we should learn to *prefer* the difficult experiences of aridity in prayer to what seems more desirable in the experience of consolation. This advice goes beyond merely a recommendation of renunciation toward seeking delight in prayer. It urges a shift in perspective by which we now lean our inclination in prayer toward experiencing harsh aridity as the way of greater love. From what we now know of his teaching, this should really not be too surprising. In his view, consolation in prayer, if not clearly denied as a desire in prayer, will be sought implicitly by our natural inclination. The pleasing experience in prayer is naturally sought, not the painful experience. The experience of dry dissatisfaction is bound to provoke frustration, unless, in a radical shift of approach, we consciously choose to prefer it as our desire. This is a significant choice in itself, certainly not to be glossed over. It means, first, to accept that dry dissatisfaction is a fine and healthy state of prayer. That advice entails an approach to prayer quite contrary to our natural inclination. But Saint John of the Cross takes this understanding even farther. He insists that we should *prefer* dissatisfaction in prayer. And why? This condition leads, by way of poverty and nakedness of spirit, to an interior emptiness in our soul that God can fill with himself in contemplation. The recommendation here is not to make prayer into a penitential practice. Rather, it is to open our soul to a naked detachment from self, precisely because this path opens us to deeper graces of contemplation. "For on this road there is room only for self-denial (as our Savior asserts) and the cross. The cross is a supporting staff and greatly lightens and eases the journey" (AMC 2.7.7). Those words pertain to prayer as much as to the exercise of self-denial in actions outside of prayer. The demands of love are indeed formidable. The following passage puts on display this understanding of self-denial that must penetrate our interior life of prayer. It can be read as an example of the purest strain of radicality in Saint John of the Cross' teaching:

> A genuine spirit seeks rather the distasteful in God than the delectable, leans more toward suffering than toward consolation, more toward going without everything for God than toward possession, and toward dryness and

affliction than toward sweet consolation. It knows that this is the significance of following Christ and denying self, that the other method is perhaps a seeking of self in God —something entirely contrary to love. Seeking oneself in God is the same as looking for the caresses and consolations of God. Seeking God in oneself entails not only the desire to do without these consolations for God's sake, but also the inclination to choose for love of Christ all that is most distasteful whether in God or in the world; and this is what loving God means. (AMC 2.7.5)

This chapter began with the remarkable letter treating the purity of the will in giving all its desire only to God. The will's operation in love is indeed distinct from the will's experience of feeling. What we have been hearing now, from these selected passages of *The Ascent of Mount Carmel*, is a confirmation of this teaching. The purity of a naked will fixed only on God requires an attitude in prayer that is extremely demanding. Yet it must be cultivated despite its uncompromising nature if we aspire to contemplative relations with God. A divestment and stripping away of self-love can take place in prayer only as we renounce the desire for our own enjoyment and consolation in prayer. This emptying of desire allows our will to be inclined in a purity of inflamed desire for God himself. Contemplation has preliminary phases of surrender that must be met if our soul is to open itself to the undercurrents of longing that take prayer into deeper regions of an encounter with God. The great surrender initially required is to let go of all our desire for satisfaction and consolation, which may have motivated prayer at one time in our lives. This surrender in turn allows our soul to forget itself more completely—a central need in contemplation. To enter into a loss of concern for self proves a great benefit for the receptivity essential to contemplation. Letting go of self occurs because nothing is sought for ourselves. This opens our soul to wanting only what God wants to give us on any day. The will wanting God alone can then permeate the time of prayer more and more. Saint John of the Cross expresses this task as a receptive acceptance of the annihilation of our soul for the sake of a love for God in these striking words from this same section of *The Ascent*:

> David says of him: *Ad nihilum redactus sum et nescivi* [I was reduced to nothing and did not understand] [Ps. 73:22], that those who are truly spiritual might understand the mystery of the door and way (which is Christ) leading to union with God, and that they might realize that their union with God and the greatness of the work they accomplish will be measured by their annihilation of themselves for God in the sensory and spiritual parts of their souls. When they are reduced to nothing, the highest degree of humility, the spiritual union between their souls and God will be an accomplished fact. This union is the most noble and sublime state attainable in this life. The journey, then, does not consist in consolations, delights, and spiritual feelings, but in the living death of the cross, sensory and spiritual, exterior and interior. (AMC 2.7.11)

Brought to nothing, annihilated in a love for God, empty of desires except an intense desire for God—these phrases cannot convey what nonetheless must become the compelling need at the depth of our prayer. The path to sanctity is exactly as Jesus described it in the Gospel—to take up our cross and follow him, losing ourselves out of great love for him. This ultimate demand of love leads us always onward to Calvary and must be heard at the heart of our prayer. "Where I am, there shall my servant be also" (Jn 12:26). Inevitably, on this path, we are invited to draw closer to our crucified Lord hiding within the silence of our prayer.

14

WOUNDS OF LOVE: BRANDING MARKS OF CONTEMPLATION

We have a deeper appreciation now for both the hard demands of contemplation and its undeniable attraction. But we have not yet fully exposed the interior challenge. The concealment of God's presence, mysteriously near to our soul, yet known only by love, is at the heart of contemplation. The *hidden* presence of God is a truth of inescapable provocation, never fully lifted or overcome in a lifetime, showing many variations in the experience of a soul. Sometimes the hidden presence of God is stronger in the silence of prayer; other times it is met outside prayer in the sudden opportunity for sacrifice or in the disguised face of Jesus hiding in a poor person. God as elusive, hiding behind shadows, speaking in quiet whispers, disappearing from sight even in the encounter with him, is all a realization of greater faith. His presence has no predictable quality and offers no promise of an easy recognition. Shadows and darkness can become for lengthy periods the ordinary ambiance of prayer. When the darkness stretches over time and is greater, the thought of God's withdrawal can trouble souls in their silent prayer, despite how close they may be to God.

The contemplative paradox of darkness as the setting for a very personal contact with God implies a need at times for reassurance. This comes as we deepen a calm certitude of faith in prayer and continue to long for our Lord in love and yield to him in surrender. All the while, over years of committed daily prayer, God works to bring a soul to a greater surrender to his mysterious personal love. One definite requirement for advancing in contemplation is that he remains the Beloved throughout all events in life, including the most distressful, and within all the uncertain experience of prayer itself. The readiness to accept everything that God permits or chooses for us must be fostered at all costs. God communicates his love to our soul, even in darkness, when we seek, not our own will, but conformity with the will of God. This desire for conformity with his desires is the secret of every great love for God. Whether he remains truly the Beloved who is sought in everything, his will guiding our deeper desire of soul, is an essential condition for the contemplative quest for God. In words quoted earlier, but worth recalling for their great challenge and promise, Saint John of the Cross expresses this need in *The Spiritual Canticle*, in his commentary on the first stanza:

> When God is loved he very readily answers the requests of his lover. This he teaches through St. John: *If you abide in me, ask whatever you want and it shall be done unto you* [Jn. 15:7]. You can truthfully call God Beloved when you are wholly with him, do not allow your heart attachment to anything outside of him, and thereby ordinarily center your mind on him. . . . Some call the Bridegroom beloved when he is not really their beloved because their heart is not wholly set on him. As a result their petition is not of much value in his sight. They do not obtain their request until they keep their spirit more continually with God through perseverance in prayer, and their heart with its affectionate love more entirely set on him. Nothing is obtained from God except by love. (SC 1.13)

The clear demand in these words is for an uncompromising commitment to love. Not surprisingly, for a soul aspiring to advance in contemplation, this demand can lead in time to a suffering for love, even a kind of martyrdom by love. If God is to remain the Beloved, the quest for him requires a perseverance in abnegation and self-emptying in our interior life. The martyrdom in contemplation, if that is not too strong an expression, is due largely to a deeper encounter over time with the Beloved's concealment. No one who loves God intensely can but suffer from an inability to feel his presence in love. Often, for a contemplative soul, this experience may be interpreted—indeed, wrongly —as a choice on God's part to distance himself from close contact and for no reason that can be perceived. Even when a soul accepts this trial, the concealment of God, when our Lord seems silent, withdrawn, or absent for a longer duration of time, wounds the soul that loves him with intensity. It may seem that it will never find the resting in love that it seeks in God. Any visits of consolation from the Lord, if they occur, are ordinarily brief and serve only to return the soul afterward to the pain of its solitary hunger. This, too, is a mark of contemplative grace. The hunger carves deep fissures into the caverns of the soul. The soul longs and lies in waiting, only to be left in dissatisfaction. The interior wound of emptiness, with no other desire but to belong to God, refines the soul for the greater gift of God himself. Saint John of the Cross has striking passages in the stanza commentaries of *The Spiritual Canticle* on the soul wounded in love by God. But his poetry is perhaps the first evidence of this painful effect of loving God intensely. An example is the second stanza of "The Spiritual Canticle":

Shepherds, you who go
up through the sheepfolds to the hill,
if by chance you see
him I love most,
tell him I am sick, I suffer, and I die. (SC stanza 2)

The "wound of love" is a special phrase for Saint John of
the Cross. This wound can become a kind of silent companion in the interior life of prayer as a soul engages the
hard contemplative experience of God hiding from its love.
Indeed, the concealment of God, when actually he *is* present
within the soul, can wound the soul more than if God simply departed and left it alone. There are many possibilities
for experiencing in prayer this wounding of the soul, all
of which are linked to a soul's intense love for God. The
bitter taste in prayer of a long silence from God, with perhaps nothing of Scripture speaking so personally, can seem
as though the soul is undeserving of communication from
God. The scraping down of the heart to a raw state of aridity
is another type of wound. It is not something a soul simply
ignores. These trials are not just a suffering in prayer, but
can make a trial as well of everything outside of prayer. It
can draw some souls into a sense of futility in everything
they seek to do for God. They may become blind to the
actual fruits they are bearing for God. No relief, no human
comfort, may intervene to alleviate this condition. At the
same time, Saint John of the Cross makes clear that no soul
moves forward to union with God except by means of the
wounds of love in some form or another. The soul walking
the road of contemplation can be like a person with an illness of the heart, unable to release itself from a steady suffering as long as the healing touch of the Beloved remains
absent. Yet the wounding of the soul becomes, in effect, the
manner in which God takes captive the soul that has great

love for him. Saint John of the Cross invokes this state of soul in writing of the heart stolen by God, a moving image central to another stanza of "The Spiritual Canticle":

> Why, since you wounded
> this heart, don't you heal it?
> And why, since you stole it from me,
> do you leave it so,
> and fail to carry off what you have stolen? (stanza 9)

The duration of waiting for the Beloved while wounded with love for him is a decisive factor in bringing a soul to a greater love for God. We can hear that truth implicit in the cry of the bride in the stanza just read. Every longer period of waiting for God provokes more intense love; each lingering delay inflames desire in a heart "stolen" by God. God seems to make a soul wait longer, the more he desires that soul to long more intensely for himself. If a soul is fortunate, it perceives a pattern after a time. The absence of any direct encounter with God in prayer may stretch for what seems an unendurable time. Nothing a soul does in generous action and sacrifice outside prayer alters the sense of interior emptiness. But then, unexpectedly, the experience of a strong, releasing love returns and is felt again in prayer. The soul, after being wounded by love, enters more fully into a deeper love for the Beloved. As *The Spiritual Canticle* progresses, Saint John of the Cross invokes this pattern of love's absence and reappearance in the soul's search for the Beloved. In a short passage early on in *The Spiritual Canticle*, he describes the pain of a desire for God when he is "absent" as a sign of the depth of love in a soul. The wound of discontent carved into a soul is a clear sign of its consuming desire for God: "The absence of the Beloved causes continual moaning in the lover. Since she loves nothing outside of him, she finds no rest or relief in anything. This is how we recognize persons who truly love God: if they are content with nothing less than God" (SC 1.14).

There may be a need to ponder statements like this over many years in a lifetime. The usual manner of experiencing human love for someone who is much loved is to enjoy a great satisfaction. Being in the presence of someone uniquely loved brings a delight beyond any comparable experience. But Saint John of the Cross is not writing about romantic love or the joys of married life. When God is the Beloved, the scales turn in the opposite direction. An increasing dissatisfaction begins to invade the soul as its love deepens for God. God cannot be possessed in love, only longed for and sought perpetually. The soul may find itself in the prayer of contemplation confronting daily the immeasurable distance it may feel from God. This frustration may extend, as mentioned, to all areas of life, where it can find "no rest or relief in anything". A kind of holy discontentment becomes the lot of the soul in love with God, which may be a surprising observation. Naturally, this does not signify a plunge downward into some kind of depressive attitude. On the contrary, the discontent becomes a stimulant for a soul to give itself more generously in all ways to God. These souls customarily become more absorbed in the desire to please God precisely in those times when God seems most removed and absent.

This holy response to interior discontent may be a primary reason why saints became saints. It is not that their efforts of sacrifice and self-giving were undertaken out of obligation or to draw God's notice and induce his favor. Rather, for the soul that loves intensely, there seems no other desirable choice than to give to God a gift in everything. The stripping away of all things outside of God as unworthy of a passionate pursuit in life is a typical reaction in the saintly life. But it is also a fruit and symptom of contemplation. The emptying of desire for things other than God becomes itself at some point a form of satisfaction for the soul. This unusual shift may occur more readily once a soul recognizes that becoming poor and empty of self is a way of pleasing the Beloved. A deeper contentment of soul begins to be found in poverty and in a dispossession of all things other than God. In a sense, every soul has to make this discovery for itself in a way that remains personal and permanent, as described in these words: "The will is content with nothing less than his presence and the sight of him" (SC 6.2). It becomes an important insight in the life of contemplation to realize the insufficiency of pursuing anything in this life for an ultimate happiness other than to please God. As Saint John of the Cross writes:

> But what am I saying, if they are content? Even if they possess everything they will not be content; in fact the more they have, the less satisfied they will be. Satisfaction of heart is not found in the possession of things, but in being stripped of them all and in poverty of spirit. Since perfection consists in this poverty of spirit, in which God is possessed by a very intimate and special grace, the soul, having attained it, lives in this life with some satisfaction, although not complete. (SC 1.14)

Some further thoughts on this theme of being wounded for love can enhance our understanding of the love that flows out of contemplation. If we think for a moment about what God does with a soul he favors, it is evident that he seeks to draw it into an *exclusive* love for himself. Nothing outside of God can be allowed to consume the soul's deepest desire and affections. The inability to find lasting satisfaction in anything, including prayer itself for long stretches, becomes a continual goad to a soul. A hunger for God then consumes the soul, and nothing else that might be sought does anything other than bring it back to a desire for God. Nothing in life satisfies so much; instead, everything causes remembrance of God. It is as though all things worth re-membering have become a memory of a time spent with God. The events even of a single day bring the soul back to its desire for him. This consuming desire within a soul is ultimately for a possession of God, and yet that possession in love proves impossible. The soul may come to know this as a truth accepted in the mind. And yet it is common that a contemplative soul in its heart does not view the desire for taking hold of God as an unattainable longing. Instead, it plunges more intensely into its desire for God, thereby inciting its own dissatisfaction.

This dissatisfaction in love is a blessed state that animates a deeper advancement in contemplative life. The wound of dissatisfied love carves itself into all contemplative striving. At the same time that such love is painful, it is increasingly sought. It is possible, in this sense, that everything in a life may serve in God's mysterious plan to inflame greater desire for God. God becomes more solicitous for such souls even as he maintains his concealment. And so he leads them to generous self-giving and a more sacrificial life by provid-ing these opportunities. Let us say it again: The saints were saints because they were contemplatives in their deeper life of prayer and souls of great sacrificial self-giving outside prayer. When God consumes the longing of the soul, the soul wants nothing but to seek for him and to prove its love for him. The holy dissatisfaction of love with its un-satiated desires plunges a soul increasingly into losing itself for love and for others. Behind these desires to give of it-self is always a longing of the soul that God show himself more fully. This disposition is captured in a passage from *The Spiritual Canticle* that we might say is equivalent to an overheard prayer:

> My Lord, my Spouse, you have given yourself to me partially; now may you give yourself completely. You have revealed yourself to me as through fissures in a rock; now may you give me that revelation more clearly. You have communicated by means of others, as if joking with me; now may you do so truly, communicating yourself by yourself. In your visits, at times, it seems you are about to give me the jewel of possessing you; but when I become aware of this I find myself without possessing it, for you hide this jewel as if you had been joking. Now wholly surrender yourself by giving yourself entirely to all of me, so my entire soul may have complete possession of you. (SC 6.6)

In effect, the *perpetual* wound of love is the unrelieved dissatisfaction within a soul that is in love with God. No experience of peace, tranquility, or satisfaction at any time alleviates for very long the chronic dissatisfaction of the soul in not possessing a greater closeness to the Beloved. This condition is not necessarily the entire journey of a life. But it has much importance in the transformation of a soul in love. The Gospel itself speaks strongly of the need to lose ourselves in order to gain the greater gift of a new life with our Lord. The interplay between the enjoyment of God's presence and the suffering at his seeming absence is a primary means by which God allows a soul to lose more of self for him. In this arena of spiritual testing, the contest is fought for the sake of love itself. In *The Spiritual Canticle*, Saint John of the Cross writes that two things wound the soul directly in profound ways: the uncontrollable feeling at times of the absence or withdrawal of God; secondly, even more, the departures of God after his visits of consolation, or as Saint John of the Cross expresses it, "the swiftness with which he shows and then hides himself" (SC 1.15). As he writes, there is divine purposefulness in these shifts of experience for the soul: "He usually visits devout souls in order to gladden and liven them, and then leaves in order to try, humble, and teach them. Because of his visits his withdrawals are felt with keener sorrow" (SC 1.15).

Saint John of the Cross expands on the theme. He stresses that the heart is "inflamed" in love by these wounds inflicted by the departure of God: "They so inflame the will in its affection that it burns up in this flame and fire of love" (SC 1.17). Simply eliciting a yearning for God is not the sole effect of this and should not be identified with an emotional desire for God. Rather, the primary effect is that the soul begins to *lose* itself in its suffering. It becomes lost to its own need, precisely in becoming consumed with a love for God. A profound transformation of soul is beginning to take place: "So intense is this burning that the soul is seemingly consumed in that flame, and the fire makes it go out of itself, wholly renews it, and changes its manner of being, as in the case of the phoenix that burns itself in the fire and rises anew from the ashes" (SC 1.17). The appetites and affections of the soul are taken up with an intense longing for God, and nothing matters to a soul so much as God himself. It wants nothing but to love; the result, predictably, may be great generosity in actions and sacrifice. "The soul, through love, is brought to nothing, knowing nothing save love" (SC 1.18).

Indeed, a grave suffering in love may thereby ensue—"a kind of immense torment and yearning to see God" (SC 1.18). The lack of any release from this pain endured for the sake of love is a dramatic spiritual truth. It speaks quite directly of God himself in his manner of loving a soul that is much loved: "So extreme is this torment that love seems to be unbearably rigorous with the soul, not because it has wounded her—she rather considers these wounds to be favorable to her health—but because it left her thus suffering with love, and did not slay her for the sake of her seeing and being united with him in the life of perfect love" (SC 1.18). But in time the fruitfulness of this love manifests itself in a particular way. The wound of love has the effect over time of making the soul "go out of herself and enter into God" (SC 1.19), which does not mean taking possession of God. Rather, entering into God causes a profound desire to please God in any way possible, which is bound to overflow into sacrifice and charity outside prayer. A spiritual departure from itself, a forgetting of self, takes place in the soul. This departure from self is a release that now animates the soul's exclusive pursuit of God. Saint John of the Cross writes in this regard that there "are two ways of going after God":

> One consists of a departure from all things, effected through an abhorrence and contempt for them; the other of going out from oneself through self-forgetfulness, which is achieved by the love of God. When the love of God really touches the soul, as we are saying, it so raises her up that it not only impels her to go out from self in this forgetfulness, but even draws her away from her natural supports, manners, and inclinations, thus inducing her to call after God. (SC 1.20)

In reading this passage, we can recall the opening stanza of "The Spiritual Canticle" and in particular its last line: "I went out calling you, but you were gone." The departure of the Beloved into hiding does not simply constrain the soul and pull it down into desolation. It also prompts a soul to go out of itself in a pursuit of him. In that sense, the inability of the soul to encounter the Beloved in prayer is not a kind of conclusive state, much less a terminal condition. It is true that the experience of the Beloved's presence, followed quickly by his disappearance, can leave the soul oftentimes in a no-man's-land of interior uncertainty. Full of inflamed longing for God, and yet feeling an emptiness within itself, a soul seems to have nothing by which to support itself. It knows only a familiar return to emptiness. But this is not all that is occurring, for love is provoked to greater intensity in the time of the Lord's seeming absence. In the following passage, we can observe a painful state of soul and view it as unfortunate; or we can perceive the great movement of love carving itself into the depth of the soul, and indeed we can wish for the same grace in our lives: "'But you were gone.' This is like saying: At the time I desired to hold fast to your presence I could not find you, and the detachment from one without attachment to the other left me suspended in air and suffering, without any support from you or from myself" (SC 1.21).

What is being described is an interior suffering of soul, certainly. It is the suffering inseparable from a great love for God in the prayer of contemplation. The soul has offered itself fully, surrendered itself, and yet experiences this emptiness within prayer. In surrendering to God, every soul likely expects in return an intimacy with God. But as part of the contemplative path, it must bear this unrelieved emptiness and the wound of dissatisfied love. And God seems to leave it in this state, "without any support from you or from myself" (SC 1.21). As a result, a soul can only feel somewhat lost, not knowing where to turn, without any option but to surrender anew. The act of surrender stretches a soul in its love for God to a greater love. This is the reality of a deepening love for God in contemplation. After surrendering itself, a waiting for God commences for a soul, a need for a perseverance in love that may continue for a long time. The desire for more intense love may not be granted despite the soul's pure offering. For who can know how God chooses to act with particular souls? This waiting is a wound of love, causing suffering in the undercurrents of desire within the soul, as Saint John of the Cross writes: "The loving soul lives in constant suffering at the absence of her Beloved, for she is already surrendered to him and hopes for the reward of that surrender: the surrender of the Beloved to her. Yet he does not do so. Now lost to herself and to all things for the sake of her loved one, she has gained nothing from her loss, since she does not possess him" (SC 1.21).

Later in *The Spiritual Canticle*, Saint John of the Cross offers additional insight into the suffering of the soul in its longing for God. The experience of being wounded for love of God in contemplation intensifies as the soul draws nearer to God. The sense of emptiness increases to the extent that a soul is more fully surrendered to God. The close proximity of God, who assuredly is pleased with such a soul, only heightens the inner heaviness of a soul still not in possession of the love for God for which it longs. There is need to confront a stark spiritual principle here. As a soul is more united to God, it ordinarily does not enjoy more consoling contact with God. Rather, it is likely to experience, at least intermittently, its own vacancy and may often suffer a heavy and purifying interior darkness. The paradox of more intense darkness occurring when God is closer to the soul can be a strange truth for us when first encountered. The nearer the soul approaches to the light of God, the thicker the interior darkness it may experience within itself. As long as God does not communicate in some clear fashion but, rather, leaves a soul without any feeling of him, a strain and tension inhabit

the experience of love. And yet all this interior purification
is marked by an apparent purpose in God's design to refine
a soul and prepare it for further gifts of grace. The following passage from *The Spiritual Canticle* does not necessarily
indicate in its context the spiritual drama of the "dark night
of the soul", which we will speak of in the next chapter.
The words express an experiential truth that accompanies
contemplation even from its beginnings in grace, although
much less so early on. Intensity of love brings the soul near
to God, yet it also crushes the soul to some degree under a
cloud of dark incomprehension. The suffering in contemplation is a pattern that can be expected simply because the
soul is intensely fixated in its love for God.

> The reason the soul suffers so intensely for God at this
> time is that she is drawing nearer to him; so she has greater
> experience within herself of the void of God, of very
> heavy darkness, and of spiritual fire that dries up and purges
> her so that thus purified she may be united with him. Inas-
> much as God does not communicate some supernatural
> ray of light from himself, he is intolerable darkness to her
> when he is spiritually near her, for the excess of supernat-
> ural light darkens the natural light. (SC 13.1)

Immediately after hearing the words of this passage, the
stanza quoted earlier from "The Spiritual Canticle", the
ninth, in which the wounding of the human heart is likened
to the heart seized and stolen, is worth some further attention. The soul that loves with intensity loses possession of
its own heart, an experience familiar to all great love. But
when the love in question is for God himself, the implications are immense. God tends to allow great suffering in
the depth of the soul, a "very heavy darkness", becoming
himself "intolerable darkness to her when he is spiritually
near her", as we just read. The drama of spiritual intensity

in contemplation carries weighty implications. Contemplation is not for a soul lacking in courage. The martyrdom of love is a real prospect in the experience of a love for God himself. Let us hear again the evocative ninth stanza, followed by Saint John of the Cross' own insights on the wounding of the soul by love:

> Why, since you wounded
> this heart, don't you heal it?
> And why, since you stole it from me,
> do you leave it so,
> and fail to carry off what you have stolen? (stanza 9)

Somewhat like the first stanza read at the beginning of the book, these words of complaint lay bare the pain of a loving soul impatient for the Beloved to show some gesture of his love, namely, by manifesting his presence. Instead, there is only the affliction of an unhealed wound and his continued absence. As Saint John of the Cross comments at this point, however, the soul feels as though robbed of its essence inasmuch as love is its deepest truth. Now that its love has been given away entirely, it is empty and bereft. The teaching on love here is striking in the context of contemplation. The nature of love is that it ''lives in'' whatsoever is loved; in this case, in the person of the Beloved. But the Beloved has departed, it seems, to some faraway place of immeasurable distance. As a result, the soul suffers a terrible emptiness in which it possesses not even itself. It can claim no security, no substance, even of its own truth. The soul's truth is in its love for the Beloved, but he has disappeared and forsaken it, stripping it. The pain leaves it with no recourse but to go out seeking for the Beloved. The dissatisfaction and pain that takes it out in search of the Beloved is nonetheless a salutary state. The soul truly in love with God goes out from itself in hunger, forgetting itself, and searches for ways to please God. It longs for him, and nothing else satisfies it but to find ways to show love for him, even though he seems absent. In one sense, it is an empty vessel of painful craving; in another sense, it is a soul of expectation. It becomes, in the best sense of the term, a "driven" soul in its seeking, intensely desirous of God, steady in its determination to remain on this path of a great love for the Beloved. Saint John of the Cross writes beautiful words in his commentary on this stanza about what being in love with God does to a soul:

> Lovers are said to have their heart stolen or seized by the object of their love, for the heart will go out from self and become fixed on the loved object. Thus their heart or love is not for themselves but for what they love. Accordingly, the soul can know clearly whether or not she loves God purely. If she loves him her heart or love will not be set on herself or her own satisfaction and gain, but on pleasing God and giving him honor and glory. In the measure she loves herself, that much less she loves God. (SC 9.5)

These comments on the effect of being in love with God deepen in their intensity in the treatment of Saint John of the Cross. The seizure of the heart stolen by God may become an unmanageable state of pain. The heart in love with God no longer has peace, precisely because of its love. It is restless in its craving for the Beloved, anxious for him, desirous for any sign of his presence. The soul cannot live without returning continually to the thought of the Beloved. It lives with a sense of perpetual incompletion and in frustration of its deeper desire. A kind of spiritual sickness seems to overtake it, but of course this is not an unhealthy condition. For the frustration plunges a soul into a greater desire for self-giving and generosity. In this section of his commentary on the ninth stanza, Saint John of the Cross writes a moving paragraph on the heart stolen by God in love. The last lines are especially memorable:

> Whether the heart has been truly stolen by God will be evident in either of these two signs: if it has longings for God or if it finds no satisfaction in anything but him, as the soul demonstrates here. The reason is that the heart cannot have peace and rest while not possessing, and when it is truly attracted it no longer has possession of self or of any other thing. And if it does not possess completely what it loves, it cannot help being weary, in proportion to its loss, until it possesses the loved object and is satisfied. Until this possession the soul is like an empty vessel waiting to be filled, or a hungry person craving for food, or someone sick moaning for health, or like one suspended in the air with nothing to lean on. Such is the truly loving heart. (SC 9.6)

What are we to make of such a description of love? Where does all this lead? And what is he teaching us about love in prayer? For Saint John of the Cross, an essential truth of contemplation, even in the experience of darkness and interior trial, is the manner of God's communications of love. In the soul's undercurrents, in the deeper unperceived yearnings within the soul, God speaks his love. The experience of a longing to love, piercing the deeper "layers" of the soul, is a better indication of an encounter with God than any sense of direct experience. Desires, longings, the wounds of an impatient love for God—these are the means by which God informs the soul that he is near. The experience of a longing for God in dissatisfaction may seem to contradict the idea of his close presence. But this is incorrect. The soul has to learn the ways of God, so contradictory in some ways to human love, and to choose to accept them, not becoming discouraged or downtrodden by the difficult path of love. The short statement that follows can bring benefits both to our efforts outside prayer and to the contemplative quest to remain fixed on the Beloved in prayer despite difficulty. "She loves him more than all things when nothing intimidates her in doing and suffering for love of him whatever is for his service" (SC 2.5).

The great spiritual task, in a sense, is stated here; namely, not to be intimidated by the essential demand to please God in any way available. A pure love for God, if that is what we really seek, requires a deep persevering faith over a long lifetime. Every touch to the Heart of God, even the smallest, moves him despite what can seem as an action to be a mere nothing in magnitude. The realization that love often consists in small things done with great love has to be embraced for any significant love of God in this life. The most intimidating thought may not be that we must do extravagant or exorbitant things for God; rather, that we must accept being reduced to doing apparently insignificant acts that hide a deep love, because these, too, penetrate the Heart of God. It is difficult for many people to think that a great love consists in faithfulness to small details in a day. And yet a loving service of God must include small acts of heroism as much as the acts more publicly acclaimed. When the love is great, nothing is small. But we can be intimidated by the erroneous thought that these are worthless things that occupy our small lives, which have never advanced to important feats of spiritual greatness. The contrary is perhaps true in the eyes of God. The embrace of the small act with profound love is a way to overcome the heaviness of dissatisfaction in not arriving at possession of a consoling love for God. In *The Sayings of Light and Love*, Saint John of the Cross includes a splendid statement on the value of the hiddenness of small actions:

God is more pleased by one work, however small, done secretly, without desire that it be known, than a thousand done with the desire that people know of them. Those who work for God with purest love not only care nothing about whether others see their works, but do not even seek that God himself know of them. Such persons would not cease to render God the same services, with the same joy and purity of love, even if God were never to know of these. (SLL 20)

In his commentary on stanza 35 of "The Spiritual Canticle", Saint John of the Cross offers yet another keen insight into what happens as the soul's interior desire to love is taken up exclusively with God. The dissatisfaction with everything less than God places the soul more and more in a kind of enclosed interior solitude. The soul is alone in its desire, with no other companionship, because nothing in this world really attracts its greater desire. Nothing but God offers a satisfaction worth pursuing with any so-called passion of soul. The solitude of the soul of which Saint John of the Cross speaks is not an absence of human companionship. It is an interior state of being separated from any satisfaction other than for God. To be without a desire for anything but God is to be alone with one's desire for God. Nothing else enters that solitude within the soul. In the view of Saint John of the Cross, this dissatisfaction that the soul feels in not possessing God becomes in turn immensely attractive to God, a wonderful thought indeed: "Insofar as she desired to live apart from all created things, in solitude for her Beloved's sake, he himself was enamored of her because of this solitude and took care of her by accepting her in his arms, feeding her in himself with every blessing, and guiding her to the high things of God" (SC 35.2).

It is a striking notion that God finds the withdrawal of the soul from comfort and satisfaction in anything other than himself as a solitude in the soul that he then desires to fill with his own companionship. It is beneficial to linger on that thought. The satisfactions we seek in the things of this world become, as it were, companions of the soul while they remain for us desirable. But the soul that empties itself of desires for comfort or human companionship longs more intensely for the divine companionship that still awaits it. "There is no companionship that affords consolation to the soul that longs for God; indeed, until she finds him, everything causes greater solitude" (SC 35.3). The solitude here is the emptiness of the interior soul without the comforts of any satisfaction, including possibly the companionship of close human relations. Indeed, this does occur in some lives. God then finds in the soul a solitude open and alone for himself when it is in this state of withdrawal from all things and all favors. "He is taken with love for her and wants to be the only one to grant her these favors" (SC 35.6). In a beautiful thought, Saint John of the Cross writes that God himself is then wounded with love for the soul. As God sees the soul wounded in love for him in its solitude, he in turn is wounded with love for the soul. It is a remarkable spiritual thought. The emptiness of desire in the soul for everything other than God draws an immense desire of God wounded in love for that soul. The wound of love present in God will seek then to relieve the wound of love in the solitary soul. This is a deep contemplative insight. The following is a striking passage of Saint John of the Cross commenting on two lines from stanza 35 of "The Spiritual Canticle", reflecting what has just been said of these mutual wounds within the Heart of God and in the heart of a soul:

> [he alone, who also bears]
> in solitude the wound of love.

That is, he is wounded in love for the bride. The Bride-groom bears a great love for the solitude of the soul; but he is wounded much more by her love since, being wounded with love for him, she desired to live alone in respect to all things. And he does not wish to leave her alone, but wounded by the solitude she embraces for his sake, and observing that she is dissatisfied with any other thing, he alone guides her, drawing her to and absorbing her in himself. Had he not found her in spiritual solitude, he would not have wrought this in her. (SC 35.7)

We may find these kinds of passages far beyond our strength, too elevated for our present state of spiritual aspiration. But who can say where God will lead a soul in the course of a life in which prayer has been a consistent need? The desire of a soul to love God and consider everything else of little or no importance compared to him perhaps does not occur until a late stage in many lives. Yet this desire leads to an increasing loss of self-interested pursuit, as the Gospel demands. Love for God has always the effect of detaching the soul from excessive interest in itself and from the passing things that do not remain after this life. The soul, for instance, no longer seeks to shine outwardly for others or to draw the attention of interested eyes. Only God matters; vain pursuit seems frivolous and without value. There is no gain for the soul but in drawing closer to him and in pleasing him. Saint John of the Cross describes this exclusive love for God in the following words that can serve as almost a testimony of contemplative endeavor. But this is also the program for a saintly life: "The one who walks in the love of God seeks neither gain nor reward, but seeks only to lose with the will all things and self for God; and this loss the lover judges to be a gain" (SC 29.11).

The twenty-ninth stanza of the poem presents yet another

beautiful image, especially after hearing these last words, in this case of the soul becoming lost to itself when nothing of worldly endeavor and satisfaction is sufficient to uphold a life:

> If, then, I am no longer
> seen or found on the common,
> you will say that I am lost;
> that, stricken by love,
> I lost myself, and was found. (stanza 29)

Saint John of the Cross, in commenting on this stanza, affirms that the works of the soul become increasingly hidden works when a strong love animates it with intense desire for pleasing God. Dissatisfaction of soul leads in time to a consuming desire to give only to God and to perform all its works for his eyes alone. No care or concern is for the sight of others seeing anything. This in turn leads to the soul becoming "lost". It disappears into its own concealment, withdrawn from the eyes of others. Nothing is now on display; nothing is pursued for its own satisfaction. Everything is only for the attention of the Beloved, who alone sees. Saint John of the Cross affirms, pointedly, that few people can be found who execute their works with "perfection and nakedness of spirit"; most people "think about what others will say or how their work will appear" (SC 29.8). These former souls are lost to themselves, while others are not. In the latter case, the desire of souls for satisfaction in themselves and in the good works they perform for God becomes a hindrance to their pursuit of God and an obstacle to contemplation. This purity of seeking in a concealed manner only to please God is an immense challenge. The hidden soul finds in its concealment the secret path to the realization of God's eyes resting upon the soul more continually. Lost to themselves, they are found in him. This pure intention of the soul, not deviating from the path of naked emptiness, is essential for love. The passage that follows conveys the beauty of this endeavor in a striking way:

> In order not to fail God she failed all that is not God, that is, herself and all other creatures, losing all these for love of him. Anyone truly in love will let all other things go in order to come closer to the loved one. On this account the soul affirms here that she lost herself. She achieved this in two ways: she became lost to herself by paying no attention to herself in anything, by concentrating on her Beloved and surrendering herself to him freely and disinterestedly, with no desire to gain anything for herself; second, she became lost to all creatures, paying no heed to all her own affairs but only to those of her Beloved. And this is to lose herself purposely, which is to desire to be found. (SC 29.10)

A last thought is perhaps important on the nature of dissatisfaction in the soul's relations with God. This has to do with the wound of incomprehension that a soul experiences in its love for God. As Saint John of the Cross writes on the soul seeking to know God: "All the knowledge of God possible in this life, however extensive it may be, is inadequate, for it is only partial knowledge and very remote" (SC 6.5). In the experience of a soul that loves much, there is never a knowledge of God in prayer that seems enough, never a satiation that arrives, even temporarily, at an adequate awareness of God. Some degree of a frustration of awareness is the customary completion of prayer, even after a soul's love has grown much. Love is simply never satisfied when the love is for the divine Beloved, as we have encountered before. Now Saint John of the Cross will describe this experience of unsatisfied love as a kind of dying for the soul in this life. A death by love takes place while the soul still lives this life. The death is the slow, deepening encounter with the immense incomprehension our soul must accept in its inadequate knowledge of God. Always there is more to meet in God. Prayer itself is the arena for this struggle with an uncomprehending experience of love: "She lives by dying until love, in killing her, makes her live the life of love, transforming her in love. This death of love is caused in the soul by means of a touch of supreme knowledge of the divinity, the "I-don't-know-what" that she says lies behind their stammering. . . . And she dies the more in realizing that she does not wholly die of love" (SC 7.4).

This description is not meant simply to reaffirm an apophatic aspect in the pursuit of God in prayer. A wounding of the soul takes place with every glimpse it is given into the immense reality of divine love. The incapacity of the soul to arrive at God, and the dying this imposes on the soul, intensify the wounds of love. And yet this experience takes a soul ever more into the depth of contemplation. Saint John of the Cross goes on to comment about the cryptic phrase just used: "There is a certain 'I-don't-know-what' that one feels is yet to be said, something unknown still to be spoken, and a sublime trace of God as yet uninvestigated but revealed to the soul, a lofty understanding of God that cannot be put into words. Hence she calls this something 'I-don't-know what.' If what I understand wounds me with love, what I do not understand completely, yet have sublime experience of, is death to me" (SC 7.9).

We can affirm, from this passage, that in contemplation the apophatic dimension of God's infinitude of love, always beyond the soul's grasp, is really a wound to the soul's love more than it is a frustration to the intellect. The soul wants intimacy with God and encounters his love as a vast immensity stretching far beyond the reach of its most intense desire. A soul wants his presence, and yet it finds that the presence of God is overwhelming in its inaccessibility. The soul would like to see, but is stricken with blindness and suffers this darkness. It would like to feel God close and to touch him if that were possible, and it knows too well this impossibility. Saint John of the Cross affirms that on a rare occasion the soul may be given an experience and a favor from God that makes it "understand clearly that everything remains to be understood" (SC 7.9). The affirmation is actually of a starkly dissatisfying realization. Yet that understanding is precisely a favor beyond all others. "This understanding and experience that the divinity is so immense as to surpass complete understanding is indeed a sublime knowledge" (SC 7.9). The soul becomes aware of the absolute truth of God's infinite being beyond the reach of its meager understanding. In effect, the soul enters by a kind of blind, staggering step into the clearest truth. This favor, despite its dissatisfaction, alters all subsequent prayer for a soul. God becomes utterly personal in his near presence and yet stretches into the vast infinite reaches of the heavens beyond any enclosure of human love. The following words convey eloquently the experiential nature of this "apophatic" aspect of contemplation:

> One of the outstanding favors God grants briefly in this life is an understanding and experience of himself so lucid and lofty that one comes to know clearly that God cannot be completely understood or experienced. This understanding is somewhat like that of the Blessed in heaven: Those who understand God more understand more distinctly the infinitude that remains to be understood; those who see less of him do not realize so clearly what remains to be seen. (SC 7.9)

Our Lord himself and our knowledge of him are described continually by Saint John of the Cross in such terms. We never reach the end point in our knowledge of Jesus. The Gospel offers clear historical testimony of his words and actions. Yet the truth of who he is as our God extends beyond our possession and grasp for a lifetime. The quest is endless because love never arrives at a conclusive knowledge of the Beloved who died on a cross in Jerusalem for us. The only entryway into this greater knowing is to be wounded with love for him. We may have to suffer a perpetual wounding of the soul to open a door repeatedly into the unlimited treasures concealed in the Heart of our Lord. The image used by Saint John of the Cross in the following passage captures both the incomplete encounter felt by a soul and the wounding of the soul that thereby ensues. It can serve as a fitting conclusion to this chapter. As he writes, most impressively:

> There is much to fathom in Christ, for he is like an abundant mine with many recesses of treasures, so that however deep individuals may go they never reach the end or bottom, but rather in every recess find new veins with new riches everywhere. On this account St. Paul said of Christ: *In Christ dwell hidden all treasures and wisdom* [Col. 2:3]. The soul cannot enter these caverns or reach these treasures if, as we said, she does not first pass over to the divine wisdom through the straits of exterior and interior suffering. For one cannot reach in this life what is attainable of these mysteries of Christ without having suffered much and without having received numerous intellectual and sensible favors from God, and without having undergone much spiritual activity; for all these favors are inferior to the wisdom of the mysteries of Christ in that they serve as preparations for coming to this wisdom. (SC 37.4)

15

SUFFERING FOR LOVE
OF A CRUCIFIED BELOVED

Certainly an atmosphere of great challenge pervades the writings of Saint John of the Cross. It is possible that the recurring accent on purification, interior trials, dissatisfaction in prayer, or the wounds of love in certain sections of Saint John of the Cross' writings has a jarring or intimidating effect. His attention to painful experiences may seem to propose a spirituality of endless burdens and impossible endurance. From our perspective, this focus may be too excessive. It is not that we lack struggles and tribulations. Who does not experience them? Yet our own thought may be that matters of trial and difficulty should be kept to a minimum and brought to a conclusion as quickly as possible. For many people, even of strong religious conviction, the common experiences of fatigue and pain compete with the pursuit of pleasures and comforts. We often find a way to compensate ourselves with worldly enjoyment if for a time we have faced trial and difficulty. Perhaps we do not ponder the Gospel deeply enough. Suffering for the sake of a profound love of God can be a neglected notion in our understanding of love, though clearly not for Saint John of the Cross: "Let Christ crucified be enough for you, and with him suffer and take your rest, and hence annihilate yourself in all inward and outward things" (SLL 92). That kind of advice is not commonly heard at any time in the Church.

For Saint John of the Cross, writing to those who seek
sanctity, a need to suffer for love cannot be evaded on
the path to union with God. Indeed, he will insist that
a threshold of understanding must be crossed in perceiv-
ing the blessed effects of bearing suffering. Exterior trials
strengthen the soul, and interior struggles grant to the inner
spirit a depth otherwise unattainable. A refinement of the
soul occurs as a soul exercises fortitude in trials. Detachment
begins to become a kind of "second nature" within a soul.
This detachment from self always accompanies greater love,
as another aphorism proclaims: "Love consists not in feeling
great things but in having great detachment and in suffering
for the Beloved" (SLL 115). In other words, we suffer well,
deepening our love, when a detachment from self allows
us to turn our attention more fully toward Another. The
opposite, by contrast, is clearly debilitating. Human repugnance and fear toward suffering, especially in the thought
of suffering in some unknown manner, is an obstacle to
advancing spiritually. It is one of the essential favors God
bestows in grace when a soul begins to offer its suffering
courageously for others and accepts it without resentment.
A soul soon perceives a strength quite new and unprece-
dented in its experience. There are two striking passages
from *The Living Flame of Love* on suffering that can enhance
our awareness of God's presence in trial. Let us recall that
this treatise was written, not for cloistered Carmelites, but
for a Spanish laywoman. The first passage speaks in effect of
God's hands being tied when he sees a soul unable to bear
suffering for love of him, which may involve the refusal to
embrace even smaller voluntary mortifications. We cannot
advance in prayer unless we are ready to forgo the pursuit
of satisfaction in prayer, as we have seen. But this detach-

ment from self requires also an ability to bear deprivation and hardship outside the time of prayer.

> And here it ought to be pointed out why so few reach this high state of perfect union with God. It should be known that the reason is not that God wishes only a few of these spirits to be so elevated; he would rather want all to be perfect, but he finds few vessels that will endure so lofty and sublime a work. Since he tries them in little things and finds them so weak that they immediately flee from work, unwilling to be subject to the least discomfort and mortification, it follows that not finding them strong and faithful in that little [Mt. 25:21, 23], in which he favored them by beginning to hew and polish them, he realizes that they will be much less strong in these greater trials. As a result he proceeds no further in purifying them and raising them from the dust of the earth through the toil of mortification. They are in need of greater constancy and fortitude than they showed. (LF 2.27)

The second passage, which was memorized by another great Carmelite, Saint Thérèse of Lisieux (1873–1897), affirms the profound benefits that accrue to the soul that does not resist the path of suffering for love of the Beloved. The realization that all serious love demands a companionship with the Beloved in his suffering is an essential insight. But it must also become an actual experience within our interior soul that carries us across a threshold in our relations with God. We hear again in the following passage the need to relinquish the desire for consolation in love. The true path of love is one of self-emptying and humble interior poverty. This is a costly venture in contemplation. Only the turn away from ourselves opens us to the gift God wants to give of himself. The realization that blessings, abundant and untold blessings, lie ahead if a soul is willing to let go and surrender itself to all that God asks is an inestimable grace. The sense of crossing a threshold and forever changing is at times strong in passages of Saint John of the Cross, as in this one, a paragraph dear to Saint Thérèse of Lisieux:

> O souls who in spiritual matters desire to walk in security and consolation! If you but knew how much it behooves you to suffer in order to reach this security and consolation, and how without suffering you cannot attain to your desire but rather turn back, in no way would you look for comfort either from God or from creatures. You would instead carry the cross and, placed on it, desire to drink the pure gall and vinegar. You would consider it good fortune that, dying to this world and to yourselves, you would live to God in the delights of the spirit, and patiently and faithfully suffering exterior trials, which are small, you would merit that God fix his eyes on you and purge you more profoundly through deeper spiritual trials in order to give you more interior blessings. (LF 2.28)

If we turn even somewhat randomly to passages of Saint John of the Cross, we find repeated insistence on this importance of suffering for love of the Beloved. The mature desire to suffer for Jesus Christ introduces a soul into the deeper mystery of divine love. Yet how difficult such a demand is, and how much courage it may require. No concern for an easier human acceptance among our confreres and friends, no negligence of actions asked by God, no objection protesting our incapacity for demands coming from God: in short, nothing can be permitted to halt our pursuit of God. Not simply love, but the *intensity* of love must compel the quest for greater love: "Since the desire in which she seeks him is authentic and her love intense, she does not want to leave any possible means untried" (SC 3.1).

We hear in this statement a truth perhaps not acknowledged sufficiently. The contemplative life is anything but passive; it demands an *active* generosity by means of which the soul deliberately stretches itself in self-giving, even beyond its human strength, so that grace may uphold it. Works must abound outside prayer if prayer is to be permeated with love. As we have seen, a *blessed* state of dissatisfaction pervades a soul that loves much. The soul that loves much becomes self-forgetful and generous in action, and yet it finds these actions still painfully insufficient to express the true depth of its love. These brief words from *The Spiritual Canticle* convey the concealed truth of holiness: "The soul that truly loves God is not slothful in doing all she can to find the Son of God, her Beloved. Even after she has done everything, she is dissatisfied and thinks she has done nothing" (SC 3.1).

The motivation of every great love for God is contained in this passage. We have to do what is possible by our efforts in action, and with an implicit motive: We want our Lord to know that he is much loved. This is not a pious remark or exhortation. The soul's desire for our Lord to know how much he is loved, at least by our own soul, can become a compelling drive affecting all else in a life. Perhaps it is this passion for God that is missing in many lives committed to religious principles and spiritual practices. It is the *passion* for God in a soul that accounts for a desire for more sacrificial self-giving. To live for souls, and to mortify one's own life for the sake of others, is essential to sanctity: "A soul must through its own efforts do everything possible" (SC 3.2)— that is, everything possible for the good of souls. On the other hand, it is perhaps common for religious people who may claim to have given all to God to maintain a cautious generosity, not stretching their capacity for self-giving. The secret of saintly lives is altogether different. In these lives, sacrifice and charity are united in a partnership and even in-distinguishable. The self-emptying of the one is inseparable from the self-giving of the other. Saint John of the Cross, in one of his most sharply worded passages, reproaches those who are unwilling to pay this greater price for the sake of love:

> Many desire that God cost them no more than words, and even these they say badly. They desire to do for him scarcely anything that might cost them something. Some would not even rise from a place of their liking if they were not to receive thereby some delight from God in their mouth and heart. They will not even take one step to mortify themselves and lose some of their satisfactions, comforts, and useless desires. Yet, unless they go in search for God, they will not find him, no matter how much they cry out for him. (SC 3.2)

The costly search for God, in and out of prayer, is a nar-row path, as we hear strongly in these words. But let us recall from the second chapter the image of the caverns of the soul and "*the vast emptiness of their deep capacity*" (LF 3.18; emphasis added). In the grace of contemplation, the suffer-ing of love for the Beloved descends into these vast depths of the soul. A limitless hunger for God drives the passionate search for God in prayer. There is an endless depth in the soul that can be given over to God. This is the reality be-hind the sharp words that we just heard from Saint John of the Cross. A hunger without limits must rise up from the "vast emptiness" of a soul's inward recesses. But for that to occur, a costly purging of desire must take place in our soul, so that God alone is sought with deepest longing. It is the limitless, vast immensity within the soul that demands the need for self-emptying and that accounts for the suffering of the soul in contemplation. The suffering of love intensifies inasmuch as the hunger to love finds little or no satiation. We cannot live without this hunger to possess God in love if we are to walk the path of contemplation. The hunger, if it is to sustain our prayer, is like a muted cry of the soul, unanswered if not unheard, a cry for God to lift the barrier of his hiddenness within the interior caverns of the soul. If at times a more tangible encounter with God takes place in prayer, it is always inadequate for a soul longing with a boundless hunger for our beloved Lord to show himself more fully. Yet Saint John of the Cross assures us that this frustration *is* a sign of progress in contemplation and increases the soul's love. The soul gains in love and intensifies its love precisely by suffering for love. In *The Spiritual Canticle*, Saint John of the Cross writes of the mysterious process at work in contemplative love:

> It is noteworthy that any soul with authentic love cannot be satisfied until it really possesses God. Everything else not only fails to satisfy it but, as we said, increases the hunger and appetite to see him as he is. Every glimpse of the Beloved received through knowledge or feeling or any other communication (which is like a messenger bringing the soul news of who he is) further increases and awakens her appetite, like the crumbs given to someone who is famished. Finding it difficult to be delayed by so little, she pleads: "Now wholly surrender yourself!" (SC 6.4)

With no slaking of hunger, love nonetheless continues to stir the unseen depths of the soul in a steady discomfort. The insufficiency of what is experienced in prayer may characterize long periods of prayer. The trying aspect of prayer is due precisely to the vast depth of the soul as a receptacle for God himself. "Boundless goods" are the never reached "end point" of this reception. For the soul's capacity to be filled by God is likewise endless—"*anything less than the infinite fails*

to fill them" (LF 3.18; emphasis added) The one thing needful, namely, greater love, may become the one thing experienced as most painful. The reason is the incapacity of the
soul's love to extend and stretch into these limitless depths.
"Love is incurable," writes Saint John of the Cross, "except
by things in accord with love" (SC 11.11). The mystery of
contemplative relations with God is in this statement if we
understand it in the light of the vast capacity of the soul to
love. For any soul in love with God, the wound of love is
incurable unless it can arrive at a love for the Beloved that
fills the inner regions of soul.

   But does that ever take place? It is not that the soul desires
primarily an *experience* of love. Rather, it learns by means of
the depths within it to suffer in a hunger of love for the
Beloved. This contemplative demand to love for the sake of
love itself, not for a subjective experience of love, becomes
the compelling inner drive in contemplation and in holiness.
The soul with intense hunger is led by grace continually to
want to love more. And yet it may find itself almost as though
paralyzed at times in an incapacity to love more, trapped in
what it may consider its own meager desire. Saint John of
the Cross writes that, despite the suffering, this can be a
fortuitous juncture on the contemplative path. When the
soul comes to acknowledge its own lack of love, it arrives
at a graced insight. It is now ready for greater love, which
often comes after the painful sense of the insufficiency of its
love. The awareness of lacking love is a recognition that can
inflame the urgent need for a healing by love itself. As Saint
John of the Cross describes this understanding of the soul:
"Those who feel in themselves the sickness of love, a lack
of love, show they have some love, because they are aware
of what they lack through what they have. Those who do
not feel this sickness show they either have no love or are
perfect in love" (SC 11.14).

The demand to seek an endless journey in love is, in a sense, the contemplative code of conduct. We heard earlier, in the last chapter, that "God makes use of nothing other than love" (SC 28.1). It is the kind of statement that can provoke a regular self-examination, especially in lives too busy to give more time to God in prayer. And what might the thought of God using "nothing other than love" imply? It is precisely a costly love that God makes use of in contemplative lives for the sake of other souls. The comfort of a love warming our heart in peace is not the gift we should expect from the crucified Lord Jesus Christ. He may prefer instead that our lives become united to his own Passion in order to bear greater fruitfulness for other souls. The great effort of contemplative love is to persevere in a love that draws us closer over time to the crucifixion of Jesus Christ. "Bear fortitude in your heart against all things that move you to that which is not God, and *be a friend of the Passion of Christ*" (SLL 95; emphasis added). No routine recommendation is urged in such words. The endurance necessary for a great love of Jesus Christ crucified is without limit. The measure of completion for such love can be found only in the Passion of Jesus at Calvary. All the while we ought to keep our eyes on the prize of love, which is to give ourselves away to the Beloved nailed to a cross in Jerusalem. This driving desire—to show him how much he is loved—is for a lifetime that stretches always before our lives. The centrality of love in the contemplative quest is certainly on display in these words:

> For the wages of love are nothing else neither can the soul desire anything else than more love, until perfect love is reached. Love is paid only with love itself. . . . The soul that loves does not await the end of her labor but the end of her work. Her work is to love, and of this work, which is love, she awaits the end, which is the perfection and

completeness of it. Until this work is accomplished . . .
she considers her days and months empty and counts her
nights as long and wearisome. (SC 9.7)

It can be a promise arousing a profound desire in us that
one day we may take hold of a great love, as the first words of
this passage affirm. The suffering of love descending into the
limitless depths of the soul has its reward, if love is tenacious
in its longing and committed in action. "For God repays the
interior and exterior trials very well with divine goods for
the soul and body, so there is not a trial that does not have
a corresponding and considerable reward" (LF 2.31). The
one condition necessary for moving forward in love, especially in trial, is to give all to God: "It is the property of
perfect love to be unwilling to take anything for self, nor
does it attribute anything to self, but all to the beloved" (SC
32.2). We hear in these words a holy secret about the path
of love. Continually, there must be a giving away of self,
a loss and immolation of self, an ultimate offering of self,
because we have come to know that personally, for us, the
Beloved is all that matters. The determination to give ourselves in this manner calls for the heroism of a saintly life.
But who should say that this saintliness is not meant for our
own lives? It is more than just an admirable beauty that is
present in saintly lives. They are the great victors precisely
in losing all for the sake of a love beyond any other love
possible in this life. They pierced the ultimate wisdom of
offering themselves to a love for God and caught hold of
the true purpose of life. There is an unlimited variation of
possible circumstances in these holy lives, but they nonetheless display a certain common quality. It is invoked in this
passage near the end of *The Spiritual Canticle*:

> The power and the tenacity of love is great, for love cap-
> tures and binds God himself. Happy is the loving soul,

since she possesses God for her prisoner, and he is surrendered to all her desires. God is such that those who act
with love and friendship toward him will make him do all
they desire, but if they act otherwise there is no speaking to him or power with him, even though they go to
extremes. Yet by love they bind him with one hair. (SC
32.1)

If we place such remarks in the context of prayer, we
gain a deeper insight into contemplation. The contemplative knowledge of God that comes through love into prayer
is unlike any other notion of knowledge. As we have examined previously, it is an experiential knowledge by love.
This love, we can affirm now, depends on a tenacity of the
inner spirit to plunge ahead into unseen depths of love. A
steadfast quality of love feeds ever greater love. But let us
remember another truth taught by Saint John of the Cross:
The suffering of love necessarily engages our mind. Indeed,
our mind in prayer may need especially to be tenacious.
Contemplation does not entail an expansive stretching of
thought or vision into impressive depths of awareness. On
the contrary, it brings the experience of a poverty in what
we know of God, even by love. A pause on occasion in
prayer is advisable to recall how vast is the capacity of our
soul for God. When our mind is silenced in blindness, this
awareness may be needed. There is always a depth of hidden
action in prayer that can remain unperceived. Great graces
may go unseen in prayer itself, closed to the view of our
blind eyes. In Saint John of the Cross' expression, we enter
with our mind by contemplation into the "thicket" of God's
wisdom. As an image in this context, a "thicket" suggests
the dense impenetrable obscurity in contemplation that we
can traverse only by small steps. We walk at best darkly
in love, in a blindness led by love, drawn by a great sense
of mystery to the Person of the Beloved whom we seek.

Unknown to the soul, with no means of an exact measure, the tenacity of love takes us inwardly over time to the wisdom of knowing the incomprehensible love of God. He is known by love precisely as One who is unknown in his infinite love. We never fully understand, and yet this wisdom of love is granted to those who persevere in love and suffer for love. The truth of wisdom gained in love cannot be conveyed adequately, because it is never concluded: "This thicket of God's wisdom and knowledge is so deep and immense that no matter how much the soul knows, she can always enter it further; it is vast and its riches incomprehensible" (SC 36.10).

This contemplative encounter with the incomprehensibility of God as infinite love—captured in the image of "the thicket of God's wisdom"—is an experience of a suffering that does not disappear because the soul simply accepts it or becomes accustomed to it. The demand of love in facing the mysterious depths of God requires a determination of soul that never at some point relaxes. Our encounter with God, in which we do not understand him even while longing for him in love, is a journey through a dense thicket of mystery. A refusal to halt in seeking God with love, despite his incomprehensibility, assumes great perseverance. It is this tenacious love that perhaps attracts God even more to a soul. If the knowledge by love in contemplation surpasses all other knowledge that we can have of God, it does so precisely by taking us more and more, even in ways unknown to us, into the inner unfathomable depths of the soul. God hides himself in the deeper caverns, as it were. There, in the exercise of our love for him, the knowledge of God given to our soul is not the knowledge of scholarly insight and investigation, but the recurring sense of a mysterious presence in love concealed within our own surrender of heart to

God. It is a knowledge of his presence gained only through a willingness to suffer for love of it. The soul must be ready to plunge humbly into the thicket of its own limitless blindness and lack of comprehension, despite the suffering this may entail. Suffering for love is as such the threshold into a great love for God. A great desire for God must animate this movement of the soul in love.

> Yet the soul wants to enter this thicket and incomprehensibility of judgments and ways because she is dying with the desire to penetrate them deeply. Knowledge of them is an inestimable delight surpassing all understanding. . . . Hence the soul ardently wishes to be engulfed in these judgments and know them from further within. And, in exchange, it will be a singular comfort and happiness for her to enter all the afflictions and trials of this world and everything, however difficult and painful, that might be a means to this knowledge, even the anguish and agony of death, all in order to see herself further within her God. (SC 36.11)

This passage affirms more than simply the value of suffering. The interior longing of the soul is always for the sake of greater entry into a knowledge of God as the Beloved. ''Dying with desire'' invokes a vibrant longing in the soul, but it also implies a kind of martyrdom for the soul in love. The martyrdom of love occurs as the soul's love enters into the boundless depths where love is never satiated fully. Yet nothing will stop the soul from returning again and again to seek there the impenetrable mystery of God. If darkness increases, nonetheless love intensifies as the soul suffers this darkness at deeper limits within the caverns of the soul. The knowledge it embraces is a knowledge that God surpasses in love all that is known. It is a knowing by love that can claim only the blind certitude of a mysterious encounter with God. Yet a soul at a certain point realizes that this is enough, even if it entails a suffering. If it loves in purity, this love is all that is needed on any day of prayer. A great wisdom is received in such a realization. The purest interior suffering is inseparable from the purest experience of profound love. It is striking again to meet words of Saint John of the Cross that can be reread countless times and yet seem never to arrive at their ultimate impact:

> Suffering is the means of her penetrating further, deep into the thicket of the delectable wisdom of God. The purest suffering brings with it the purest and most intimate knowing, and consequently the purest and highest joy, because it is a knowing from further within. . . . Oh! If we could but now fully understand how a soul cannot reach the thicket and wisdom of the riches of God, which are of many kinds, without entering the thicket of many kinds of suffering, finding in this her delight and consolation; and how a soul with an authentic desire for divine wisdom wants suffering first in order to enter this wisdom by the thicket of the cross! (SC 36.12, 13)

The link between suffering for love and an entry into deeper contemplative knowledge is profoundly expressed in this passage. The "purest suffering" becomes the open door into the "purest and most intimate knowing" by love. In a sense, we are at the heart of Saint John of the Cross' contemplative teaching. What will it mean, then, to penetrate more deeply by means "of many kinds of suffering . . . into the thicket of the delectable wisdom of God"? The hope of every contemplative soul is that God should touch the soul more and more with his *loving* presence. But clearly this does not mean what we might think before understanding better the road of contemplation. We are now more familiar with what to expect. Darkness is certainly an unavoidable aspect; indeed, that the intellect undergoes a purging experience of spiritual darkness is a basic contemplative principle: "When the divine light of contemplation strikes a soul not yet entirely illumined, it causes spiritual darkness . . . it also deprives the soul . . . and darkens it" (DN 2.5.3). The spiritual darkness in prayer is a form of suffering, but there is another darkness that can afflict the soul, troubling its depths in profound ways, extending beyond prayer itself. This is the shocking experience, due to the overwhelming light and purity of God filling the soul, of being seized with the thought of a possible rejection by God. The conviction of being not just unworthy of God but of considering oneself *rejected* by him because of the soul's incorrigible impurity is a terrible affliction for a soul that loves God with intensity. The suffering can be acute, piercing into the depths of the soul. Yet if a soul does not halt on its path of love, persevering in faith, this suffering, too, is fruitful. The following words from *The Dark Night* are an introduction into the intense suffering that an advanced life of prayer can bring. But they also provide an insight into why this occurs to a soul so committed and tenacious in its love for God. God desires to burn away the impurity of a soul, still weighed down in deeper regions of the soul by self-love.

> The soul, because of its impurity, suffers immensely at the time this divine light truly assails it. When this pure light strikes in order to expel all impurity, persons feel so unclean and wretched that it seems God is against them and they are against God. . . . Clearly beholding its impurity by means of this pure light, although in darkness, the soul understands distinctly that it is worthy neither of God nor of any creature. And what most grieves it is that it thinks it will never be worthy, and there are no more blessings

for it. This divine and dark light causes deep immersion
of the mind in the knowledge and feeling of one's own
miseries and evils; it brings all these miseries into relief so
the soul sees clearly that of itself it will never possess anything else. (DN 2.5.5)

This most serious suffering on the contemplative path
to God has been called in later spiritual theology the "dark
night of the soul". It is not the exact phrase Saint John of
the Cross uses. He speaks rather of the night of the spirit.
But the concept and description are his own. It can be helpful to expose some remarks on this grave spiritual trial, because in certain lives, there may be some lesser taste of a
suffering that can resemble this depiction. The impact of
this notion is important to know if we intend to take prayer
seriously over the long duration of a lifetime. The passage
below from book 2 of *The Dark Night* conveys the violent
sense of upheaval that a soul might experience as it grows in
a more consuming love for God. The affliction, as the previous quotation shows, is due to the pure touch of the divine presence upon the impurity of the human soul. When
God pierces the soul more fully with his presence—a soul
that has already opened deep caverns within itself to him
—a profound purgation is bound to occur. Ordinarily, we
may expect a blessing and comfort in the thought of being
"touched" in grace by God. But the actual reality in contemplation, and much more so in this case of a grave spiritual
purgation, is an encounter of the soul's meager capacity to
love with the vast magnitude of divine love. The darkness
that encloses the soul at all stages of contemplation is due
in part to the incomprehension it experiences of God. This
darkness, in turn, may at times leave the soul alone within
itself in its own misery. Now, in this discussion of the dark
night of the soul, we see a much more intense display of

this pattern. What follows is only an initial description of the dark night of the soul, as Saint John of the Cross depicts the meeting of two extremes in the divine and the human:

> The divine extreme is the purgative contemplation, and the human extreme is the soul, the receiver of this contemplation. Since the divine extreme strikes in order to renew the soul and divinize it (by stripping it of the habitual affections and properties of the old self to which the soul is strongly united, attached, and conformed), it so disentangles and dissolves the spiritual substance—absorbing it in a profound darkness—that the soul at the sight of its miseries feels that it is melting away and being undone by a cruel spiritual death. . . . It is fitting that the soul be in this sepulcher of dark death in order that it attain the spiritual resurrection for which it hopes. (DN 2.6.1)

The great suffering of the soul just described may crystallize, as Saint John of the Cross writes, into a "conviction that God has rejected it, and with abhorrence cast it into darkness" (DN 2.6.2). These are remarkably strong words if we think that such a person is very holy at this point in life. One wonders also if such a condition of soul may be related to personal events in a saintly life. In his providential designs, God works through converging effects to accomplish his purposes for the interior life of souls. A saintly life, for instance, might have mishaps and mistakes in external affairs that convince the soul strongly that its failures have disappointed God in a terrible manner. One might consider, for example, the pain to a foundress of a religious order who suffers acutely from the loss of Sisters who leave the congregation for reasons that could have been prevented with greater care or by timely interventions. The saintly foundress might suffer badly with self-doubt that her own negligence or personal failing caused these departures and thereby wounded

the Heart of God. These personal experiences can accentu-
ate what then begins to invade the soul as part of a burning
refinement of its love. The soul in this dark night, as Saint
John of Cross describes it, becomes utterly convinced, despite its great love, that God has rejected it because of its
unworthiness or failure. The feeling of God's abandonment
may become so undeniable, carved so deeply in the heart,
that nothing a soul contemplates in thought seems able to
reverse this conviction. His absence each day in the darkness
of prayer seems only to confirm this truth. Let us remember
that these are souls with the depths of their souls opened
already in love and so for that reason vulnerable to wounds
of love in a far more intense manner.

We might pause for a comment that can shed light on the
spiritual meaning of what is taking place in such descriptions. For souls serious with God, the mystery of suffering
for the Beloved may cross a threshold of love at a certain
point in life. The threshold of significance is to realize that
the indwelling of the Lord within the soul is an interior
presence of the Christ of the Passion. Jesus crucified lives
his Passion in a mysterious manner in a soul of great love
and, in a particular manner, through the gift of contemplation. The soul does not simply become united to God in
the vast longing it has for our Lord within itself. It comes
to know quite personally within itself an ongoing imitation
and replication of Jesus' Passion. Naturally, this is a mere
taste of the suffering of Christ, but it is a real taste nonetheless. The words of Jesus that we might abide in him, and
he abide in us (Jn 15:4–5), now take on a different quality
and meaning. It is no longer simply his presence that draws
a soul's attraction in these words. Now it understands that
these words mean to abide in his Passion, so that his Passion may abide in the soul. This secret realization, utterly

personal and direct, awakens a soul to a different capacity for love. The communication of love from God to a soul is now expressed in the taste of his Passion mysteriously united to the soul's own life and existence. This can take place in prayer, but also outside prayer. No longer is the Passion of Christ then an event from the past, pondered with love while standing apart from it. The soul now experiences as a mysterious truth that Christ himself lives elements of his Passion over again in the life of the soul. This contemplative threshold, once crossed, places all prior purification and struggle in a new light. The abiding presence of Christ himself in his Passion now permeates the spiritual path. And love may leap forward as a result into great depths within the boundless caverns of the soul.

The most forbidding feature described in the dark night of the soul is surely the sense of a rejection by God. The conviction of being lost, permanently lost and forsaken, is not described adequately if considered solely as a grave purification stripping the soul down to its nothingness. The truth is rather, as just suggested, that the experience replicates in a mysterious manner Jesus' own Passion; in this case, the experience of Jesus' forsakenness on the cross. The dark night of the soul is understood properly only in union with Jesus' sense of abandonment at Calvary. Saint John of the Cross writes that this experience for a soul, admittedly uncommon and rare, nonetheless informs the genuine path to a union with God. There is no deeper spiritual progress except that the soul moves in a kind of holy alignment with Jesus Christ as "the way, and the truth, and the life" (Jn 14:6). He is not simply Teacher and Lord in these words, but the Beloved who offers his Passion to those souls who are beloved to him as their way, their truth, and their life. A mystery of union with him takes place under the sign of the Passion, as it were. In book 2 of *The Ascent of Mount Carmel*, in the section on faith, Saint John of the Cross writes thus of the annihilation undergone by Christ as a model and example for the soul in its own self-offering. The spiritual truth of a union with our Lord is not of separate experiences and events, standing parallel and distinct, that is, a suffering undergone by the soul apart from Christ. Rather, a union of Christ with the soul in its suffering takes place as our Lord relives his Passion in that soul. The second half of the following passage, which we quoted earlier, is worth reading again in this context. The dark night of the soul, when a soul is reduced to nothing, is a union with Christ's own experience on the cross at Calvary.

> At the moment of his death he was certainly annihilated in his soul, without any consolation or relief, since the Father had left him that way in innermost aridity in the lower part. He was thereby compelled to cry out: *My God, My God, why have you forsaken me?* [Mt. 27:46]. This was the most extreme abandonment, sensitively, that he had suffered in his life. And by it he accomplished the most marvelous work of his whole life. . . . That is, he brought about the reconciliation and union of the human race with God through grace. The Lord achieved this, as I say, at the moment in which he was most annihilated in all things. . . . David says of him: *Ad nihilum redactus sum et nescivi* [I was reduced to nothing, and knew nothing] [Ps. 73:22], that those who are truly spiritual might understand the mystery of the door and way (which is Christ) leading to union with God, and that they might realize that their union with God and the greatness of the work they accomplish will be measured by their annihilation of themselves for God in the sensory and spiritual parts of their souls. When they are reduced to nothing, the highest degree of humility, the

spiritual union between their souls and God will be an accomplished fact. (AMC 2.7.11)

Saint John of the Cross extends his discussion and remarks in *The Dark Night* to say that often it happens that in this night of the spirit "such persons also feel forsaken and despised by creatures, particularly by their friends" (DN 2.6.3). Again, we hear the sharp echo of Jesus' own Passion in this severe trial of the soul. God has his way of bringing the full brunt of a stark stripping down of the soul into prayer *and* into the external circumstances of a life. But the true significance of these unique circumstances and the inner desolation is a great personal mystery for the soul. It is a true taste for a soul of a union with our Lord at Calvary. The soul's poverty at such a time is not simply the self-emptying detachment from human satisfaction of earlier times, but something much deeper and more oppressive. Poverty becomes a grief at the core of the soul, which it suffers alone. And yet at the same time a different quality of humility is being forged in the depths of a soul. The soul's nothingness is in no way now an abstract notion of piety. It is a real experiential misery. The soul is reduced to nothing, and yet it is quite alive in God's gaze of love. What is especially important to insist upon is that a soul does not doubt its love for God. On the contrary, it knows this love intensely and is active in manifesting it in action. What it suffers is the interior sense of losing God's love:

> Although persons suffering this purgation know that they love God and that they would give a thousand lives for him (they would indeed, for souls undergoing these trials love God very earnestly), they find no relief. This knowledge instead causes them deeper affliction. For in loving God so

intensely that nothing else gives them concern, and aware
of their own misery, they are unable to believe that God
loves them. They believe that they neither have nor ever
will have within themselves anything deserving of God's
love, but rather every reason for being abhorred not only
by God but by every creature forever. They grieve to see
within themselves reasons for meriting rejection by him
whom they so love and long for. (DN 2.7.7)

The amazing insight in reading Saint John of the Cross
is to realize that in these words he is describing a soul that
is in a most fortunate condition. The person does not perceive this, obviously, but the reality is that such a soul is
very close to God in its love. A contemplative soul may be,
indeed, very near God, despite its troubled interior state,
when it seems unable to lift up its mind to God or draw
out any affection for him. In a striking image, Saint John of
the Cross writes that at such a time, "it seems as it did to
Jeremiah that God has placed a cloud in front of the soul
so that its prayer might not pass through [Lam. 3:44]" (DN
2.8.1). The image of a barrier to contact with God himself is a difficult notion. Even at earlier stages of contemplation, the encounter with darkness is more than simply
a trial to endure with forbearance. Rather, our inability to
comprehend God or to understand at times what happens
in prayer calls for an acceptance by the soul of its essential
incapacity before God. The poverty experienced in darkness
can always become the path to great unseen graces. But for
contemplative graces to penetrate more deeply, a soul must
allow itself to be brought low in a prostration of spirit. It
must give way in prayer to its own incapacity before God,
a helplessness completely open before God, exercising its
certitude of faith in darkness. The fruitfulness of this suffering does make itself known in due time. Saint John of

the Cross offers a brief comment on a soul's prayer while in this condition of soul. The statement recommends in particular the humbled prayer of a prostrated soul: "Indeed, this is not the time to speak with God, but the time to put one's mouth in the dust, as Jeremiah says, that perhaps there might come some actual hope [Lam. 3:29], and the time to suffer this purgation patiently. God it is who is working now in the soul, and for this reason the soul can do nothing. Consequently, these persons can neither pray vocally nor be attentive to spiritual matters, nor still less attend to temporal affairs and business" (DN 2.8.1).

Distressing words, surely, conveying the acute consciousness of a soul's inability to help itself; yet this path of prostration in prayer—"to put one's mouth in the dust"—is the embrace of a deeper humility before God. The trial of darkness calls always for humble surrender. The soul is being purified in the burning light of God's purity. And the experience of this burning is necessarily harsh and forbidding for any soul. A basic contemplative principle is at work: "The clearer and more evident supernatural things are in themselves, the darker they are to our intellects" (DN 2.8.2). The interior affliction of the dark night of the soul is not primarily a penitential notion in this treatment. Affliction is the path of entry into the consuming light of divine love cast on the limitless depths of the soul. Purity of heart, in Saint John of the Cross' understanding, extends far beyond a chaste avoidance of sinful inclination to an absolute immolation of the soul before the radiance of God. "Cleanness of heart", writes Saint John of the Cross, "is nothing less than the love and grace of God." That statement may seem ordinary until we hear what follows: "The pure of heart are called blessed by our Savior [Mt. 5:8], and to call them blessed is equivalent to saying they are taken with love, for blessedness is derived from nothing else but love" (DN 2.12.1). These words are located in the midst of a treatment on the nature of a severe trial in the interior life. The purity sought by God may have no end point in burning the soul with a boundless need for God. Yet this is not regretted, certainly, for the soul that loves. God does not leave a soul in ashes but, rather, fortifies it with the presence of his divine love. A concluding statement on the vehemence of love from this section on serious spiritual trial offers a provocative last word: "The strength and vehemence of love has this trait: Everything seems possible to it, and it believes everyone is occupied as it is; it does not believe anyone could be employed in any other way or seek anyone other than him whom it seeks and loves; it believes there is nothing else to desire or to occupy it and that everyone is engaged in seeking and loving him" (DN 2.13.7).

The passages quoted in this chapter are a long distance from commenting on the initial struggles of a soul beginning to receive the grace of contemplation. Yet the descriptions are important to ponder for anyone desiring to advance in love for God. The gift of contemplation only progresses as love deepens for a Beloved who is our Lord Jesus crucified. Only after much time, perhaps, does this truth come fully to light. Yet from the outset in the journey of contemplation, we are invited to a different awareness of the encounter with God. This path is not a sublime ascent to heights of breathtaking views. Contemplation finds its home more in the gaze of a loving soul on the disfigured face of Jesus at Calvary, who asks if we can keep ourselves longer before his eyes. The idea of suffering has a repugnant quality until we perceive that it has become the open fissure within our soul into the real presence of divine love in its deepest truth. The experience of suffering becomes precisely the realization of a great love in deeper regions of the soul. And love is always the last word in the pursuit of deeper prayer.

We might also remark that the possibility, not just of suffering for love, but of dying for love of God is the great prospect that Saint John of the Cross ultimately offers us. The sufferings of the contemplative path have this secret purpose: to die for love of the Beloved. An impatient, constrained, passionate need for God consumes a soul that suffers for love of God. It is the manner in which the grain of wheat falls into the earth and dies, so that it may bear fruit. We may question how intensities of this sort can be present in lives. In fact, they may be concealed to a large extent. How true it is that our lives in the context of the daily circumstances we face can never be equated with the hidden fires of desire that can inflame us in ways beyond measure. Certainly, the hidden love of souls for God is unsuspected in the view of others around them. To love God impatiently, even desperately, is the urgent lesson that Saint John of the Cross continually teaches. Perhaps a last statement of this saint says it best at the end of this chapter: "Accordingly, God makes the soul die to all that he is not, so that when it is stripped and flayed of its old skin, he may clothe it anew" (DN 2.13.11). Out of love for a soul, Jesus clothes that soul with his own Passion. The soul that loves must come to recognize this as an immense favor granted in love. In short, it is the constancy of an immolation offered up in love, if we are willing to accept it, that leads to the great contemplative encounter with God—namely, the realization of our Lord allowing his Passion to take place again within us. This mysterious fruit is the consequence only of intense contemplative love. Clearly a great courage in love is a primary need in the contemplative quest for God.

16

PARTING ADVICE: LOSS OF SELF FOR THE GREATER LOVE

The advice that Saint John of the Cross gave in letters and in some short instructions to Carmelite nuns and friars is informative and, not surprisingly, often rigorous in its demands. We do not have to be a religious or a priest to profit from these recommendations for living a holy life. The demands are those of the Gospel, if a soul is desirous to lose itself, to give itself away, for love of God. The same principles of holiness, if not always in the exact detail and application, will be pertinent in every life that aspires to closer union with our Lord. The personal guidance Saint John of the Cross gave to souls can serve as a last chapter, revealing other traits of his heart and soul and easing our way back down the Mount of Carmel that we have been vigorously climbing in the preceding chapters. It is best to begin with some of the comments contained in the letters. Unfortunately, there are only thirty-three letters that survived his death. Many were destroyed, in part because of fears generated by suspicions and persecutions directed toward him at the last period of his life. Late in life, he suffered much within his own order from misunderstanding, but also from the ecclesial turbulence in this period of the early Protestant Reformation when so-called mental prayer raised questions and was sometimes disparaged and mistrusted. From the quality of the extant letters, we can only regret the sad loss of the many other letters he wrote.

Saint John of the Cross, as we have observed, was a master of the pointed remark. He writes in 1582 to a Carmelite prioress in Caravaca, Madre Ana de San Alberto, "not to walk with fears that intimidate your soul" (L3). We do not know what caused this anxiety, but we do know that it is not unusual in our very human lives to be drawn on occasion into fear and helplessness. Saint John of the Cross insists that she should not draw back, intimidated, but exercise confidence in appealing to God. And then a great remark in this letter: "Return to God what he has given you and gives you each day. It seems you want to measure God by the measure of your own capacity, but it will not be so" (L3). The words identify a problem often seen in souls. A focus on ourselves leads us to think God can only do so much, given our limitations and inabilities. The thought can seem a humble one in assuming that we are unworthy of larger favors. But this may be a deceptive pretext for not seeking a greater generosity toward God. There are no boundaries, no limits, to what God can give our souls. We ought not to limit him by the measure of our own capacity, but simply expect much from him and then give back all that is given. Saint John of the Cross concludes this letter in words surely uplifting to this Carmelite prioress: "Prepare yourself, for God desires to grant you a great favor" (L3). Anyone reading Saint John of the Cross regularly might consider a need as well to prepare for unexpected favors from God.

To the Carmelite community of Beas, for whom he had a lasting love and whom he visited often as a spiritual guide and confessor, he writes in 1586, exhorting these nuns to mortify the human tendency to seek their own satisfactions in their spiritual pursuits. Their goal must be to become "unencumbered" in order to receive from God what he desires to give, which is often not at all what is expected or predictable but, rather, something costly that will take the soul more deeply down the path of surrender to God. He reminds them that the search for inner peace and contentment, so common to spiritual people, may be an impediment to the emptiness that God wants to see within a soul so that he might fill this emptiness. The key phrase is uncompromising: "Those who seek satisfaction in something no longer keep themselves empty that God might fill them with his ineffable delight" (L7). The end of this letter is an encouragement to keep their eyes fixed on our Lord and to follow "in his footsteps of mortification, in utter patience, in total silence, and with every desire to suffer, *becoming executioners of your own satisfactions*, mortifying yourselves, if perhaps something remains that must die and something still impedes the inner resurrection of the Spirit who dwells within your souls" (L7; emphasis added).

Almost to the day one year later is a follow-up letter of sorts to the same Carmelite community of Beas. The mortification he urged in the early letter in that unusual phrase —to become "executioners of your own satisfactions"— is now directed at the practice of silence. Perhaps he had received some complaint on the matter from the Mother Prioress, Ana de Jesús, who had some years earlier, as mentioned, requested from him the commentary of *The Spiritual Canticle*. Although his advice cannot be so surprising to Carmelites, it might be worth pondering in our own lives: "Speaking distracts one, while silence and work recollects and strengthens the spirit" (L8). The silence he recommends is an interior silence that will draw the soul more fully into the presence of our Lord. He suggests that Jesus loves to approach the soul that loves silence. This silence is not just a kind of external practice; it is a way of interior detachment and of losing self—the silence of self-forgetfulness, the silence of mental austerity, turning away from unnecessary preoccupation with external affairs that trouble one's thoughts and cannot, in any case, be solved for the moment. The urgent need of silence is a strong teaching in this letter. Silence is in itself a holy path to God because it leaves us alone with God, as these comments in this letter affirm:

> Never, whether in adversity or in prosperity, cease to quiet your heart with deepest love, so as to suffer whatever comes along. . . . Keep this in mind, daughters: the soul that is quick to turn to speaking and conversing is slow to turn to God. For when it is turned toward God, it is then strongly and inwardly drawn toward silence and flight from all conversation. For God desires a soul to rejoice with him more than with any other person, however advanced and helpful the person may be. . . . Our greatest need is to be silent before this great God with the appetite and with the tongue, *for the only language he hears is the silent language of love.* (L8; emphasis added)

In 1588, Saint John of the Cross wrote some memorable words to another Carmelite, an ex-prioress, Madre Leonor Bautista, living in the community of Beas. He returns in this letter to the expression of receiving a "great favor" from God, which in her case is the favor of being able to enjoy God in solitude, despite her grief at some unnamed trial. As an ex-prioress, this sorrow may be due to her removal from a place she loved and the new adjustment she now faces at a later stage of life. His advice is again uncompromising; in this case, it concerns the need to accept a trial coming from others: "For love of him have no care that they do to you what they will, *since you do not belong to yourself but to God*" (L9; emphasis added). The last phrase captures an essential demand of holiness. We belong to God, and he must be free to do what he wants, even to the extent of costly suffering coming into our lives. All must be surrendered to God, all must be follow-up offered to him and for souls. Charity can be exercised always, even without a return of love. In a similar vein of thought, in a magnificent statement, written five months before his death, when he was undergoing a grave trial of calumny and persecution within his own congregation, he wrote in a letter to another Carmelite prioress in Segovia, Madre María de la Encarnación: "Think nothing else but that God ordains all, and where there is no love, put love, and you will draw out love" (L26).

In another letter from 1589 to a Carmelite prioress, Madre Leonor de San Gabriel, who had also been transferred and may also have been suffering on that account, he writes two years before his death of the importance of a radical self-emptying, a giving all to God, if we are to allow God to fill our soul with himself. The words recall the great importance of the first operation of desire in the will that we treated earlier. God is very active in touching with grace the desires of the will. "The more he wants to give, the more he makes us desire—even to the point of leaving us empty in order to fill us with goods" (L15). He comments to Madre Leonor that her change of location is surely in God's plan, that it ought to be seen as a gift to strip her down for the sake of a pure self-offering to God. God's personal solicitude for the soul that loves him intensely is often to lead that soul to a depth of solitude in which the soul's only companionship is God himself. He insists in his customary manner on the need for self-emptying:

> Since the immense blessings of God can only enter and fit into an empty and solitary heart, the Lord wants you to be alone. For he truly loves you with the desire of being himself all your company. . . . Strive carefully to be content only with his companionship, so you might discover in it

every happiness. Even though the soul may be in heaven, it will not be happy if it does not conform its will to this. And we will be unhappy with God, even though he is always present with us, if our heart is not alone, but attached to something else. (L15)

Perhaps in reading such comments in these letters, we may consider that they are meant only for intensely religious souls enclosed in cloistered convents. Saint John of the Cross did not just write to Carmelites; two letters survive to a laywoman from Granada, Doña Juana de Pedraza, in which memorable comments are made. The first letter, in 1589, is an answer to some "grief, afflictions, and loneliness" that this woman is suffering. Saint John of the Cross writes initially that these experiences of pain "are all comparable to knocks and rappings at the door of your soul so it might love more" (L11). Then, as he continues, he returns to the familiar advice of a necessary emptying and detachment: "In what concerns the soul, it is safest not to lean on anything or desire anything. . . . Let not the soul be attached to anything . . . I see this with myself: The more that things are mine, the more I set my heart and soul and care on them" (L11). From the perspective of Saint John of the Cross, even when writing to a laywoman living in the world, it is not surprising that God should allow suffering to come from the things that are most dear to our lives. Making reference to the famous story in Genesis of Abraham about to offer his son Isaac as a holocaust in sacrifice (Gen 22:1–19), he writes to her: "But because it behooves us not to go without the cross, just as our Beloved did not go without it, even to the death of love, God ordains our sufferings that we may love what we most desire, make greater sacrifices, and be worth more. But everything is brief, for it lasts only until the knife is raised; and then Isaac remains alive with the promise of a multiplied offspring" (L11).

Nine months later, in October 1589, he writes a very moving spiritual letter to this same woman, who at this time is undergoing a trial of interior darkness and has written to him with some helplessness regarding her ordeal. The letter of Saint John of the Cross does not attempt to comfort her in her state of anguish. Rather, he offers a sharp contradiction of what he considers to be the misinterpretation of interior darkness she seems to be experiencing. The thought that God has disappeared and abandoned her soul, as she has apparently written, is met by a strongly voiced commentary on the actual favor God is extending to her soul. Her soul is being invited to a greater trust and confidence in God, who is indeed close to her, in this time of interior darkness. Darkness is simply the experiential realm of an interior trial. The true reality underneath any experience of darkness is the actual close presence of God, forging a deeper union with the soul. A longer quotation from this beautiful letter is worth our attention. Who in a lifetime cannot profit at some time from these words?

> Since you walk in these darknesses and voids of spiritual poverty, you think that everyone and everything is failing you. It is no wonder that in this it also seems God is failing you. But nothing is failing you, neither do you have to discuss anything, nor is there anything to discuss. . . . Those who desire nothing else than God walk not in darkness, however poor and dark they are in their own sight. And those who walk not presumptuously, or according to their own satisfactions, whether from God or from creatures, nor do their own will in anything, have nothing to stumble over or discuss with anyone. You are making good

progress. Do not worry, but be glad! Who are you that you should guide yourself? Wouldn't that end up fine! You were never better off than now because you were never so humble or so submissive, or considered yourself and all worldly things to be so small. . . . What need is there in order to be right other than to walk along the level road of the law of God and of the Church, and live only in dark and true faith and certain hope and complete charity, expecting all our blessings in heaven, living here below like pilgrims, the poor, the exiled, orphans, the thirsty, without a road and without anything, hoping for everything in heaven? Rejoice and trust in God, for he has given you signs that you can very well do so, and in fact you must do so. (L19)

We turn now to another form of writing. Saint John of the Cross wrote as well a few pages of instructions, which have been entitled *The Precautions*, to the Carmelite nuns of Beas, which, as mentioned, was a much loved convent for him. This is not a letter *per se*, but a short instruction containing practical comments on living a holy religious life with dedication. Of interest to know is that he wrote these instructions in his mid-thirties only a few short months after his escape from imprisonment with the Calced Friars in Toledo. Perhaps we are hearing lessons for the interior life that he learned himself in those hard nine months. It can be read with great benefit for all who want to appreciate the serious demands of holiness, and not just those who might be in a cloister, monastery, or a serious religious community. It introduces us, as well, to the human struggles that carry over into the private world of dedicated religious life outside the eyes of the public. The work is divided into three sections that address impediments from the world, the devil, and the flesh, with three precautions identified against each of these "enemies" of the soul.

He addresses what he considers an immediate task for those who have entered the religious life. The need, writes Saint John of the Cross, to avoid worldliness requires a soul to "have an equal love for and an equal forgetfulness of all persons" (P 5). He strongly urges these sisters to withdraw from attachment to relatives, not because the families are not loved, but because the natural weakness of the heart can be easily preoccupied with blood relations. He urges these religious Sisters to "regard all as strangers" (P 6), even inside the convent, which is a way to avoid getting caught up in seeking for friendships that will relieve a natural human hunger but will only impede a pure love and dedication for God. He writes in a manner that may seem somewhat severe for our ears: "Do not love one person more than another, for you will err; the person who loves God more is the one more worthy of love, and you do not know who this is" (P 6). The need felt by some people for close relationships in the context of a cloistered convent opens souls to a serious error of thinking that they love more if they cultivate special love for one or another person. He insists that one must live ultimately for God alone in such a setting and love others with a calm evenness for the sake of charity. In communal relations, the goal must be a high standard of charity, and not a sentimental love for others that is unstable and uneven. The second precaution against worldliness is to "abhor all manner of possessions and not allow yourself to worry about these goods" (P 7). Again, in the context of a convent, concern for food or clothing or personal possessions is contrary to the poverty that must be present in such lives. The third precaution against worldliness is more subtle, but nonetheless strong in its warning. He urges the nuns to remain detached from the turmoil and disturbance that may occur even in a convent among people meant for holiness. He writes on that precaution:

> Very carefully guard yourself against thinking about what happens in the community, and even more against speaking of it, of anything in the past or present concerning a particular religious. . . . Never be scandalized or astonished at anything you happen to see or learn of, endeavoring to preserve your soul in forgetfulness of all that. . . . Even were you to live among devils you should not turn the head of your thoughts to their affairs, but forget these things entirely and strive to keep your soul occupied purely and entirely in God, and not let the thought of this thing or that hinder you from so doing. And to achieve this, be convinced that in monasteries and communities there is never a lack of stumbling blocks, since there is never a lack of devils who seek to overthrow the saints; God permits this in order to prove and try religious. (P 8, 9)

In his instructions about the direct assaults of the devil, he begins by alerting souls to the wiles and trickery of the evil one in convents. The devil knows that these kinds of souls will not ordinarily choose evil; yet they are capable of being deceived by the appearance of good. His recommendation is foremost to seek proper counsel whenever in doubt and to be "suspicious of what appears good, especially when not obliged by obedience" (P 10). His first precaution against the devil is not to take on any work other than the obligations that are part of the life without the command of obedience. The value of obedience for a religious is perhaps little appreciated by the outside world, in his day and our own. The fading of this virtue from religious life has led to the diminished quality evident in many congregations that not so long ago, some decades previously, were thriving. For Saint John of the Cross, the loss of self in a holy manner, so integral to the Gospel and to holiness, takes place especially through obedience. "The actions of religious are not their own, but belong to obedience, and if you withdraw them from obedience, you will have to count them as lost" (P 11). The second precaution in this section is surely surprising to the ears of most laity: "Always look on the superior as though on God, no matter who he happens to be, for he takes God's place" (P 12). The need, then, to avoid gazing on the faults of a superior, on her character and contradictions as a person, is likewise essential. Otherwise, the danger arises that obedience will be motivated "by the visible traits of the superior, and not by the invisible God whom you serve through him" (P 12).

We can learn much here, perhaps to our surprise. A great mental austerity is called for in genuine religious life, but this is equally true in every life. In the convent, writes Saint John of the Cross, there is a continual need to mortify the suggestive appeal of interpretations that are overtly human perceptions. The effort must be to remain sacrificially fixed on the reality of God's will expressed through the preferences and commands of a superior. All this difficult submission is for the sake of giving to God a more generous offering of oneself. Saint John of the Cross, no doubt from his own experience with nuns, stresses that too many allow the unpleasant aspects of a superior to undermine their obedience. Or, conversely, they allow the appealing personality of an attractive superior to undermine a pure motivation in obedience. In this case, they do all to please simply another human person instead of God. As he writes, "If you do not strive, with respect to your personal feelings, to be unconcerned about whether this one or another be superior, you will by no means be a spiritual person, nor will you keep your vows well" (P 12). The third precaution against the devil is the need for practicing serious humility. A religious can do this especially by "desiring that [others] be given precedence over you in all things" (P 13). This is tested in particular when those not admired or attractive are given preference. The absolute demand to lose self for God is the undercurrent in all these remarks.

The first of the three precautions against the impediment of the flesh begins with a truly memorable passage. To our ears it may sound as though the entry into the enclosure of religious life must be a masochistic feat of endurance. But, of course, this is not the case. Saint John of the Cross understands the loss of self to be central to the advancement of a life with God; thus he writes as if there should be nothing but agreement with him. It should be no surprise, then, if God allows the soul to be stripped down quickly. The first precaution on the impediment of the flesh deserves an extended quotation; admittedly, he is perhaps exaggerating the conduct of convent life, but nonetheless his point is clearly stated. The desire to give oneself fully to God is certainly going to be tested:

> Understand that you have come to the monastery so that all may fashion you and try you. . . . You should think that all in the community are artisans—as indeed they are— present there in order to prove you; that some will fashion you with words, others by deeds, and others with thoughts against you; and that in all this you must be submissive as is the statue to the craftsman who molds it, to the artist who paints it, and to the gilder who embellishes it. If you fail to observe this precaution, you will not know how to overcome your sensuality and feelings, nor will you get along well in the community with the religious or attain

holy peace or free yourself from many stumbling blocks and evils. (P 15)

The second precaution against the flesh is not to give up works and exercises because there is an absence of satisfaction in them. Likewise, one should not do works simply because they procure delight and satisfaction for oneself. The need to remain constant and persevering in all types of spiritual work requires a willingness to continue in actions that bring no apparent benefit to oneself or any satisfaction. The third precaution is similar, and a familiar one for us at this point. The soul should not look for the satisfaction of pleasant feelings in prayer and spiritual exercises or go to them for this reason. Otherwise, this desire for our own satisfaction will become in time the motive for prayer. Soon, when this satisfaction is not forthcoming, we are likely either to curtail spiritual exercises or to treat them simply as a burdensome obligation in life. The recommendation of Saint John of the Cross is the customary advice focused on fruitfulness in the long term: "seek the arduous and distasteful and embrace it. By this practice sensuality is held in check; without this practice you will never lose self-love or gain the love of God" (P 17).

There is one other similar work of Saint John of the Cross, written again almost like a letter, and in this case to an unknown Brother of his own order. It was likely written when he was serving as a vicar provincial sometime between 1585 and 1587 and is entitled "Counsels to a Religious on How to Reach Perfection". In this short work, he offers four counsels regarding resignation, mortification, the practice of virtue, and solitude. The counsel on resignation recommends that the Carmelite Brother "should live in the monastery as though no one else were in it" (CR 2). That sounds stunning at first, contrary to the need to maintain a communal spirit of charity. But apparently Saint John of the Cross was aware of the danger of becoming drawn into the all too human curiosities and interest in the internal affairs within a monastic environment. The need is to be detached and mentally austere, not getting involved in matters that do not concern one's own life of dedication to God alone. "And thus you should never, by word or by thought, meddle in things that happen in the community, nor with individuals in it, desiring not to notice their good or bad qualities or their conduct" (CR 2). The advice is to guard and protect a tranquility and quietude of soul for the sake of the greater offering to God. The second counsel concerns mortification, and here we have again a memorable quotation that can seem excessive in its tone unless perhaps we realize how realistic is the understanding of Saint John of the Cross. We hear an echo, but in sharper tones, of the first precaution against the flesh recently quoted. Again, it may seem exaggerated. On the other hand, people do not leave behind their weakness because they close a heavy wooden door behind them on the day they enter a convent or monastery. The thing to note is that it is essentially a counsel about interior mortification. For Saint John of the Cross, the primary effort in this regard is to temper the interior passions that might be provoked in human relations. And so he writes:

> You should engrave this truth on your heart. And it is that you have not come to the monastery for any other reason than to be worked and tried in virtue; you are like the stone that must be chiseled and fashioned before being set in the building. Thus you should understand that those who are in the monastery are craftsmen placed there by God to mortify you by working and chiseling at you. Some will chisel with words, telling you what you would

rather not hear; others by deed, doing against you what you would rather not endure; others by their temperament, being in their person and in their actions a bother and annoyance to you; and others by their thoughts, neither esteeming nor feeling love for you. You ought to suffer these mortifications and annoyances with inner patience, being silent for love of God and understanding that you did not enter the religious life for any other reason than for others to work you in this way, and so you become worthy of heaven. (CR 3)

It is of interest to observe that Saint John of the Cross stresses the inevitability of trials in religious life, precisely because God wants to use them for the sake of sanctification. The encounter with trials allows souls to prove themselves before God. If a more self-interested motive has brought a person into a religious life, it becomes transparent in time by a repugnance to the harder path. It may be that before entrance into religious life, people do not anticipate a deeper suffering to be a reality in that life. They are ready for the physical austerities and deprivations, but do not expect other forms of hard trial in the close communal context of human living. The desire for a kind of perpetual peacefulness evaporates quickly as an illusion of sentimentality. Interior peace in religious life, for Saint John of the Cross, depends on a great detachment from self. "Since many religious do not understand that they have entered religious life to carry Christ's cross, they do not get along well with others. At the time of reckoning they will find themselves greatly confused and frustrated" (CR 4). In short, they expect too much from others. We can assume that the opposite disposition is also true. Those who can carry the cross with fortitude, patience, and a spirit of offering manage to live with the human aspects of such a life far better in charitable fruitfulness.

One might pause to think that the same principles can inform a healthy spiritual approach to the vocation of marriage and its own testings. The fundamental principles of holiness in every vocation are rooted in the Gospel demand to lose ourselves for love of our Lord. The third counsel concerns the practice of virtue in a setting of religious life. Here Saint John of the Cross urges especially a constancy in religious observances and obedience, living only for God. "You should never set your eyes on the satisfaction or dissatisfaction of the work at hand as a motive for doing it or failing to do it, but on doing it for God" (CR 5). Pleasing God in all we do, living daily a sacrificial offering for souls, is the only worthy motive for actions. The following recommendation is a clear echo from his words in *The Ascent of Mount Carmel*:

> You should take care always to be inclined to the difficult more than to the easy, to the rugged more than to the soft, to the hard and distasteful in a work more than to its delightful and pleasant aspects; and do not go about choosing what is less a cross, for the cross is a light burden [Mt. 11:30]. The heavier a burden is, the lighter it becomes when borne for Christ. You should try, too, by taking the lowest place always, that in things bringing comfort to your brothers in religion they be preferred to you. (CR 6)

The last counsel regarding solitude is not directed simply to physical solitude in a monastery. The desire of Saint John of the Cross is to see the soul detached and empty, no longer dependent for security or any other interest upon the outside world. "You should deem everything in the world as finished. . . . Pay no heed to the things out in the world, for God has already withdrawn and released you from them. . . . It is very fitting for you to desire to see no one and that no one see you" (CR 7, 8). Naturally, duties may require dealings with the world, but the religious man should remain focused on a task, not seeking to entertain himself by contact with the outside world. An inner solitude must be cultivated that remains separated from indulgence in unnecessary interests of curiosity. Saint John of the Cross urges the Carmelite Brother to take care with his thoughts so that a solitary fixation on God may be uninterrupted as much as possible. "This is very necessary for inner solitude, which demands that the soul dismiss any thought that is not directed to God" (CR 9). This last counsel is too much for most of us surely in our circumstances of distraction and busy occupations. But let us not be too dismissive. A forgetfulness of worldly concerns has the reward of bringing a soul mysteriously into the proximity with God in the midst of common occupations. We can assume that Saint John of the Cross was speaking from his own experience, as evidently he did on every page of his works.

A last comment might be made on the importance of the ascetical aspect of the interior mortifications we have encountered in these letters and instructions. The advice we have been hearing is not without a direct link to the possibility of contemplative graces. The refusal to indulge the self, to withdraw into self, or to turn inward on the needs of self is at the heart of all these recommendations. This refusal of self-indulgence in all forms can become a cultivated attitude of soul with a deep effect over time. It is essentially a choice to give the self away for God. On this condition being met, the grace of contemplation finds an open pathway into the caverns of the soul. Contemplation is a gift from God by which he fills an emptiness receptive to him alone. This principle is equally operative in all the advice and recommendations we have just been hearing.

In these letters and instructions, we are reminded, as we have seen often, that self-denial extends far beyond physical sacrifices; likewise, its fruits in a life stretch far beyond mere bodily discipline. The soul that submits itself to self-emptying opens itself to the Heart of God. And certainly a good part of self-emptying in a life takes place in the context of human relations. These letters and instructions offer an implicit commentary on our Lord's words in Saint John's Gospel: "Every branch that does bear fruit he prunes, that it may bear more fruit" (Jn 15:2). The pruning of the soul for a greater union with God takes place especially in the things we do not choose for ourselves. The unforeseen testing that comes within religious communal life or, indeed, from living with a spouse in marriage is inevitable. God's providential hand is certainly present in this pruning. If we desire contemplative graces to thrive, we must be vigilant to perceive the loving hand of God in all forms of the pruning of our soul and submit to his gestures with a great love.

EPILOGUE

> Now I occupy my soul
> and all my energy in his service;
> I no longer tend the herd,
> nor have I any other work
> now that my every act is love. (SC stanza 28)

When Saint John of the Cross met Saint Teresa of Ávila in September 1567, only weeks after his priestly ordination, he was thinking strongly of a transfer from the Carmelite Order to a life of more complete solitude and silence in the Carthusians. He mentioned this possibility to her in their initial conversation. Saint Teresa shared with him on that day her plan for a contemplative reform also of the men's branch of the Carmelites. She proposed that he should give this a try first. After all, she commented, he had joined the Order of the Blessed Virgin, wearing her scapular as a sign of his special bond with her. Would it really be a good thing, she asked, to "desert" our Lady's Order? That was enough persuasion, apparently. Saint John of the Cross reversed tracks and agreed, on the condition, as he put it, that he did not have to wait too long. And, indeed, he did not have to wait long at all to discover how solicitous Mary is for the gift of contemplation to souls.

The hidden mantle of Mary covers the entirety of the contemplative pursuit. We can affirm that all that Saint John of the Cross wrote is enclosed in her as the exemplary figure of contemplation. And yet this is largely a concealed truth

373

in his treatises; she does not occupy a prominent focus in an explicit way. Nonetheless, she is the primary guide and teacher to his soul and every contemplative soul. Her quiet presence is as real in these writings as her motherly companionship with her Son in his life. And what does she teach us, if we desire this grace of contemplation? Perhaps we should hear her voice at times in some of the words of Saint John of the Cross, such as these, now familiar to us: "When evening comes, you will be examined in love. Learn to love as God desires to be loved and abandon your own ways of acting" (SLL 60). If we desire to love as God wants to be loved, an essential condition for love must be faced. We can only love much if we pursue relations of depth with God in prayer. Contemplation is essentially a mark of love, the fruit of a soul that seeks God with a passion. And a passion for God translates always into a hungry need for prayer. Surely at all times in the Church, Mary never tires of seeing new children coming hungry to her table so that she can instruct them in a prayer of greater depth and of more intense love.

Her first lesson on this path is simply to choose a dedication to committed prayer. Every age in history confronts what might be called the dilemma of prayer, which is essentially the lack of deeper attraction for serious prayer. Naturally, there are always souls who find at some point in life a great love for prayer, but sometimes the number is far fewer and sparse. This question of a deeper commitment to prayer has grave repercussions. If a crisis of faith takes place in the Church, as for some decades is notable in our time, it is bound to have complex causes. But at its core, every crisis of faith is a crisis of prayer and spirituality. This difficulty is not unanswerable; the loss of greater desire for God need not continue endlessly. Mary might insist, however, that a choice is necessary, the same choice for prayer that once may have been abandoned in lives. The discovery of the beauty of prayer before a tabernacle in a silent chapel or church does not just quickly transform an individual life. If contagious among souls, the attraction for silent prayer is capable of unleashing a quiet revolution of recovery in Catholic faith and fidelity. It did so in other times and can do so again. Indeed, it is a sound wager that no crisis of faith outlasts the power of souls of contemplation in their exercise of hidden prayer. The truism has been repeated often that the history of the Church is in part the concealed history of the contemplative lives upholding the Church. Perhaps now we simply need more of these souls, and not just in cloisters or monasteries. Certainly a return to the importance of prayer in the priesthood is a crucial need, in respect both for the sacredness of the Mass and for private prayer before a tabernacle. The conversion of priests to a greater love for prayer, if widespread, would have an untold impact on souls. The following quotation from Saint John of the Cross, who lived also in a time of turbulent crisis in the faith during the period of the Protestant Reformation, would seem, then, especially pertinent to place in an epilogue. We can assume that he would say exactly the same words today:

> After all, this love is the end for which we were created. Let those, then, who are singularly active, who think they can win the world with their preaching and exterior works, observe here that they would profit the Church and please God much more, not to mention the good example they would give, were they to spend at least half of this time with God in prayer, even though they might not have reached a prayer as sublime as this. They would then certainly accomplish more, and with less labor, by one work than they otherwise would by a thousand. For through

their prayer they would merit this result, and themselves be spiritually strengthened. Without prayer they would do a great deal of hammering but accomplish little, and sometimes nothing, and even at times cause harm. God forbid that the salt should begin to lose its savor [Mt. 5:13]. However much they may appear to achieve externally, they will in substance be accomplishing nothing; it is beyond doubt that good works can be performed only by the power of God. (SC 29.3)

If, instead of neglecting prayer, we remember the rewards of prayer, we are reminded that the benefits have no limits or end. Our Lord has instructed us to ask for blessed favors; we should ask with some real fervor for this gift of a love for prayer—through Mary's intercession. Then we may find that far greater truths come our way. Inevitably, God himself will begin to show his mystery of presence to us in a different manner. Saint John of the Cross understood well the gift we can desire and conveyed it in these striking words: "For as Moses declares in Deuteronomy, *Our Lord God is a consuming fire* [Dt. 4:24], that is, a fire of love that, being of infinite power, can inestimably consume and transform into itself the soul it touches" (LF 2.2). This interior fire of divine love, which refines by its touch, burns away dross, and ultimately divinizes, invokes the mystery of contemplation. Let us be drawn to seek and desire it. The soul that gives way to God and releases a deep interior longing for God has a clear promise. The consuming fire of God will fill a sacred emptiness at its depths with the mystery of his immediate presence.

There is another instruction, more secret this time, that we might learn from Mary the Mother of contemplative souls. The fire of God's touch burns mysteriously in us on the basis of a further condition: We must learn how to receive the humility of God. This does not mean simply to practice the virtue of humility as a received grace. Mary knows and wants to teach us a truth more profound than human humility; namely, that God himself is an all-holy humility. In contemplation, he offers us a mysterious encounter with this truth of his divine humility. Humble himself, he descends to what is small and meager, full of emptiness, and offers himself in humility to be loved. Mary knows well this revelation of divine humility. The small child conceived in her Virgin's womb, the hidden years in Nazareth of divine humility, the embrace of powerlessness and abandonment at Calvary, united to her own silent suffering—she remains perpetually in adoration and wonder at God's descent upon lowliness. A pure receptivity to God's humility remains forever in her soul. She wants us to know it as well, especially when we pray before the concealed humility of our God present in the Holy Eucharist. Contemplation in the presence of the Eucharist can absorb us mysteriously into the immolation of our Lord's humility that he continually offers to the Father's will.

If we desire, then, the grace of contemplation, our soul needs a profound "yes" to this humility of God in the depths of our prayer. The "*fiat*" of Mary at the Annunciation echoes down the centuries for our emulation and opens the way to these depths. Each day in silence a servant's great "yes" that all be in accord with the divine will can ignite the initial flame in our prayer. Over time we can learn to become more fully one with her continual "yes" to God. Then, like her, we can ponder, admire, and adore the humility of God, who descends inside our lowliness and allows us to rest before his eyes in a prayer of deeper love. In a humble love, we find within us the One who is infinitely humble. The humility of God may become, indeed, the great unspoken truth of our prayer. Even a poor recognition of his humility in giving himself to our interior nothingness allows us to know his closeness in the hour of hiding. God, who is utterly personal, does not wait long, even in his hiding, to fill these blind glimpses of his humility with his presence. Nothing else we do may be more fruitful for souls than such prayer. For God seems not to refuse the requests of those who, poor and humble, acknowledge the power in his humility. May Saint John of the Cross provoke in us a passionate need to become souls with a great desire to intercede for others in the current day.

APPENDIX

O Lord, my God, who will seek you with simple and pure love, and not find that you are all one can desire, for you show yourself first and go out to meet those who seek you? (2)

God values in you the inclination to dryness and suffering for love of him more than all the consolations, spiritual visions, and meditations you could possibly have. (14)

The fly that clings to honey hinders its flight, and the soul that allows itself attachment to spiritual sweetness hinders its own liberty and contemplation. (24)

If you lose an opportunity you will be like one who lets the bird fly away; you will never get it back. (32)

One human thought alone is worth more than the entire world, hence God alone is worthy of it. (35)

What you most seek and desire you will not find by this way of yours, nor through high contemplation, but in much humility and submission of heart. (40)

Reflect that the most delicate flower loses its fragrance and withers fastest; therefore guard yourself against seeking to walk in a spirit of delight, for you will not be constant. Choose rather for yourself a robust spirit, detached from everything, and you will discover abundant peace and sweetness, for delicious and durable fruit is gathered in a cold and dry climate. (42)

If you wish to attain holy recollection, you will do so not by receiving but by denying. (52)

Souls will be unable to reach perfection who do not strive to be content with having nothing, in such fashion that their natural and spiritual desire is satisfied with emptiness; for this is necessary in order to reach the highest tranquility and peace of spirit. Hence the love of God in the pure and simple soul is almost continually in act. (54)

Since God is inaccessible, be careful not to concern yourself with all that your faculties can comprehend and your senses feel, so that you do not become satisfied with less and lose the lightness of soul suitable for going to him. (55)

How is it you dare to relax so fearlessly, since you must appear before God to render an account of the least word and thought? (74)

Preserve a habitual remembrance of eternal life, recalling that those who hold themselves the lowest and poorest and least of all will enjoy the highest dominion and glory in God. (83)

Preserve a loving attentiveness to God with no desire to feel or understand any particular thing concerning him. (88)

Enter within yourself and work in the presence of your Bridegroom, who is ever present loving you. (90)

Let Christ crucified be enough for you, and with him suffer and take your rest, and hence annihilate yourself in all inward and outward things. (92)

Have great love for trials and think of them as but a small way of pleasing your Bridegroom, who did not hesitate to die for you. (94)

The soul that walks in love neither tires others nor grows tired. (97)

The Father spoke one Word, which was his Son, and this Word he speaks always in eternal silence, and in silence must it be heard by the soul. (100)

To be taken with love for a soul, God does not look on its greatness, but on the greatness of its humility. (103)

Wisdom enters through love, silence, and mortification. It is great wisdom to know how to be silent and to look at neither the remarks, nor the deeds, nor the lives of others. (109)

If a soul has more patience in suffering and more forbearance in going without satisfaction, the sign is there of its being more proficient in virtue. (120)

Detached from exterior things, dispossessed of interior things, disappropriated of the things of God—neither will prosperity detain you nor adversity hinder you. (125)

The devil fears a soul united to God as he does God himself.
(126)

The purest suffering produces the purest understanding.
(127)

The soul that desires God to surrender himself to it entirely
must surrender itself entirely to him without keeping anything for itself. (128)

Old friends of God scarcely ever fail him, for they stand
above all that can make them fail. (130)

My Beloved, all that is rugged and toilsome I desire for myself, and all that is sweet and delightful I desire for you.
(131)

The submission of a servant is necessary in seeking God. In
outward things light helps to prevent one from falling; but
in the things of God just the opposite is true: It is better for
the soul not to see if it is to be more secure. (133)

The soul that desires God to surrender himself to it entirely
must surrender itself entirely to him without keeping anything for itself. (128)

Love to be unknown both by yourself and by others. Never
look at the good or evil of others. (135)

To lose always and let everyone else win is a trait of valiant
souls, generous spirits, and unselfish hearts; it is their manner to give rather than receive even to the extent of giving themselves. They consider it a heavy burden to possess

themselves, and it pleases them more to be possessed by others and withdrawn from themselves, since we belong more to that infinite Good than we do to ourselves. (137)

It is seriously wrong to have more regard for God's blessings than for God himself: prayer and detachment. (138)

Be silent concerning what God may have given you and recall that saying of the bride: *My secret for myself* [Is. 24:16]. (153)

Whoever knows how to die in all will have life in all. (160)

The humble are those who hide in their own nothingness and know how to abandon themselves to God. (163)

If you desire to be perfect, sell your will, give it to the poor in spirit, come to Christ in meekness and humility, and follow him to Calvary and the sepulcher. (165)

Whoever flees prayer flees all that is good. (169)

What does anyone know who doesn't know how to suffer for Christ? (175)

∼

BIBLIOGRAPHY

John of the Cross, Saint. *The Ascent of Mount Carmel, The Dark Night, The Spiritual Canticle, The Living Flame of Love, The Sayings of Light and Love*, Special Counsels, The Letters. In *The Collected Works of Saint John of the Cross*. Translated by Kieran Kavanaugh, O.C.D., and Otilio Rodriguez, O.C.D. 1991. Revised ed. Washington, D.C.: ICS Publications, Institute of Carmelite Studies, 2017.

Balthasar, Hans Urs von. *The Glory of the Lord: A Theological Aesthetics*. Vol. 3, *Studies in Theological Style: Lay Styles*. Translated by Andrew Louth, John Saward, Martin Simon, and Rowan Williams. Edited by John Riches. San Francisco: Ignatius Press, 1986.

Brenan, Gerald. *St John of the Cross: His Life and Poetry*. With a translation of his poetry by Lynda Nicholson. Cambridge: Cambridge University Press, 1973.

Bruno, Father, O.C.D., *Saint John of the Cross*. Edited by Fr. Benedict Zimmerman, O.C.D. London: Sheed & Ward, 1936.

Chapman, Dom John, O.S.B. *The Spiritual Letters of Dom John Chapman*. Edited by Dom Roger Hudleston, O.S.B. London: Sheed & Ward, 1935.

385

Crisógono De Jesús, O.C.D. *The Life of Saint John of the Cross*. Translated by Kathleen Pond. London: Longmans, Green, 1958.

Dubay, Thomas, S.M. *Fire Within: Saint Teresa of Avila, Saint John of the Cross, and the Gospel—on Prayer*. San Francisco: Ignatius Press, 1989.

Gabriel of Saint Mary Magdalen, O.C.D. *Saint John of the Cross: Doctor of Divine Love and Contemplation*. Translated by a Benedictine of Stanbrook Abbey. Cork: Mercier Press, 1946.

———. *Union with God: According to Saint John of the Cross*. Translated by Sister Miriam of Jesus, O.C.D. Eugene, Ore.: Carmel of Maria Regina, 1990.

Garrigou-Lagrange, Reginald, O.P. *Christian Perfection and Contemplation: According to Saint Thomas Aquinas and Saint John of the Cross*. Translated by Sister M. Timothea Doyle, O.P. Saint Louis: Herder, 1937.

Gaucher, Guy. *John and Thérèse: Flames of Love: The Influence of Saint John of the Cross in the Life and Writings of Saint Thérèse of Lisieux*. Translated by Alexandra Plettenberg-Serban. Edited by Bernadette Frenzel. New York: Alba House, 1999.

Herrera, R. A. *Silent Music: The Life, Work, and Thought of Saint John of the Cross*. Grand Rapids, Mich.: Eerdmans, 2004.

Maritain, Jacques. *The Degrees of Knowledge*. Translated under the supervision of Gerald B. Phelan. New York: Charles Scribner's Sons, 1959.

Matthew, Iain, O.C.D. *The Impact of God: Soundings from St John of the Cross*. London: Hodder & Stoughton, 1995.

Peers, E. Allison. *Saint John of the Cross and Other Lectures and Addresses 1920–1945*. London: Faber and Faber, undated.

Stein, Edith (Saint Teresa Benedicta of the Cross, O.C.D.). *The Science of the Cross*. Translated by Josephine Koeppel. Edited by Dr. L. Gelber and Romaeus Leuven. Washington, D.C.: ICS Publications, Institute of Carmelite Studies, 2003.

———. *Edith Stein: Selected Writings*. In *The Classics of Western Spirituality*. Edited by Marian Maskulak, C.P.S. New York: Paulist Press, 2016.

Wojtyła, Karol. *Faith according to Saint John of the Cross*. Translated by Jordan Aumann, O.P. San Francisco: Ignatius Press, 1981.